Bathroom

Titles in the *Objekt* series explore a range of types – buildings, products, artefacts – that have captured the imagination of modernist designers, makers and theorists. The objects selected for the series are by no means all modern inventions, but they have in common the fact that they acquired a particular significance in the last 100 years.

In the same series

Aircraft
David Pascoe

Bridge
Peter Bishop

Chair
Anne Massey

Computer
Paul Atkinson

Dam
Trevor Turpin

Factory
Gillian Darley

Motorcycle
Steven E. Alford, Suzanne Ferriss

Railway
George Revill

School
Ian Grosvenor, Catherine Burke

Ship
Gregory Votolato

Theme Park
Scott A. Lukas

Bathroom

Barbara Penner

REAKTION BOOKS

Published by Reaktion Books Ltd
33 Great Sutton Street
London EC1V 0DX, UK

www.reaktionbooks.co.uk

First published 2013

Printed and bound in China by 1010 Printing International Ltd

A catalogue record for this book is available from the British Library

ISBN 978 1 78023 193 8

Contents

Introduction

We shall deal here with humble things, things not usually granted
earnest consideration, or at least not valued for their historical import.
But no more in history than in painting is it the impressiveness of the
subject that matters. The sun is mirrored even in a coffee spoon . . .
Modest things of daily life, they accumulate into forces acting upon
whoever moves within the orbit of our civilization.[1]
Sigfried Giedion, *Mechanization Takes Command* (1948)

In the summer of 2009, I went on a pilgrimage. My destination: the
John Michael Kohler Arts Center in Sheboygan, Wisconsin, celebrated
for its artist-designed washrooms. The institution itself has a long history of bringing together art and plumbing through its Arts/Industry
programme, which offers artists the opportunity to produce work in the
company's pottery (one of the world's largest), iron and brass foundries
and enamel workshop. In this sense, the Kohler washrooms can be seen
as the consummation of the company's interest in uniting the most
basic of human needs – the need to urinate and defecate – with the
most elevated of our faculties – the ability to appreciate beauty.

The coordinator of the Arts/Industry programme, Mike Ogilvie,
offered me a tour. The washrooms were a revelation. One highlight

Ann Agee, *Sheboygan Men's Room*, John Michael Kohler Arts Center, Wisconsin, 1999. Detail
featuring the blue-on-white tile work.

was Merrill Mason's women's room, *Emptying and Filling*. In a series of marble niches Mason had installed an array of delicate objects – gloves, lipsticks and combs – all cast in iron, capturing perfectly the tensions of the female toilette and the discipline required to achieve beauty. Mike then guarded the door as I inspected the men's rooms, though the precaution was probably not necessary (at the Center, women and men routinely trespass into each other's washrooms to view the art). Matt Nolen's *The Social History of Architecture* was an art historical tour de force: each fixture, representing a particular period in history, playfully riffed on the idea of the toilet as a 'seat of power'. But it was in Ann Agee's *Sheboygan Men's Room* that I experienced my 'eureka' moment, when different ideas for this book all coalesced.

On entering *Sheboygan Men's Room* my first impression was of a rather bijou space, filled with details that evoked times past: delicate hand-painted, blue-and-white tiles showing picturesque views. Initially taken in by the prettiness of it all, I became aware only gradually that the space was anything but an exercise in nostalgia. As I contemplated an image of what at first glance seemed to be a quiet pond, the penny finally dropped: the 'pond' was actually a tank, part of the city's water treatment works. Looking closer, I realized that all of the *Men's Room* vignettes depict Sheboygan's water system in action. And, in case one misses the point, a diagram of the system is located on the wall above the paper towel dispenser, functioning as a key to the whole.

Quite apart from their artfulness, Agee's images inspired me because they portray things that we regularly use or experience in a fragmented and remote way – a lake, a swimming pool, a car wash, a water gun, a sprinkler, a treatment plant – and makes their interconnectedness clear. By organizing these episodes into a single space and into a single decorative scheme, the vignettes replicate the way in which water and sanitation infrastructure enables and links disparate moments in our daily lives, both mundane and pleasurable, small and grand. Standing in *Men's Room* we understand that we are implicated too: even our most basic actions – flushing the toilet, turning on a tap – makes us a part of the scenes on the walls.

In the way that it links Sheboygan's water system to the Arts Center's washroom and situates users within it, Agee's work captures in images what I hope to convey in this book. Like Agee, I do not intend to consider the bathroom as a discrete and enclosed site. I want to make sense of how the bathroom meets the world outside, how it moves between different sites, scales and conditions, and how it hooks the human body up to technology, individuals to infrastructure and private to public realms. In so doing I aim to break down what is sometimes referred to as the 'disconnect' between the architecture of the water system and reality of its use to allow for a more holistic and situated understanding of this humble yet complex space.

Small rooms, big systems

While the task of connection seems easy enough on paper, it goes against deeply ingrained habits and conventions, not to mention the design of the water system itself. For the 'disconnect' is actually plumbed into the developed world's water networks, which are created to render not only the user but also the impact of use invisible. They are literally 'flush and forget', removing the sight and the smell of our waste. The vast majority of people take it for granted that treated, potable hot and cold water will be on tap 24 hours a day and that waste can be flushed speedily away. Our everyday routines, our standards of hygiene and our understanding of civility are all constructed around these ordinary facts. We tend to assume that access to water and its unfettered use is our right and do not give much thought to what enables it.

This feeling of disjunction is further emphasized by our tendency to treat the bathroom as private, even as the most private space in the house, where we are able to indulge in the most personal of all our routines. We refer to the bathroom as 'the smallest room' to reflect both its small scale and its direct relationship to our bodies; in short, we value it precisely because it is so good at shutting the world out. Yet, as the interconnected episodes in *Men's Room* remind us, the 'smallest room' depends on and is plugged into the vast infrastructural network beyond. The bathroom thus is a hinge between private and public realms, the place where bodies, technologies, domestic interiors and urban systems most intimately interact.

In order to understand these interactions, we first need to counteract the system's plumbed-in invisibility, its taken-for-grantedness. But how do we move our understanding outwards from the smallest room to the big system on which it depends? The difference in scale between these worlds is immense. Aesthetically, too, they are miles apart: the decorative surface of the bathroom bears little relation to the industrial architecture of the system – dams, reservoirs, water towers, sewers, pumping stations and treatment plants – mostly located on the peripheries of cities. As Agee's installation highlights so cleverly, decoration works *against* connecting the bathroom to infrastructure, precisely because the exoticism and prettiness of its detailing distract from the utilitarian world beneath.

Even when we turn to more conventional renderings of bathrooms, for instance in trade catalogues, we find fixtures represented in perspective views as discrete objects, free of context or the reality of use. The one exception is the sanitary section, in which we see a

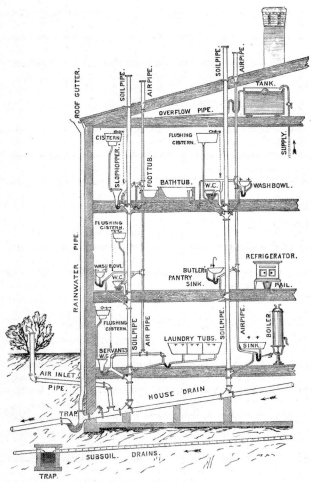

FIG. 17.—A properly plumbed house—Woman's sphere.

Harriet Plunkett, 'Woman's Sphere', in *Women, Plumbers and Doctors* (1885).

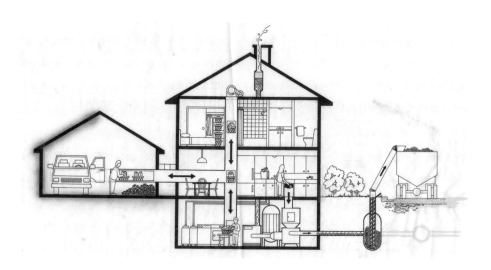

building sliced through vertically, walls and all, to reveal its network of pipes and drains. This form of representation emerged in the nineteenth century as a way of dealing with the new complexity of infrastructural systems. As pipes proliferated, houses were increasingly likened either to machines, designed to regulate the flow of services, or to living organisms. The idea of the house as a biological organism in particular has persisted into the modern era: take the industrial designer Bill Stumpf's 'Metabolic House' (1989), where the home breathes, eats and excretes, taking in oxygen, food and water and expelling it again.

The metabolic metaphor has not only been used to make sense of the home: since the nineteenth century it has also been deployed to conceptualize the layers of the modern city, as so many arteries, veins and organs. The film director Alfred Hitchcock drew on this long-standing tradition when he revealed to François Truffaut his desire to make a film about a day in the life of a city, which would focus on food – its arrival, distribution, sale, purchase, preparation

Bill Stumpf, 'The Metabolic House', 1989.

and consumption – and would end by following the waste into the sewers and out into the sea. 'So there's a cycle,' he explained, 'beginning with the gleaming fresh vegetables and ending with the mess that's poured into the sewer.'[1] Like many others, Hitchcock believed that this ongoing cycle of in-flows and out-flows embodied the entire story of modernity.

The metabolic view rightly underscores the fact that most modern infrastructural improvements share one critical goal: improved circulation. Above all else, capitalism and industrialization demand efficient circulation to enable the free movement of goods and people; the primary role of local government is to regulate the movement of water, goods, traffic, people and waste. As part of this remit, from the mid-nineteenth century onward, authorities intervened more actively in city workings to provide public services such as paving and street lighting and, crucially, water and sewerage systems. Britain was at the forefront of the move to pass public health legislation to ensure that private homes and businesses were properly connected to these centralized systems. It is at this moment that the story of the modern bathroom truly begins.

But the metabolic view can only take us so far in conceptualizing modern infrastructure. Its main limitation is that it tends to treat infrastructural systems as a logical and natural response to a host of functional requirements rather than to more contingent and historically specific factors.[2] By contrast, this book maintains that the growth of these systems is never simply driven by functional needs or technologies, but that larger political and social processes and attitudes always play a role too. Society cannot be separated from technology; instead, society and technology are bound together in overlapping and intertwined networks that mutually shape each other and which produce new hybrids of features, fixtures and spaces in their turn.

Flush with ideology

Perhaps the easiest way to describe a sociotechnical view of the bathroom is to note that, just as turning on a tap plugs us into a 'hard' network of pipes and plants, it also plugs us into a 'soft' network made up of social attitudes and beliefs. This is (at least partially) what provocateur-theorist Slavoj Žižek had in mind when he asserted: 'As soon as you flush the toilet, you're in the middle of ideology.'[3] By this Žižek means that ideology follows us even into those spaces we consider separate from the outside world and that it shapes the equipment that we use so unthinkingly. He develops this theme further through graphic descriptions of the variations in toilet design in Germany (where excrement falls on to a ledge), France (where excrement falls straight down into the water) and America (where excrement falls into the water but floats). If, as modernist histories hold, technology is neutral and its form is purely determined by rational or functional considerations, then how do we account for such national variations? Žižek's point is that they cannot be explained without referring to social factors, ideas, beliefs and habits, which are equally significant in determining design.

Chief among these social factors in Žižek's account are ideas about health: the understanding of the causes of illness and the regimes adopted in order to prevent them (for instance, the reason German toilets have ledges is to allow stools to be inspected). At a collective level, Žižek is no doubt correct that evolving understandings of public health and fear of disease and contagion have been the most significant factor in bathroom provision and design. As is well understood, it was only as a result of devastating outbreaks of cholera and typhoid in the nineteenth century that governments began to take responsibility for sanitation and to fund the construction of sewers. And theories about hygiene have continued to influence the appearance and maintenance of the bathroom and its fittings. Just consider the shift in the early 1900s from the richly furnished bathroom of the Victorian period to the spare, white one, in order to better expose and eradicate dirt – and to symbolize a cultural commitment to doing so.

This last is a crucial point. For as the anthropologist Mary Douglas suggested in her seminal work *Purity and Danger* (1966), what we are doing when cleaning and decorating is 'positively re-ordering our environment, making it conform to an idea'. It is surely not coincidence that Douglas introduces the ritualistic nature of domestic activities through a toilet anecdote: she describes her discomfort at using a friend's bathroom that is perfectly clean but which occupies a corridor space. Contemplating the gardening tools and gumboots that share the space, Douglas notes: 'It all made good sense as the scene of a back corridor, but as a bathroom – the impression destroyed repose.'[4] To her surprise, Douglas discovered that she was unsettled by the fact that the space didn't much *look* like a bathroom, with a tiled floor and walls and smooth surfaces. The episode led her to conclude that bathroom decor and behaviours carry a heavy symbolic load: they reflect and express social ideas of purity and pollution.

It soon becomes apparent, however, that other ideas have exerted nearly as much power over bathroom design as have health, hygiene and purity, notably the emphasis in the West since the eighteenth century on bodily privacy. No less than the rise of the field of public health, privacy should be seen as a modern invention that decisively broke with attitudes towards the body that had prevailed for much of human history. Historically speaking, most bathing cultures have been public ones, and bathing complexes themselves have been important sites of sociability. The most famous public bathing culture was that of the ancient Romans, which was extended across their empire to Europe and North Africa, but it has been an integral

feature of other civilizations as well. Think of Turkish hammans, Japanese sentō bathhouses and onsen, and Finnish saunas. And European bathhouses and thermal baths continue to thrive, from venerable old establishments like Munich's Müller'sches Volksbad to stunning new ones such as Therme Vals in Switzerland, designed by the architect Peter Zumthor.

The rise of privacy has resulted in the general privatization of Western bathing culture, though this did not happen evenly or all at once. Given that 'private' was increasingly equated with 'exclusive', it is not surprising that private and often very luxurious bathrooms first appeared in Europe in aristocratic or bourgeois homes. Until the 1920s, and sometimes well after that, rural or poor urban inhabitants were mostly left to carry on as before, with

Julia Baier, 'Sentō – the Japanese Bathhouse', 2005.

Outhouse, Alabama, USA, n.d.

outhouses and communal privies (which were often sites of socializing), public bathhouses, showers and swimming pools. But privacy
and related concerns about decency left their mark on these establishments, too. Communal privies were downsized and public baths
were more rigorously subdivided to ensure the segregation of men
from women and, with partitions, doors and cubicles, men from
other men and women from other women.

Highly atomized bathing arrangements are now so naturalized
throughout much of Europe and North America that we have trou-
ble imagining them any other way. The ancient communal latrine
still visible at Hadrian's Wall, for instance, or even the two-seater
privy in the garden of William Morris's Kelmscott Manor in the
Cotswolds seem quite alien to visitors who come upon them now –
amusing curiosities from a distant past. But there are many parts of
the world, such as Southeast Asia, India and Africa, where open or
communal bathing and toileting arrangements remain the norm.[5]
These arrangements are often flagged up in travel guides and are
regularly the subject of amazed commentary in travellers' blogs. For
better or worse, many travellers' most memorable encounters with
the Other – those moments when they feel their otherness most
keenly – still take place in the bathroom.

Far from being straightforward pieces of technology, then, bathrooms are culturally determined and historically specific. Social
factors like gender, class, race and religion influence their design and
shape their use. Their arrangements directly reflect the dominant
political ideology and its shifts: at the first sign of perestroika, for
instance, Russians almost immediately began making 'Euro-repairs'
to their homes, replacing communal toilets and baths with private
ones.[6] Bathrooms also uphold and actively enforce what Mary
Douglas called society's 'cherished classifications', particularly
through their segregation of users. Even today, when few other

sex-segregated facilities remain in our cities, we still expect to be presented with two doors, one marked 'Ladies' and the other 'Gents'. Consider, however, that in the American South until the 1960s and in South Africa into the 1990s, users would have been presented with two doors marked 'Whites' and 'Blacks' (or, simply, 'Non-whites') in addition to the division by sex. That bathroom arrangements and divisions change according to the prevailing social structure underscores the reality that there is nothing 'natural' about them.

By preventing 'promiscuous' social mixing or activities, these segregated spaces not only reflect and shape relations between men and

Toilets and a Tenant of "Douglas Flats," the Largest Tenement in Washington; Supposed to Have Been Erected as a Model.

[Photo by Hine]

Lewis Wickes Hine, 'Toilets and a Tenant of "Douglas Flats"', c. 1908.

women, but also the 'proper' relations between people of the same sex. Segregated bathrooms are spaces of discipline in the sense that Michel Foucault defined the term: as well as keeping users apart, they are often designed to enable external surveillance and policing. But no matter how effective stalls and walls may be, just as powerful are the mechanisms of discipline that users have internalized (not least through 'toilet training') and which significantly influence everyday bathroom behaviour. Think, for instance, of the complicated etiquette of avoidance that governs men's gazes at public urinals.

Far from resenting the disciplining design of bathrooms, many users see it as necessary, to protect them from physical attacks, bullying or contamination of various kinds. While it is important

Martin Jones, sponsored public urinal, India.

Be concerned about getting HIV.
But don't worry about getting it here.

One million Americans have HIV. And not one of them got it from a coffee pot, a water fountain, a toilet, or any piece of office equipment touched by someone with HIV. So don't worry about getting HIV through casual contact at work.

For more information on HIV and AIDS, call the CDC National AIDS Hotline at 1-800-342-AIDS.

BUSINESS
RESPONDS
TO AIDS

U.S. DEPARTMENT OF HEALTH AND HUMAN SERVICES · Public Health Service CDC

not to dismiss these concerns, this book will make clear that they do not always stem from real threats so much as from broader social anxieties. When people say they might 'catch something' in a public convenience, they often have in mind an illness or disease transmitted by a stigmatized social group (for example minority ethnicities, homosexuals, homeless people). In the 1980s and early '90s toilet seats were wrongly believed to be breeding grounds for the HIV virus. Erroneous or not, these fears can have real consequences as they are often used to brutally enforce the status quo. As the sociologist David Inglis rightly reminds us, toilet habits are very often used to assert the cultural and biological inferiority of subaltern groups and classes: as an example, he observes that

Business responds to AIDS, advertising campaign poster, USA, 1993.

discrimination against British gypsy communities is frequently justified by the stereotype that they live in squalid conditions with filthy toilet facilities. As in the colonial period, the perception that certain groups are dirty or 'excrementally uncontrolled', in Inglis's words, remains a powerful tool of denigration and exclusion today.[7]

Unless we recognize the part bathrooms play in enforcing order and existing power relations, it is hard to make sense of why they are often such bitterly contested spaces. The recent 'toilet wars' in South Africa, when the provision of substandard toilets to township residents led to violent protests and politics clashes, provoked some astonished remarks from journalists.[8] But should they have been surprised? Public facilities have often been at the front line of civil rights challenges; they are places where claims for equality are made and tested – and sometimes aggressively put down. It should not be forgotten that one of the first deaths of the American civil rights movement occurred when black activist Samuel Younge Jr tried to use a whites-only restroom at a filling station in Alabama: he was shot and killed by the attendant, who was subsequently cleared by an all-white jury.[9] And restrooms would prove to be crucial sites for the Freedom Riders, who travelled across the southern states in 1961 to test whether interstate train stations, bus depots and airports had been desegregated in compliance with recent Supreme Court decisions.

The very real threat of violence has not stopped a steady parade of marginalized or disadvantaged social groups from staking their claims for equal rights in the bathroom, from people with disabilities to the transgender community today.[10] In fact, campaigns for improved access have been around for almost as long as public facilities themselves. Those for women's conveniences have been the longest running and most far-reaching, having taken place in countries from the United Kingdom to Belgium to New Zealand. Protests have now reached Asia, too, as female activists

WOMEN
WHITE

in Guangzhou demonstrated in 2012 with their Occupy Men's Toilets campaign.[11] Some important victories have been scored in the last two decades, such as 'potty parity' laws in the United States, which mandate that for every one male toilet, two female toilets should

Freedom rider Gwendolyn Jenkins attempts to desegregate facilities at Jackson Municipal Airport, Mississippi, 7 June 1961.

be provided; similar laws have since been adopted in Singapore and Hong Kong. And New Zealand has declared that under human rights legislation, no woman should wait more than three minutes to go to the loo.[12] For all these gains, however, the queue for the Ladies is in no immediate danger of extinction.

Of course, many acts of social and political resistance are performed not collectively, but individually. Even the most utilitarian bathroom can serve as a place for small transgressions, where one can temporarily escape the routines and pressures of life. This is beautifully captured in *Modern Times* (1936, dir. Charlie Chaplin) when the Tramp, struggling to keep up with a factory assembly line, retreats to the washroom. Assuming he is unobserved, he perches on

Charlie Chaplin, *Modern Times*, 1936.

the edge of the sink and gratefully lights a cigarette, only to have the company president appear on a giant two-way screen behind him and order him back to work. The President's invasion of the washroom, the one place where the Tramp might reasonably expect some peace (he even clocked out at the door), exposes the company's ruthless drive to control its workers' bodies and time. Interestingly, the essence of this scene rings true in the sense that washrooms in American factories and in institutions were frequently not fully enclosed or had stalls without doors, presumably to discourage shirking or illicit activities. As Chaplin no doubt well knew, in the same way that privacy in the bathroom reflects class privilege and status, its absence reflects disenfranchisement and subjection.

Marcel Duchamp, *Fountain*, 1917, replica of 1964, porcelain, 360 x 480 x 610 mm.

Judy Chicago, *Menstruation Bathroom*, from *Womanhouse*, 1972, mixed media installation.

When they occur, the temporary moments of release or liberation offered in bathrooms are often intensely personal, but they can also destabilize larger social norms and taboos. The inspiring Iranian documentary *Zananeh* (*The Ladies Room*, 2003, dir. Mahnaz Afzali) focuses on the social life fostered by a women's restroom in a public park in Tehran. The bathroom in Laleh Park offers its users, mostly homeless women or prostitutes, a space for sociability and for uncensored conversation. In the shelter of the public toilet they can smoke, discuss forbidden topics and even remove their veils in violation of Iranian conventions.[13] As well as fostering camaraderie among people of the same sex, public facilities can equally shelter forbidden sexual acts and are central to the queer practices of cruising and cottaging.

As this brief survey reinforces, bathrooms are impossible to decisively categorize. They are among the most regulated spaces in contemporary society and the most potentially liberating. They are emblems of civility and containers of social threat. In them we confront our basest bodily needs, even as we transcend them or flush them away. They are places of passage and of transformation: one enters the bathroom dirty and leaves it clean. Hence even when functionalist attitudes were strongest, in the first half of the twentieth century, bathing retained the sense of a purification ritual. Indeed, one of the most iconic works in the history of modern art, Marcel Duchamp's *Fountain* (1917), teasingly asserted the quasi-spiritual aura of the urinal. But, by turning it upside down and leaving it unplumbed, Duchamp made it unusable, perversely denying us the release that encounters with urinals – and with art – are meant to provide.

One legacy of Duchamp's work is that generations of artists have been inspired to use sanitary fittings in their works or have sited their work in bathrooms. Some have reworked *Fountain* itself, such

Alex Schweder, *Bi-Bardon*, 2001, mixed media installation.

as Sherrie Levine's version cast in bronze of 1991. Many, however, have simply drawn from Duchamp the lesson that bathroom fittings are ambiguous in meaning. They unsettle. They provoke. In short, they are anything but 'plain pieces of plumbing', as Duchamp's supporters ingenuously maintained.[14] Artists today use the bathroom to probe personal and collective repressions and the way these affect identity, especially female or queer identity. In their works, the bathroom emerges as a classic 'backstage' space: a place that hides the messy realities of the female body (such as in Judy Chicago's *Menstruation Bathroom*, 1972), contains sexual desire (Terence Koh's sculpture *Medusa*, 2006, for example) or permits moments of revelation and remaking (tropes beautifully enacted in some of Cindy Sherman's *Untitled Film Stills*, 1977–80).

The acknowledgement of these artworks is important because they speak powerfully of the body, experience, and bathroom use and abuse – subjects that are often suppressed in polite discourse and which emerge instead in euphemisms or jokes. We cannot ignore the fact that, rather than being too inconsequential for words, bathrooms remain embarrassing, even unspeakable subjects for many, even for those in the design professions. Artwork that re-imagines the bathroom and its fittings, like Alex Schweder's 'Siamese' urinal *Bi-Bardon* (2001), addresses these strategic silences, often with wit and humanity. They open up questions: why are bathrooms designed as they are? Could they be designed differently, and if they were, how might our society be transformed?

The bathroom goes global

Most histories of bathroom design have downplayed questions of distribution and dissemination, as well as issues of use and consumption. The spread of bathroom equipment or the waterborne infrastructural model that underlies it have not been adequately explained. The unspoken assumption seems to be that 'superior' forms of technology naturally supersede existing ones through a process of evolution. In these accounts, superior varieties take over and now-obsolete ones wither away in a one-way parade of progress. Yet this doesn't stand up when we look more closely at the world in which we live. The best refutation of the 'Darwinian' model is the fact that now, over a century since the waterborne infrastructural system 'triumphed', traditional dry sanitation systems are making a comeback in some regions in the face of global concerns about water scarcity. And as already noted, in many countries they have never gone away or been replaced at all.

One of the revelations of my research was to discover that many alternative models of waste removal, from earth closets to vacuum systems, actually remained in use for many decades after the apparent triumph of waterborne sewerage systems in the developed world. Another revelation was just how many doubts about conventional sewerage and plumbing arrangements have been aired over the past century and a half by diverse thinkers from Karl Marx to Buckminster Fuller. Since the beginning of modern plumbing, many have questioned the wisdom of a system that uses the same water sources for drinking and for waste disposal. Just as nineteenth-century reformers could not understand the logic of a system in which local waterways were turned into local sewers – and inevitably became dangerously polluted – today some critics fail to understand the logic of treating all water to a potable standard, even that used for flushing toilets. One critic damningly sums up the paradox:

> If I urinated and defecated into a pitcher of drinking water and then proceeded to quench my thirst from the pitcher, I would be undoubtedly be considered crazy. If I invented an expensive technology to put

my urine and feces into my drinking water, and then invented another expensive (and undependable) technology to make the same water fit to drink, I might be thought even crazier.[15]

In the face of such criticisms, we have to ask not only how a particular technology and system is established but also how it becomes so 'locked in' that change comes to seem impossible. Sewerage is, in fact, frequently cited as the quintessential example of a self-perpetuating system, mainly because the initial investment it requires is so large that alterations become prohibitively expensive, even if evolving circumstances makes change desirable. As urban planner Eran Ben-Joseph writes, 'Historical decisions . . . have locked our current practice into a specific mode of operation.'[16]

This is no less true of bathroom interiors. As the sociologist Harvey Molotch has argued, even the most modest bathroom interior has been shaped by many actors: organizations that set national standards and write model building and plumbing codes; governmental bodies empowered to adopt these standards and codes (or make up their own); public health and planning boards; water companies; bathroom manufacturers; sanitary engineers; architects; industrial designers; retailers; developers; plumbers; activists of all kinds; and, last but not least, users and consumers.[17] Occasionally a single historical event has a strong and immediate impact, such as the Americans with Disabilities Act of 1990, which mandated that bathrooms in public buildings throughout the United States be made accessible to people with disabilities. More typically, however, bathroom design evolves over long periods of time in response to many, largely anonymous, forces.

This goes some way towards explaining why some of a bathroom's most common features can, on reflection, seem strange or inexplicable. Something that bemused me, a North American, when I first moved to England, was the prevalence of pillar taps. Why did the English so often have separate taps for hot and cold water – which means that freezing cold and scalding hot water has to be swilled around to the right temperature in the basin – instead of a mixer tap that ensures water comes out at the desired temperature? Attempting to unravel this mystery, Molotch, another transplanted North American, quizzed the British Bathroom Council, two British designers of bathroom fixtures, several bath shops and numerous English friends, before concluding that pillar taps were simply a 'style preference'.[18] Style is undoubtedly part of it, but if I consider the case of my own pillar-tapped bathroom in London, the explanation is more prosaic. We kept the taps because changing them would have meant changing our sinks, too, and we wanted to spend our limited budget on new tiles and a heated towel rail instead. So the taps stayed; we adjusted.

While much valuable recent scholarship has analysed the inadequacies or inequities of existing bathrooms, too often it fails to question how and why these environments came into being in the first place. Understanding the mundane realities of inherited spaces, standardized designs, limited budgets and deeply ingrained conventions makes it possible to see why certain features endure in our domestic and public bathrooms, thwarting even the most determined of activists. And, equally important, the fact that the different needs and desires of users are often in conflict means that it can be difficult ever to agree on a coherent agenda for change. Molotch sums it up perfectly: musing on his largely failed attempt to erect unisex restrooms in his own queer- and trans-friendly department at New York University, Molotch concludes that, for any innovation to happen, 'A whole lot of stars need to be aligned' – that is, many actors need to believe in and show 'love' for the project for it to succeed.[19]

Although there may not always be obvious answers as to why modern bathrooms operate and look the way they do, identifying the various forces at play in their production and dissemination is essential – and here architectural and design history can make a real contribution. Yet the anonymity and complexity of bathroom spaces poses some challenges for the historian. How can we do justice to the many different forces shaping bathroom spaces? How do we understand the motivating factors that drive each one? Accepting that the goal of completeness is unrealistic, I have opted to focus on how and why the waterborne model of sanitation and its associated spaces and equipment emerged, and how they were subsequently locked in locally, nationally and beyond. On the one hand, this is a story of mass production and of standards and codes of various kinds. But on the other, it is also one of how a particular model of sanitation and hygiene was 'sold' internationally. World expositions, hygiene fairs, model dwellings, trade catalogues, bathroom showrooms, Hollywood films – the entire modern apparatus of sales and promotion – are central to the story of the bathroom and extend it beyond physical space or the discourses of engineering and production.

Many of the innovations, companies, standards and events that I focus on initially are British and later American, for the simple reason that, until very recently, Britain and the United States have been the two most influential shapers of modern bathroom culture. Many bathroom elements have existed for millennia – baths and lavatories, for example – but it was British inventors and manufacturers who, from the 1850s onwards, first began to make high-quality goods at scale, lowering costs and making them affordable for a wider cross-section of the populace. Moreover, the British were the acknowledged world leaders in the most genuinely revolutionary sanitary technology of all: the water closet. And from the nineteenth century it would be not only specific British bathroom products and technologies but also the country's entire

sanitation model that were adopted by, and exported to, cities across Europe and to its colonies.

For the story of how Western bathrooms came to be locked in is not only a story of trade but also a story of empire, colonial expansion and war. Many countries' water infrastructure dates back to colonial times and was built with reference to the 'home' nation. In 1927 the Columbia University political scientist Parker Thomas Moon described such infrastructural interventions (approvingly) as 'sanitary imperialism'.[20] As American and European sanitary models reshaped colonial cities from Mumbai to Manila, colonial subjects were themselves 'modernized' through their encounters with new sanitary technologies and theories of hygiene.[21] It is important not to overstate the practical success of these projects, but scholars have argued that the symbolic importance of infrastructure and the

Showroom for F. Bolding, Davies Street, London, 1934.

accompanying fear of dirt and disorder retain a firm hold on post-colonial governmental policy-making. And the flush toilet itself remains a potent indicator of progress.

Despite the widespread dismantling of empires after the Second World War, the exportation of the Western bathroom continued as part of the process of Americanization. In tracing the rapid change in Japanese bathroom culture following the Second World War, Rose George notes the influence of American troops who expected to use the same facilities overseas as at home. (The transformation was likely well advanced by this point: already in 1933 the writer Jun'ichirō Tanizaki was elegaically lamenting the replacement of the dim, camphor-scented, outdoor toilet with the glaringly lit, white-tiled, indoor one.[22]) Increasingly, however, American-style sanitation and hygiene were carried abroad by multinational businesses. McDonald's was the most influential in this regard, as the fast-food chain sparked what the anthropologist James L. Watson describes as a public hygiene 'revolution' among East Asian consumers.[23] Mean-while, Western manufacturers of sanitaryware were themselves becoming more international. Although they had long exported vast quantities of their goods, in the 1950s and '60s they opened factories in countries such as South Africa, Malaysia and India to serve new markets. Starting in the 1980s the situation shifted again, as even the most venerable companies were consolidated into larger, multi-national entities: the British company Twyford, for instance, is now owned by the Icelandic bathroom giant Sanitec, while American Standard is owned by the private equity firm Sun Capital, with Mitt Romney's former company, Bain Capital, as a minority partner. And the majority of sanitaryware companies now manufacture a large portion of their products in Asia.

Another significant factor in the bathroom's spread has been the rise of mass tourism and of global events such as world expositions

公共卫生间
PUBLIC TOILETS

and the Olympics. Standardized pictograms to represent 'men' and 'women' were first introduced at the 1964 Tokyo Olympics. Since then, the installation of sex-segregated public facilities complete with pictograms and throne-style toilets has become a crucial way for countries to make their claims to civility and world-class status. Just consider the initiatives to build Western-standard public toilets in preparation for global sporting events, such as for the 2002 South Korea and Japan World Cup or the 2008 Beijing Olympics. These events have left a lasting imprint, and Southeast Asian countries now lead the international crusade for sanitary facilities. The former mayor of Suwon, South Korea, Sim Jae-duck, founded the World Toilet Association; such was his belief in the cause that, in advance of the WTA's inaugural meeting in 2007, he built a US$1.1

New public facility constructed in advance of the Olympics, Beijing, China, 2008.

million house shaped like a toilet. The WTA has since been joined by the Singapore-based World Toilet Organization, run by social entrepreneur Jack Sim, who fully deserves his reputation as the planet's most dynamic campaigner for sanitation. Sim is also planning yet another monument to toiletry: the World Toilet Museum, shaped like three interlocking toilet rolls.

Preparations for the World Expo in Shanghai in 2010 also featured the by-now-familiar push to remake the city's bathroom culture. Expo 2010 drew over 72 million visitors and was reputed to be most expensive global event ever staged. In the same way that thousands of Olympic Toilets were installed throughout Beijing (with five-star models at tourist sites), Model Toilets were installed throughout Shanghai, with an impressive barrage of signage to enable people to locate them. And on the exhibition site itself, bathrooms were everywhere, queue-less, clean and available in 'Western' (throne) or 'Asian' (squat) models. However, appropriately enough in an event devoted to intercultural communication, a large number of Chinese visitors seemed not to discriminate. In the Ladies, many women entered whatever stall was nearest and went about their business with the doors wide open, the legacy of using communal facilities without doors. Through one open door I caught a glimpse of an older woman perched acrobatically on the seat of a throne toilet, transforming it into an instant squat.

As this anecdote reminds us, Western-style bathrooms and their associated fixtures and behaviours are not always embraced or translated exactly into other contexts. In the case of China, for instance, villagers resist indoor bathrooms because, sensibly enough, they don't wish to bring dirt into their homes (hence confirming historian Dominique Laporte's remark that the 'privatization of waste' – the shift from outdoor to indoor toilets – is a process 'whose universality is not a historical given'[24]). And when Western bathrooms are introduced into middle-class homes, from Ankara to Jakarta, Moscow to Karachi, they are usually modified to suit local customs or traditions. Religion is a particularly important influence in the production of hybrids: one example is that, in Islamic countries, Western-style bathrooms are installed with 'Muslim showers' (bidet-like hand sprays for washing oneself after toilet use).

The bathroom unlocked

As the discussion of cultural hybrids and civil rights suggests, this book not only traces how certain assumptions and codes came to be locked into place, it also considers cases where assumptions and codes have been 'unlocked' – at least in part. The later chapters focus on two phenomena in particular. The first considers the rise from the 1960s onward of the inclusive bathroom and the many social and legal shifts that combined to bring the needs of a far greater range of users, including the aged, women and people with disabilities, on to the design agenda. The second considers efforts to rethink waterborne sewerage. While this has a long history, the question has taken on a new urgency in the face of the sanitation crisis that faces the Global South.

Today no fewer than 2.6 billion people are estimated to lack access to basic sanitation; thousands of children under five continue to die every day due to faecal transmission of disease, deaths that basic sanitation could do much to prevent. Such shocking figures have served to nudge sanitation higher up the agenda of the international development community. In 2010, the United Nations declared access to clean water and sanitation to be a basic human right. And the UN's Millennium Development Goals set the target of halving by 2015 the number of people living without basic sanitation. Although this goal still looks very far away (indeed, it is the

Enviro Loo Dry Toilets at Equinisweni Primary School, KwaZulu-Natal, South Africa, 2012.

most off-track of all MDG targets), the field has lately been energized by the arrival of new champions with fresh approaches. Long one of the most unloved and moribund areas of government sponsorship and NGO support, sanitation now has the strong backing of organizations such as Unicef and WaterAid.

Recently too, and with great effectiveness, the Bill and Melinda Gates Foundation has thrown its heft behind the cause through its 'Reinvent the Toilet' challenge. As the programme's name suggests, the Gates Foundation and many others are going back to the drawing board to attempt to solve the sanitation crisis. The idea of conventional sewerage is now subject to serious questioning, since it is seen as inappropriate for many areas of the world due to the high cost of new infrastructure as well as water scarcity. And in the quest to 'reinvent the toilet', new tools are being deployed with a visionary verve that would have warmed Buckminster Fuller's heart, from 3-D printers (used to manufacture toilets from recycled materials) to tiger worms (used to break down excreta for compost).

Innovations in water conserving or on-site systems are relevant to the developed world, too, where certain communities still have very poor quality infrastructure – for instance First Nations peoples in Canada or poor rural communities in America – existing sewer systems are aging and natural disasters are occurring more frequently.[25] The inherent vulnerability of infrastructure was made terribly evident following the Christchurch earthquake of 2010, when many residents found themselves without running water or flushing toilets for long periods. (Those affected, however, responded with great inventiveness and wit, for instance, designing an emergency model of compost toilet that has now been adapted for other earthquake-prone regions, or humorously decorating their privies.[26]) More generally, concerns about water supplies and conservation are also beginning to bite: recent building regulations

THE SEWAGE *is received*
from 1,000,000 PEOPLE

Some of it has travelled
NEARLY 20 MILES

enforce the use of less water-hungry bathroom fixtures, such as waterless urinals and dual-flush toilets. But will such measures be enough?

All in all, the time seems right to try to think more carefully about bathrooms – our use of them and their place within our society. How should we regard and value them? At present, cultural views towards the bathroom might be characterized as inconsistent and ambivalent, even schizophrenic. Britain's pioneering efforts in sewerage and sanitaryware continues to be recognized as an extraordinary achievement and the source of no little pride. The historian Asa Briggs decreed the sewage system to be 'one of the

Inauguration of West Middlesex Drainage Scheme, Mogden Works, London, 1936.

biggest technical and social achievements of the [Victorian] age' and, when surveyed, a majority of medical experts and members of the public still agree.[27] As I was finishing this book, *The Economist* magazine came out with a cover that featured Rodin's *The Thinker*, seated on a toilet, musing: 'Will we ever invent anything this useful again?'[28] Similarly, in private homes, bathrooms are becoming bigger and more lavish than ever, with an 'average' spend of £5,000 easily rising to £20,000 for a master bathroom.[29]

Yet this trend towards private comfort and luxury contrasts sharply with the general condition of public facilities, which are clearly not valued in the same way; since 1995, 50 per cent of public toilets in the UK have closed, a decline which is consistent with that in other countries.[30] The lack of response – much less outrage – about a move that negatively affects so many people, especially those who are most vulnerable, would seem to assert our collective indifference. But it is difficult to reconcile the signals. On the one hand, in certain contexts, the bathroom is regularly acknowledged to be important, a key component in the creation of liveable environments and healthy cities. On the other, the bathroom is often overlooked. It is low on the list of local government priorities and is often not seen as worthy of serious discussion (or of academic study, though this is changing). And in big architectural offices, designing bathrooms remains a job for the most junior architects – the architectural equivalent of 'latrine duty' in the army.

Such schisms may well be inevitable. For in studying the bathroom, we find ourselves touching the core of modern civilization's values and ambitions, dreams and contradictions. The bathroom's complexities echo those of society at large: variations in its form and meaning reflect the different settings and conditions in which it appears and the many uses to which it is put. This, in turn, is reflected in the broad range of spaces that are discussed in this book.

While the modern Anglo-American bathroom lies at its core, it also acknowledges the many other places in which the activities of grooming, bathing, washing and excreting take place. Indeed, some of the spaces discussed radically challenge what we think a bathroom should or should not be. They are included in order to shed light on the particularity – and peculiarity – of bathroom cultures everywhere.

1 The Civilizing Bathroom

This story of the modern bathroom begins in England, at the Great Exhibition of 1851. Among many other wonders, the exhibition featured public conveniences for the use of both women and men. The experiment proved to be a popular success: at the exhibition's close, the conveniences were reported to have been used 827,820 times in total and, at a penny or halfpenny charge per use, raised £2,441, 15 shillings and 9 pence.[1]

The Great Exhibition deserves to be seen as a breakthrough moment for the modern bathroom not only because it was the first time that provisions of this kind were made for the public, but also because its organizers placed such emphasis on them. Well in advance of the Great Exhibition, its organizing body, the Society of Arts, stated its belief that such facilities should be a priority, sending a 'numerously and respectably signed' petition to pressure the Metropolitan Commission of Sewers to build more in London. Although the Public Health Act 1848 had authorized the building of public necessaries for sanitary reasons, the petitioners were less motivated by health concerns than by civic pride: they argued that conveniences should be provided because foreign visitors were 'accustomed' to them.[2] Conveniences projected an image of an enlightened city committed to its citizens' comfort. And, in an age of growing metropolitan

Charles Marville, Cabinet Dorion, avenue des Champs-Elysées, Paris, c. 1870.

Charles Marville, urinal, rue du Faubourg Saint-Martin, Paris, *c.* 1870.

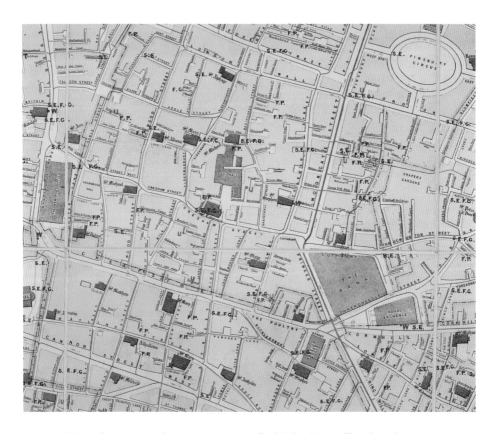

competition, there was a keen awareness of which cities offered such amenities and which ones did not. Londoners did not want to be caught short.

The feeling of metropolitan rivalry intensified as plans took shape for the Great Exhibition, itself a competitive event showcasing different countries' manufacturing capabilities. In London, one rival city loomed especially large: Paris, the host of all of previous industrial expositions of note and a place well equipped with conveniences. These ranged from elegant, privately run 'cabinets' to public urinals: thanks

William Haywood, 'General Plan of the City of London Shewing the Public Sewers', 1854. Urinals are indicated by red dots.

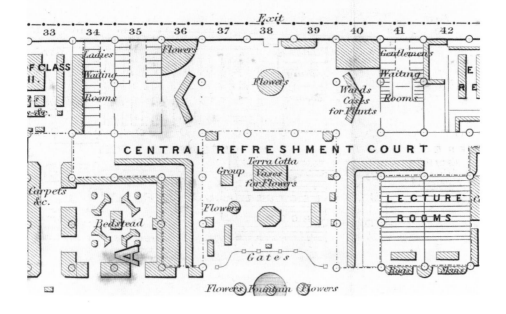

Text within the plan image:

Exit

33 34 35 36 37 38 39 40 41 42

F CLASS Ladies Flowers Gentlemens
II. Waiting Flowers Waiting E
Rooms Wards Rooms R E
Cases
for Plants

CENTRAL REFRESHMENT COURT

Terra Cotta
Group Vases
for Flowers
Carpets
&c. Flowers LECTURE G
Bedstead ROOMS

Gates

Rugs Irons

Flowers Fountain Flowers

to its energetic prefect Claude-Philibert Barthelot, Count of Rambuteau, Paris had 468 of the latter by 1843.[3] The Commissioners of Sewers of the City of London asked their surveyor, William Haywood, to study the situation. He reported that the City presently had 75 urinals, mostly located in churchyards or on public thoroughfares, and noted that it would be possible to also build public water closets were the Commissioners to deem it 'expedient'.[4] They did not, maintaining that 34 new urinals alone would meet demand.

Frustrated by the general lack of action, petitioners sent in a second, even more impressively signed letter on the subject of conveniences, this time with Charles Dickens and Thomas Carlyle lending their names to the cause.[5] When it became evident that the Commissioners of Sewers would not take action, the Society of Arts focused its reforming energies on the Great Exhibition instead. It

Detail of plan of the Great Exhibition, London, 1851, showing central Ladies and Gentlemen's Waiting Rooms.

entrusted the task of designing the Crystal Palace's facilities to leading sanitary engineer George Jennings, who fitted them up with simplified water closets (toilets), dubbed 'monkey closets', that were resilient and easy to use – the forerunners of today's one-piece pedestal models. Run by a staff of 21 attendants, the facilities were located off each of the Crystal Palace's three Refreshment Courts, conveniently close to visitors washing down their potted meats and jellies with Schweppes soda water and ginger beer. These facilities included both 'waiting rooms' (with water closets) and washing places.

It is hard to overstate the impact of these conveniences, which were used by 14 per cent of all visitors to the exhibition, 11,171 on one day alone. At least some visitors would never before have seen, let alone used, a plumbed-in water closet. Even prior to the official opening of the exhibition, Jennings boasted that his WCs had been used daily by over 4,000 workmen yet remained as 'sweet' as when first installed.[6] Many visitors from other cities and countries returned to their homes inspired by the Crystal Palace's example: for instance, after returning from the exhibition, the radical politician James Moir began a vigorous crusade to put public conveniences in Glasgow's streets.[7]

That the Society of Arts always intended to make a larger point through these facilities is obvious in its final report to Parliament on the Great Exhibition. Pointing to the conveniences' great success, the organizers urged that similar provisions be made at all future events to alleviate 'the sufferings which must be endured by all, but more especially by females . . . on account of the want of them'. Women had been provided with more water closets than men (47 versus 22) but organizers suggested that more should have been installed to meet demand. While this view was enlightened for the day, it was also financially sound: because men used the 54 urinals for free, women accounted for the bulk of revenue from the facilities – £2,084 of the total £2,441.[8]

There is a final footnote to this story. Refusing to abandon its fight with the Metropolitan Commission of Sewers, the Society of Arts invited some of its most illustrious members, the Earl of Carlisle, the Earl Granville, Sir Samuel Morton Peto and Sir Henry Cole, to oversee the establishment of two model conveniences in London in May 1852, with the aim of demonstrating that such facilities would be welcomed by the public and could be financially self-sustaining.[9] The Gentlemen's was located at 95 Fleet Street and the Ladies at 52 Bedford Street off the Strand. Both were accessed through existing businesses and were equipped with water closets, sinks, clothes brushes and full-time attendants. One penny was charged for the use of a water closet; two or three pence was charged for the use of a sink to wash and freshen up. Among others, the tile maker Herbert Minton and George Jennings donated equipment to this venture, which was publicized extensively in *The Times* and through the distribution of over 50,000 handbills.

Yet despite the triumphant precedent of the Crystal Palace, these conveniences closed after six months due to low user numbers. The committee members gave the failure a decidedly patriotic spin, thus reversing many of their previous claims. 'It would appear', they noted:

> that the English public do not really require such conveniences to the extent they are wanted abroad. There, the water-closets in private houses, and even in the most magnificent Cafes are of a most imperfect and even disgusting description, and it is the habitual custom of foreigners to frequent the 'Cabinets' established for this especial purpose. In England, on the contrary, almost every house, even the humblest, is now provided with these conveniences to an extent which strikes foreigners with as much admiration as any we may have for the establishments in their streets; and therefore, an Englishman rarely requires anything more than an ordinary urinal in the streets.[10]

These experiments to provide British men and women with public facilities helps illuminate where London stood on sanitary issues in the mid-nineteenth century. As the Society of Arts's members concluded after their second initiative's failure, bathrooms were still largely regarded as private concerns: water closets were situated in individual residences and were not integrated into a coordinated public water system. But the amount of time and energy devoted to convenience issues suggests that the mood was changing; a more civic-minded approach was on the horizon. In fact, over the next five decades the 'sanitary idea' would emerge as a major government preoccupation and the provision and oversight of water closets and conveniences, along with bath and wash houses, would be recognized as key to improving the environmental and social conditions of the metropolis. And through developments in legislation, infrastructure, plumbing, architecture, science and marketing, the bathroom was gradually hooked up to an integrated system of sanitary control.

The sanitary idea

A common starting point for histories of modern sanitation is the decision to build London's sewer system in 1858. But the above quote – where the failure of public conveniences is blamed on the prevalence of private ones – reminds us that the situation was more complicated. In reality, the rise of the water closet pre-dated the rise of a comprehensive sewer system, and precipitated the need for it.

The water closet had been a regular feature of aristocratic homes since the last decades of the eighteenth century; however, they were expensive items that required the installation of cisterns, tanks and pumps to supply a steady water supply. This situation changed when private water companies began installing water-carriage systems in London, mostly in the first decade of the nineteenth century, making a reliable water supply available to a greater number. Water closets proliferated among those who could afford them: by 1850, for instance, 65 per cent of homes in wealthy St James's parish in Westminster had one.[11] This proliferation was a disaster in public health terms. The overflow from cesspits made its way into 'sewers' that were, for the most part, natural streams and rivers that emptied directly into the Thames. (In stark contrast to most other cities, whose sewers were used for surface water only, it had been legal for London households to connect their cesspools to the common sewers since 1815.) In this way, water closets were responsible for much of the pollution of London's main water supply, which, ironically, would make a modern sewer system a necessity.

Because London was the world's largest and fastest growing metropolis, with well over 2.5 million inhabitants by mid-century, it was one of the first to confront the reality that its environmental problems needed to be dealt with in a coordinated way across the city. An important first step was taken when a single unified body, the Metropolitan Commission of Sewers, was created in 1847 to replace the eight distinct commissions that had overseen sewers previously. The next year then saw passing of the Public Health Act 1848, which laid the ground for the establishment of a General Board of Health and smaller local boards. The social reformer Edwin Chadwick, whose research and lobbying had done most to usher in these changes, was convinced that good drainage was the best means of improving public health. Like most of his contemporaries, he believed infectious diseases were transmitted through the air in miasmas bred by putrefying waste, hence the best mode of prevention would be to quickly flush or drain waste away before it stagnated. Chadwick's obsession with effective drainage would reshape the government's approach dramatically over the next decade, as resources were redirected from street cleaning and nuisance removal towards building a water system that provided clean water and sewage disposal.

The new Public Health Act's clauses regarding domestic sanitary arrangements are especially significant to this history because it marks the moment when government first entered the private bathroom in a meaningful way. As part of its mandate to prevent noxious miasmas, the Act stipulated that any newly built or rebuilt house be provided with a '*sufficient* watercloset or privy and an ashpit, furnished with proper doors and covering'. If the property owner did not comply, the local health board could build the required facility itself and recover the costs. (Some local authorities did proceed to rip out privies and replace them with water closets, with controversial zeal.[12]) The Public Health Act further stipulated that factories which employed over twenty people of both sexes provide a 'sufficient' number of water closets or privies 'for the separate use of each sex', or a fine of up to £20 would be levied. Homeowners were now legally required to notify the local board of health in writing prior to constructing a privy or cesspool, and surveyors were given the power to shut down any judged to be a nuisance or 'injurious to health'. Finally, the local board of health was empowered to erect public conveniences out of district rates, although there was no requirement they do so.[13] This resulted in the erection of at least one gentlemen's public convenience, on Rose Street in Soho in 1849 – if not the first public facility with water closets in the city, then certainly one of the first.[14]

Even though standards were still loosely defined (what constituted a 'sufficient' facility or a 'sufficient' number of water closets?) and the local boards' powers of enforcement were as yet untested by the courts, these clauses were significant, not least because they show that a form of sex segregation was built into public provision from the start. Indeed, given that the Public Health Act's provisions for factories applied only to workplaces that employed over twenty people *of both sexes*, we have to ask whether the real concern at this point was to provide adequate sanitary facilities for workers – a large number of whom worked in factories that did not meet these criteria – or if its priority was to prevent mixing between the sexes. The later Common Lodging Houses Act of 1851 suggests the latter comes closer to the truth: in this Act, local authorities were given the right to regulate the separation of the sexes to ensure the 'well-ordering' of boarding houses.[15] From the beginning, then, the aims of sanitary and moral reform intermingled.

Even though it depended on an erroneous understanding of disease transmission and did not require the retrofitting of existing buildings, the Public Health Act was a real advance, but its positive effects were partially undone by another Chadwick initiative. In order to flush waste away rapidly, Chadwick pushed the Commissioners of Sewers to banish all cesspools and replace the old, square, brick sewers with an 'arterial' system of narrow, salt-glazed stoneware pipes: Henry Doulton was the first to produce such pipes and they made his company's fortune. This mission was given great urgency in 1848–9 when the country found itself, once again, in the grip of a deadly cholera attack that killed over 14,000 in London alone. In response, the Commissioners eliminated over 30,000 cesspools in six years.[16] More cesspits were abolished as more water closets were installed, with the inevitable and deadly result that more excrement found its way to the Thames. One commentator grimly summed up the effect: 'The Thames is now made a great cesspool instead of each person having one of his own.'[17]

Before long, the contradiction bubbled to the surface in the Great Stink of 1858. Festering in unusually hot and dry conditions, the excrement-filled Thames emitted a stench so nauseating that it threatened to disrupt the workings of Parliament – and overcame any lingering governmental resistance to supporting a coordinated sewerage scheme. The newly formed Metropolitan Board of Works authorized its chief engineer, Joseph Bazalgette, to begin construction. Even though Bazalgette departed from many of Chadwick's principles, he shared Chadwick's central belief that the system's main task should be to flush sewage swiftly away from dense residential areas. His solution was to build a combined intercepting system: a network of main sewers to the north and south of the Thames intercepted effluent before it reached the central stretch of river and, with the help of gravity and four massive pumping stations, moved it downstream to be discharged into the river at ebb tide. As part of the system, embankments were also built on both sides of the Thames, 165 miles (265 kilometres) of old main sewers were rebuilt, and local authorities laid over 1,000 miles (1,600 kilometres) of new local pipes.[18]

During this same period, of course, Paris found itself in a similar position to London, with a population of over 1 million people and frequent outbreaks of cholera. Between 1857 and 1870, as part of Napoleon III and Baron Haussmann's ambitious rebuilding programme, the city's medieval sewer system was also reconstructed and extended to over 348 miles. Like London, Paris opted for a combined system that carried street water, rainwater, solid waste, waste water and (only much later) human excrement all together. The use of the combined system explains why Paris sewers were so spacious. The whole system was visitable: even the smallest sewers, the *petites lignes* installed below every street, were tall enough for sewermen to walk in to remove blockages. And from the International Exposition of 1867 onwards, genteel tourists could visit the grandest of these sewers, navigating rivers of effluent on sluice boats, and marvel at this singular, reportedly odour-free monument to progress – an almost perfect inversion of the experience of promenading on London's new embankments. The sewers are still a tourist attraction today.

With the construction of these two grand sewerage systems, the triumph of waterborne sanitation seemed assured. Yet in reality, change happened unevenly, and sewerage systems were adopted in a piecemeal, partial and at times reluctant fashion, resulting in enormous variations in take-up between different classes and neighbourhoods. Even in Paris it was not compulsory for private dwellings to connect to the mains drainage system until 1894 when, at last, the national parliament approved the plan of *tout-à-l'égout*, or 'everything in the sewers'. Property owners and landlords were a main reason for delays as they refused to pay for the necessary infrastructure or property upgrades, leading to gross inequities in provision. Factory owners were equally culpable: they provided few closets for workers (one per 60 or 70 workers was common) and left them unflushed and unventilated. In Britain, Her Majesty's Senior Metropolitan Inspector of Factories decried the water closets as 'the most objectionable feature in London workshops'.[19] He also cited an earlier, gruesome audit of bakehouses of 1881, which revealed that, among other sanitary failings (filth, dirt, open sinks, inhabitation by fowl and rabbits), several had cesspools running into them.

Illustration by Jules Pelcoq of tourists in the Paris sewers, c. 1870.

While such details were horrific in their own right, they posed a serious threat given that efforts to contain contagious diseases depended on the universal adoption of adequate sanitary technologies, habits and standards. As a result, sanitary reformers and authorities began to favour a more interventionist approach, embarking on a 'war of the community' to 'enforce upon land-owners, and house-owners and house-middlemen, obedience to the principle that "property has its duties as well as its rights"'.[20] Along with the Public Health Act of 1848, various legislative Acts and amendments were passed, covering everything from sewage to nuisance removal. Local authorities were granted greater powers over individuals, tenements, workshops and factories, permitting them for instance to enter private residences to inspect any fittings affecting water supply or drainage and to ensure that every house had a drain properly connected with a sewer.[21] Strengthened further by the Public Health Act of 1875, these interventions, which subjected domestic arrangements to increasingly specific government standards, effectively formed a parallel sanitary infrastructure to Bazalgette's – a legislative system to work alongside the physical one.

Creating 'well-ordered families'

In addition to these legal changes, sanitary reformers sought to promote the virtues of good drainage through philanthropic projects. Among the earliest of these was the full-scale Model Dwellings erected in Hyde Park for the Great Exhibition, paid for by Prince Albert and designed by the architect Henry Roberts for the Society for Improving the Condition of the Labouring Classes. Running water and a water closet was included inside each of the four flats, a pointed and radical gesture for the time. The lack of such amenities had emerged as a focus for health reformers thanks to sanitary surveys from the 1830s onward, which correlated epidemics to the poor environmental conditions of slum dwellings. The best known of these publications, Chadwick's pioneering *Report on the Sanitary Condition of the Labouring Population of Great Britain* (1842), was a catalogue of hygiene horrors. It recorded cases where a single privy was shared between 125 people or where no privies existed at all, forcing residents to defecate on dungheaps in communal courtyards. In other cases cited by Chadwick, privies, cesspools, drains and sewers did exist but were overflowing or blocked, rendering them worse than useless.[22]

As ever, the improvement of sanitary conditions was closely allied to the goal of moral reform. Henry Roberts stated that the aim of his dwellings was to provide occupants with the 'moral training of a well-ordered family'. To this end, he sought to introduce and enforce an appropriate distance between the bodies of occupants, and between bodies and their waste.[23] Water closets were preferable to privies since they flushed waste away with water from the roof cistern automatically. This was key: whereas privies and cesspools depended on the individual to be kept clean and decent, water closets took responsibility

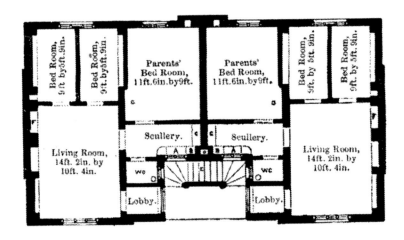

Plan of model dwellings built by architect Henry Roberts at the Great Exhibition, London, 1851, showing separate water closets.

out of the individual's hands and transferred it to a system. A perfect example of the transfer of responsibility was a later water closet, the Tipper, in which rainwater and domestic waste water drained into a tank that automatically tipped over at three gallons, flushing the closet. The inventor of the Tipper, James Duckett, proudly proclaimed that it was well suited for working-class housing because it was 'not dependent in any way on the care and cleanliness' of its user.[24]

Even more than the water closet as a piece of technology, however, the water closet as a *room* was essential to Roberts's goal of creating 'a well-ordered family'. Just as he used separate bedrooms for girls and boys to segregate occupants by sex, he used private water closets to secure a new level of visual, acoustic and olfactory privacy for individual members of the household. Accessed through the scullery, the water closet was ventilated by a window in the stairwell to help keep gases and smells out of the living space. Historians argue that, as the smell of excrement began to trigger greater levels of anxiety and disgust, the desire to contain olfactory offences generated more highly atomized interiors.[25] In these readings, the water closet helped to generate the segregationist logic of modern domestic space itself. It also helped to create a much more private subject who regarded bodily functions as a source of embarrassment or shame, to be kept hidden from neighbours and from one's own family.

It is also noteworthy that, despite the privatization of water closets, early model apartments like these did not include facilities for bathing. While cleanliness was essential – and lodgers could be evicted for 'filthy or dirty practices' – it was still assumed that labourers would make do with more impromptu arrangements like portable, sheet-metal baths or on-site communal ones.[26] And from 1846, separate establishments for bathing became more widely available to all following an Act empowering local authorities to build them at public expense. Public baths often came with swimming pools, warm and

GENTLEMEN'S PRIVATE WARM BATHS

cold tub baths, vapour baths, warm and cold shower-baths, water closets and laundries. Accommodations came in various classes and usage fees were charged: the minimum fee for a cold bath or cold shower-bath was one penny. The fee bought users clean water and a clean towel – no soap as yet.[27]

Britain's provisions served as a model for other European and American cities, which soon followed with municipal provisions of their own. The most influential alternative to the British model was

Illustration of men's public baths, Golden Lane, London, 1866. Note the edifying mottoes on the ceiling.

Dr Oskar Lassar's *Volksbad*, rough-and-ready showering pavilions built of corrugated iron which were introduced at the Berlin Hygiene Exhibition in 1883 and widely deployed throughout German and American schools and factories in subsequent years. Many sanitarians prefered showers to baths (for the poor at least) because they were seen to be more invigorating and hygienic, not to mention less expensive and easier to maintain. They were also better at washing masses of bodies at once: the American sanitarian William Paul Gerhard noted approvingly that, with a mere eighteen compartments, 300 soldiers could be cleansed in one hour.[28] Whether baths or showers, however, the provision of such public facilities meant that private ones would not regularly be included in working-class homes throughout Europe until the 1920s and sometimes much later.

As the examples of showers demonstrate, hygiene regimes were most strictly enforced in institutions, such as prisons, orphanages and asylums, where authorities had a high degree of control over individual bodies. In particular, Alain Corbin describes armies as 'laboratories' where new techniques to clean and deodorize bodies and spaces were first formulated; in France, he stresses, this was at least 50 years before similar reforms were attempted in workers' housing.[29] Already in the last quarter of the eighteenth century, soldiers' tents, ships and hospitals were models of hygiene, designed to ensure the circulation of clean air through ventilation and effective latrine accommodation. Institutional baths, showers and latrines subjected users to external supervision and policing as a matter of course. Michel Foucault noted how the toilets at France's École Militaire enabled 'hierarchical observation' to prevent inappropriate sexual behaviour, with half-doors so that 'the supervisor on duty could see the head and legs of the pupils, and side walls sufficiently high "that those inside cannot see one another"'.[30]

Similar observations apply to the British Army from the mid-eighteenth century onwards: technologies to secure clean water were

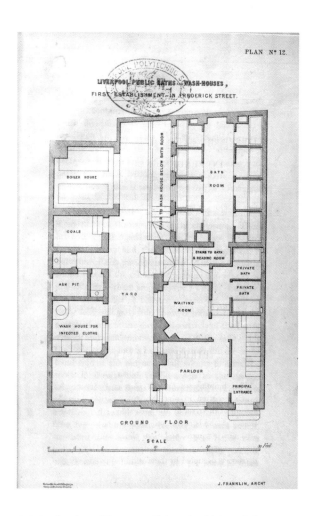

PLAN Nº 12.

LIVERPOOL PUBLIC BATHS AND WASH-HOUSES,
FIRST ESTABLISHMENT—IN FREDERICK STREET.

BOILER HOUSE

STAIR TO WASH HOUSE BELOW BATH ROOM

BATH ROOM

COALS

STAIRS TO BATH & READING ROOM

PRIVATE BATH

ASH PIT

YARD

PRIVATE BATH

WAITING ROOM

WASH HOUSE FOR INFECTED CLOTHS

PARLOUR

PRINCIPAL ENTRANCE

GROUND FLOOR

SCALE

J.FRANKLIN, ARCH.

seen as fundamental to the 'warlike expeditions' of 'the globe-per-vading British race'.[31] Many British soldiers first encountered water closets not in the streets of their village but in barracks or hospitals. At the 1,500-bed model hospital at Renkioi, built in 1855 during the Crimean War, engineer Isambard Kingdom Brunel prioritized good

The first public wash house and private baths establishment, Frederick Street Baths, Liverpool, 1842.

drainage and sanitation and insisted on flush toilets as the only way to guarantee 'comfort and cleanliness'. Brunel provided separate rooms for water closets and for baths in each ward and equipped them with George Jennings' tip-up washbasins and simplified water closets. Aware that most patients would not be familiar with the latter, he sent along printed instructions for their use.[32]

Florence Nightingale admired Renkioi's arrangements and its low mortality rate (her own hospital's much higher mortality rate was blamed in part on defective sewers). In her later writings on hospitals, Nightingale insisted on 'water-closets of the best construction', which she described as: 'A siphon water-closet of a hemispherical shape, *never of a conical shape*, and abundantly supplied with water to flush it out with a large forcible stream.'[33] Sanitarians anticipated

Bathroom at the Central Street Cleansing Station, London, 1914.

that, once soldiers were trained in correct hygiene practices and technologies, they would bring them back home and help diffuse them among the civilian population.

The prince's water closet

Inspection was vital to maintaining both military and civilian sanitary regimes. Even the British royal family's sanitary arrangements were not above public scrutiny, and one incident in particular shows how much authority the sanitary idea had gained in the decades since the 1850s. At the end of 1871, Bertie, the Prince of Wales (later Edward VII), was struck down by typhoid. The two-month saga of his illness, updated daily in every British newspaper, was as suspenseful as a detective serial. And the prince's illness did become a detective story of sorts, as identifying the source of his contagion was the focus of constant speculation and controversy. The leading medical journal *The Lancet* undertook and published a sanitary audit of both Londesborough Lodge in Yorkshire, where the prince had been a guest just prior to his illness, and his Norfolk estate, Sandringham. All the soil pipes and sewerage at Londesborough Lodge were minutely inspected and described, along with the water closet used by the prince ('The closet is of the ordinary pan construction. It is in good order, and there is depth of three inches of water standing in the pan.'[34]) Even judged against the standards of today's tabloids the report seems astonishingly intrusive, but was justified by the fact that the prince was a 'public' figure, hence his health and plumbing arrangements were fair game.

After his recovery, the chastened prince supposedly remarked, 'If I were not a prince, I would be a plumber.'[35] But given that the link between good plumbing and health had been asserted for many years (not least since Prince Albert's death in 1861 was blamed on typhoid fever), why were people still so ignorant of sanitary principles? In the wake of the prince's illness, sanitarians redoubled their efforts to improve knowledge both among builders and plumbers and among the public of all classes. Just as sanitary commissions were founded to improve the hygiene of soldiers, so too were organizations established to aid the civilian population. One such organization was the Sanitary Institute, which administered exams for sanitary inspectors (many of whom were women) and tested their knowledge of sinks, toilets, drains and ventilation pipes in preparation for house-to-house and factory visits. For the edification of the layperson, such organizations also sponsored a steady stream of lectures, hygiene fairs, journals and books. Surveying the dynamic hygiene scene in the 1870s and '80s, the engineer Samuel Stevens Hellyer concluded that Bertie's near death had done wonders 'for the advancement of the principles of sanitary plumbing'.[36]

The sanitarians' shared goal was to rid houses of sewer gas, a dangerous effluvium of gases including hydrogen sulphide and ammonia, and they had one main remedy: proper ventilation. One of the principle tenets of sanitary plumbing was that, in all houses, the soil pipe should be extended to the roof to discharge foul air, while another inlet should be provided to admit fresh air. Another important principle was that every sanitary fitting have its own waste pipe and trap rather than sharing one or being un-trapped, and that all fittings be perfectly joined to avoid leaks. In the sanitarians' writings, the house emerged as a nexus of water- and airflows that needed constant supervision, a task they assigned to the mistress of the household. She was instructed to conduct weekly inspections of every water closet, sink, housemaid's closet, scullery, dustbin or dust-hole to ensure cleanliness and to keep her family safe.[37] But what were women to look for? How could they hope to understand this new, multi-layered, gaseous world?

The question posed a real challenge because plumbing was largely buried underground and sewer gas was invisible unless revealed by

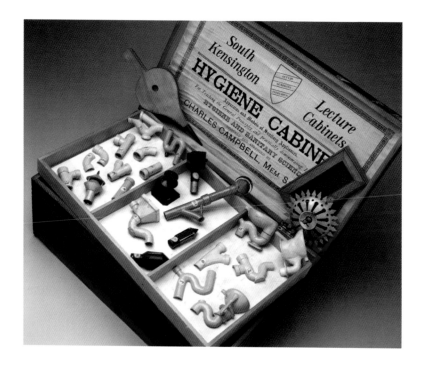

smoke or by smell in the form of peppermint oil tests. Sanitarians thus relied on sanitary sections to show the public how individual fixtures, pipes, sewers and vents formed an interconnected system and to pinpoint potential sources of leaks within it. The same principle was also applied to models of dwellings. At the International Health Exhibition in London in 1884, full-scale sections of a sanitary and an insanitary house were presented.[38] Though always done in the name of education, sanitary sections, with their depictions of plumbing gone bad, had a sensational feel, not unlike that of contemporary ghost stories, as they depicted foul air seeping into the house with deadly consequences. In contrast to the prevailing domestic ideal, where the private house was a bastion against the dangerous influences of the outside

Hygiene demonstration cabinet, English, 1895, used by Charles Campbell, a member of the Sanitary Institute, 1895.

world, these images depicted the home as inherently vulnerable to invasion, its very atmosphere charged with threat. As Annmarie Adams remarks, it seemed as if illness could pass through 'walls, water, people, and things, seemingly defying the system of physical barriers prescribed by contemporary science'.[39]

Along with sanitary sections, comparative displays were another didactic technique enlisted by sanitarians. It featured prominently, for instance, at London's Parkes Museum. *The Lancet* declared the new hygiene museum's collection of water closets to be among its most important exhibits. Asserting that water closets were 'the most common cause of unhealthiness in a modern dwelling', the journal enthusiastically set about contrasting a range of models: Jennings's Monkey Closet was compared to Hellyer's Patent Vortex Closet and Trap and to Pearson's Patent Trapless Twin-basin Closet, and so on – a useful exercise at a time when there was a bewildering array of water closets in production (pan, hopper, valve, plug or plunger,

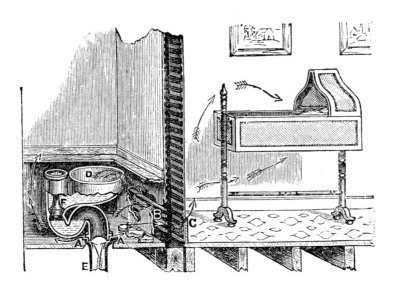

S. S. Hellyer, 'A Dangerous Water Closet', in *The Plumber and Sanitary Houses* (1887).

67

wash-out, wash-down and siphonic).[40] Bodies like the Sanitary Institute also undertook testing of water closets, traps and drains at its annual trade fairs. At the International Health Exhibition, *The Lancet* reported that a jury had flushed a 'certain number of potatoes' and papers down a variety of water closets to test the force of their flushes. The stress on effective flushing reflected sanitarians' faith in 'copious flushes' as the surest means by which to keep soil pipes and basins fresh and disease at bay.[41]

For all of this progress in sanitary matters, many people at the end of the nineteenth century remained as indifferent or hostile as before. Ratepayers were by no means always keen to fund necessary infrastructural improvements; speculative builders, landlords or factory owners still challenged sanitary laws in the courts and found 'extraordinary loopholes', which they duly exploited.[42] More fundamentally, throughout the century, the fact that a basic necessity like water was sold for commercial gain caused constant tension, especially in cases when water companies adopted practices that went against the public interest. Even though they were being written into public health legislation and promoted as key to improving the labouring classes, water companies charged users for each water closet and bath they installed in the home – a fee that, as one Member of Parliament furiously noted, would compel 'inhabitants to deny themselves the use of these conveniences, so absolutely indispensable to cleanliness, health, and decency'.[43] Private water companies were also not keen to install and maintain pipes in poorer parts of towns. Such blatant inequities and conflicts of interest led to the municipal takeover of water companies across Britain, and to the creation of London's Metropolitan Water Board in 1902. (In 1989 London's water supply was re-privatized under Margaret Thatcher's government.)

As often as water closets supported important Victorian social values, they openly clashed with others. For instance, the principles of sanitary science and the Victorian ideal of womanhood collided in London in the last decades of the nineteenth century when, in spite of vigorous campaigning from the Ladies' Sanitary Association and other bodies, some local governments resisted building women's public conveniences. There was a long tradition of objecting to public conveniences for men on the grounds that they would offend female passers-by. In 1849, the opening of the public necessaries in Rose Street immediately attracted a complaint from Warden R. J. Butler of the nearby House of Charity. Though he claimed to be 'very unwilling to disparage the feeling, which has led the Commissioners thus to provide accommodation to the public', he was apprehensive that ladies' walking by would see 'much that is disagreeable'. In the spirit of compromise, however, he suggested that a less visible sign be erected over the entrance and a spring door be installed, presumably to prevent women inadvertently catching a glimpse of men going about their business inside.[44]

Objections grew when it was proposed that conveniences should actually be provided for women. Though some conveniences for women were successfully established by the 1890s, they were far less numerous than those for men, in part due to the determined opposition of councilmen and local residents. These parties objected to them not only on the grounds that they would lower property values (a complaint levelled against male facilities as well), but also that facilities for women were 'immoral' – 'abominations'. By allowing women to move more comfortably through the city streets, conveniences undercut the ideal of femininity as static and ethereal and instead highlighted female physicality and bodily needs – clearly not a palatable option for London's ratepayers. Even when facilities were grudgingly provided, frustrated supporters like playwright George Bernard Shaw observed that their penny charge put them out of the range of the working-class women who most needed them.[45]

For all of these disparities and contradictions, however, by the end of the century, water closets, running water and baths played at least some part in the everyday lives of a large number of metropolitan dwellers. Some would have had these amenities at home; many others would have accessed them away from home. According to one report, in 1891–2 the bathhouses of London served nearly 1.5 million bathers.[46] Perhaps even more striking given the grim utilitarianism of today's provision, these facilities tended to be handsome landmarks – stone-faced buildings in the classical or Gothic style with marble wall partitions and counters, teak fittings and decorative tiles – proud statements of civic pride. And Britain's sanitary system, its waterborne sewerage and public health legislation, was increasingly the gold standard by which other countries and metropolises measured their own civility.

Britannia's bathrooms rule the waves

Britain's sanitary model was spread around the world through a variety of channels. Leading figures involved with British sanitary reform and sewerage were often consulted for their expertise. Edwin Chadwick is the single figure most often mentioned in this regard: his acolyte, William Lindley, for instance, was responsible for designing Hamburg's sewer system in 1843. Perhaps apocryphally, Chadwick is even credited with inspiring Napoleon III's interest in sewers by challenging the emperor to leave Paris smelling 'sweet'.[47] Bazalgette, too, did a considerable amount of consulting, for other British towns and for foreign communities including Budapest and Port Louis, Mauritius.[48]

Competition between cities continued to be a main spur to sanitary improvements. Metropolises actively studied the sewers and sanitary provisions of their rivals: for instance, Vienna dispatched one local councillor to London in 1861 and in 1862 to the Great London

Exhibition, to bring back different urinal models.[49] And in the 1890s, when New York City was researching different models of public baths and what were euphemistically called 'comfort stations' (public conveniences), it surveyed developments in European cities such as Vienna, Gothenburg, Milan and Berlin as a matter of course. In terms of comfort stations, the Mayor's Committee pronounced it to be most impressed by the City of London's underground conveniences, which were 'clean, inodorous, hidden from view, and attractive' and could, in theory at least, separately accommodate men and women. They were also financially self-supporting. New York City's strong preference for London was to be expected given that its public health legislation was modelled on England's; interestingly, the committee members rejected Paris out of hand, sniffing that its urinals 'disfigure the public thoroughfares and offend public decency'.[50]

As the New York example also shows, scientific papers, reports and publications played an essential role in diffusing technical information. A commission of 1857 studying how best to improve drainage in Calcutta affirmed that it had examined 'the Reports on the Drainage or Water Supply of Bombay, Madras, New York, and other Cities; and . . . the systems adopted in some European Towns, especially the views recently set forth to the London Metropolitan Commission of Sewers' – a reference to Bazalgette and Haywood's first report on intercepting sewers in 1854, which shows how rapidly information about sanitary innovations was distributed.[51] Again, it is not surprising that Britain's model carried such weight in India. Its colonies modelled their own sanitary legislation on Britain's or had it imposed on them by a cadre of colonial administrators and military authorities along with related infrastructural improvements. At the turn of the twentieth century, the British Private Secretary of the Maharaja of Mysore described their role thus: '[We, the British] cleared out the slums, straightened and widened the roads, put in a surface drainage system leading into the main sewers that discharged into septic tanks . . . and tidied up generally.'[52]

As part of these 'tidying up' efforts, British colonies such as Kingston, Kampala, Dakar, Hong Kong, Calcutta, Singapore, Toronto and Melbourne built water, drainage and sewer systems, though their benefits were certainly not equally distributed among all urban dwellers. (They could also backfire: notoriously in Mumbai, then Bombay, the disastrous combination of an overabundant supply of piped water and decrepit drainage created a marshy breeding ground for disease.[53]) The United States also actively mobilized infrastructure and hygiene to civilize and to segregate different sexes, classes and races at home and abroad in its newly acquired territories such as Cuba, Puerto Rico, Hawaii and the Philippines. When America acquired a new territory, Daniel Max Gerling observes, its Bureau of Insular Affairs immediately embarked on 'the widespread inspection of water closets in the homes of the citizens, construction of sewers, creation of new laws dedicated to proper defecation techniques, and administration of harsh punishment for those who resisted'.[54] They also sought to promote sanitary principles through education, fairs and fiestas: in the Philippines, the Americans instituted a national Clean-up Week which featured, among others, Scrubbing Day and Privy Day, when everyone was expected to build new toilets or repair existing ones.[55]

Our understanding of the spread of the sanitary idea is not complete if we do not also consider the crucial role played by British entrepreneurs, who developed and sold not simply individual fittings but whole sanitary systems. We will take two as representative: George Jennings and Walter Macfarlane. Jennings, of course, had supplied water closets to the Great Exhibition and was a very good sanitary engineer, responsible for a diverse array of patents.[56] He was also one of the first manufacturers of sanitaryware to diversify, producing everything from brass valves to stoneware pipes in his many factories. His ability to manufacture metal *and* potted goods was a real advantage, as sanitaryware had components of both: even a humble pan closet might have an earthenware basin, tinned copper pan and cast-iron receiver, not to mention the various materials needed for the cistern, trap and soil pipe. (Most other manufacturers bought some components from others – Thomas Crapper, for instance, got his bowls from Twyford's – and combined them into whole units for sale.[57])

Jennings also stands out for the way he understood and fully exploited the possibilities of publicity from the start. He excelled at 'brand placement', a tradition he began with the Great Exhibition and continued by overseeing the sanitary arrangements at other major events, including a thanksgiving service at St Paul's Cathedral to celebrate the Prince of Wales's recovery from typhoid. He enthusiastically embraced international trade fairs and won many prizes and accolades. More importantly, he used trade fairs to connect with potential buyers: after he had personally escorted Sydney's city surveyor around his stand at the 1879 International Exhibition in Australia, for instance, the city council placed a direct order for two of Jennings's stoneware urinals and later purchased twelve more.[58] Jennings also led the crusade for public conveniences or 'halting stations' as he called them, even proposing to install them for free in exchange for a charge for the use of closets and towels. By the end of the century, Jennings-designed facilities were installed throughout the City of London (possibly the same ones praised by New York's Mayor's Committee) as well as in 36 other British towns.

This summary by no means does justice to all the facets of Jennings's career or that of his firm, which after his death in 1882 carried on until the 1960s. However, it conveys a sense of the scale and international scope of the British sanitaryware business in the second half of the nineteenth century. For all his entrepreneurial acumen, Jennings was not

unique. Other manufacturers, including Thomas Twyford (followed by his son, Thomas William), John Shanks, Edward Johns, Henry Doulton and Thomas Crapper had equally notable careers. Like Jennings, they did not wait idly for customers to come to them: rather, they constantly developed new products, diversified production, improved sales through networks of agents and export trade representatives, built up their reputations through trade fairs and inspired customers with often stunning illustrated catalogues and showrooms. Their collective efforts were vital to the spread of sanitary apparatuses across the modernizing world. *The Lancet*, which faithfully reported on advances in water closet design for many decades, claimed that sanitary reformers, especially in France, owed Jennings and others a great 'debt of gratitude' for making known 'what constitutes a proper sanitary apparatus'.[59] Or, as the modernist

George Jennings's exhibit at the Centennial Exhibition, Philadelphia, 1876.

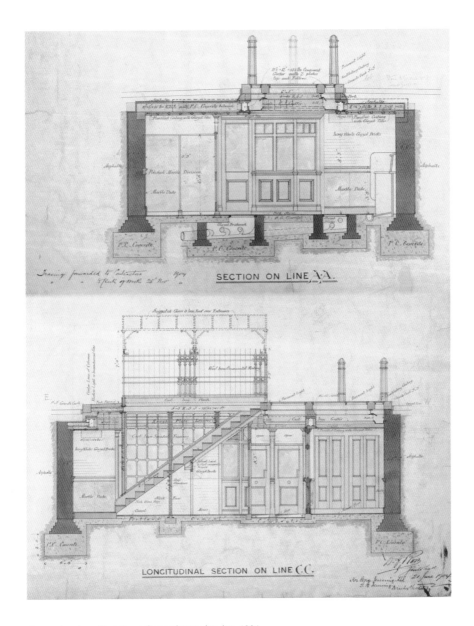

SECTION ON LINE A.A.

LONGITUDINAL SECTION ON LINE C.C.

George Jennings, Fleet Street Conveniences, London, 1904.

architect Adolf Loos more flippantly put it, in terms of plumbing, 'the English have been leading the French around on a string the whole time.'[60]

The reason English manufacturers surged so decisively ahead was that they had the strength of the British pottery and iron industries behind them. Other European countries were producing very little sanitaryware, pipes and fittings, and what they were producing was largely inferior in quality. Until the 1880s, for instance, there was still limited manufacturing capacity in America.[61] Thus British manufacturers faced minimal competition internationally and could confidently target the export market, especially in the colonies. For the Canadian market, Edward Johns designed a water closet with a trap outlet and drainpipes that went into the cellar and would not freeze during harsh winters. Appropriately, this popular closet was called 'The Empire'. Thousands were sold.[62]

The story of how Josiah Wedgwood modernized the pottery industry in Staffordshire from the mid-eighteenth century onwards is well known. At his model factory, Etruria, Wedgwood strictly divided up the labour that went into the production process and continually refined production techniques until he could reliably manufacture high-quality, uniform goods at scale – exactly what the sanitaryware industry required.[63] In the last decades of the eighteenth century, sanitaryware was a modest staple of Wedgwood's business: he made bowls for water closet manufacturers like Joseph Bramah, and simple funnel-like hoppers, bedpans, chamber pots and washbasins. Later potters carried on Wedgwood's interest in rationalized production, particularly Thomas Twyford, who built Cliffe Vale in 1887, the first purpose-built sanitaryware factory, designed to improve worker's health and productivity through the incorporation of natural light and good ventilation (to combat 'potter's rot', a pulmonary disease caused by the silica in clay dust). Twyford also carried on Wedgwood's

tradition of experimentation, constantly introducing new materials and products, as we will see in chapter Two.

The role of Britain's iron industry in supporting its sanitary revolution has been less frequently acknowledged. Yet iron foundries had played a decisive role in the development of the water system since the early nineteenth century, when cast iron supplanted lead as the preferred material for piping. (Many nineteenth-century cast-iron pipes remain in use today.) By the 1850s, iron foundries in the Midlands and in Scotland were also producing vast quantities of sanitary castings, from cisterns to urinals, for the domestic and international markets. Today we associate iron founders most immediately with the claw-foot, cast-iron bath that was ubiquitous in late-Victorian homes; however, cast iron was also favoured for

Cliffe Vale Pottery, Staffordshire, in Joseph Hatton, *Twyfords: A Chapter in the History of Pottery* (1897).

public or institutional facilities, where its ruggedness and cheapness often gave it the edge over earthenware, much like stainless steel today.[64]

Although Shanks may be most closely associated with sanitary castings for the home, Walter Macfarlane & Co.'s Glasgow-based Saracen Foundry emerged as one of the most important suppliers for the public realm. Macfarlane was certainly one of the most high-minded and articulate when it came to his products. Volume Two of Macfarlane's magnificent 1862 catalogue opened with the text of a lecture on sewerage that he had delivered to the Philosophical Society of Glasgow five years before. Macfarlane had patented a public water closet range already in the early 1850s: enclosed by cast-iron screens perforated with ventilation holes, these closets were essentially troughs that were flushed with water and emptied once a day. Although troughs were hardly sanitary given that waste could fester in them for 24 hours, they were cheap and durable enough to prevent theft or vandalism. Macfarlane claimed they could be found throughout Scotland, Continental Europe and America by the 1860s.

All Macfarlane's catalogues made a clear equation between public facilities and improved morality. As he put it in 1857: 'At present, generally speaking, no provision is made for the out-door male and female population, and thus their habits in this respect are much the same as those of lower animals.'[65] The claim that there was 'no provision' was not entirely true, but Macfarlane's disgust at outdoor urination and defecation reflects the growing lack of tolerance for such practices, not least because they involved the public exposure of genitalia ('privates').[66] To drive home the point that his facilities encouraged decency, Macfarlane's catalogue from 1882 opened with an idyllic and elegant perspective view of a city street filled with his castings – a cast-iron shopfront, water trough, lamp, railings, bollards and urinal. This particular model of urinal could be purchased with an

exterior lamp to light the surrounding roadway, serving literally as a beacon of civilization in the city's darkness.

Glasgow was comparatively well equipped with conveniences in the nineteenth century – 198 urinals by 1875 – thanks to the crusading James Moir and his seminal visit to the Great Exhibition in 1851.[67] But, by making such products affordable, Macfarlane deserves credit for their spread as well. He shaped the form conveniences took, consulting with local authorities to plan and build facilities that met sanitary legislation like Scotland's Nuisance Removal Act. Significantly, just like modern street furnishing companies such as JCDecaux, Macfarlane sold sanitary systems: that is, he sold the facility along with the necessary products for keeping it clean (cleaning hose, dustbins) and orderly (screens, roofs, partitions, lighting and signage; every Macfarlane facility primly reminded users to 'Adjust your Dress Before Leaving'). His

Cast iron urinal, possibly by Walter Macfarlane & Co., Perth, Scotland, c. 1890. Note the lamplighter trimming the gas lamp atop the urinal.

'chaste' and increasingly refined structures were designed to ennoble the streets and, it was hoped, to mollify Nimby property owners who, from Glasgow to Vienna to New York, were always the most determined opponents to public convenience construction.[68]

Even if Jennings is today far more commonly associated with sanitaryware than is Macfarlane, there are many similarities between the two men. Jennings was more innovative in terms of his designs but Macfarlane's were pragmatic responses to real-world problems (and he also won his share of prizes). Both men were canny businessmen and publicists who won contracts with British governments and with businesses who operated internationally, such as railway companies. In this way, Jennings's products could be found in Paris, Berlin, Vienna, Budapest and Philadelphia as well as cities in Argentina, South Africa, Mexico and Australia. Crucially, the success of the two men's businesses cannot be separated from Britain's military engagements abroad, since they both held contracts with the War Department; Jennings also worked with the Admiralty and the Royal Engineers. But sanitary products were not just business for either man: both were messianic about the civilizing properties of sanitary appliances and saw themselves as serving the public interest. Macfarlane would certainly have agreed with Jennings's declaration that 'the Civilisation of a People can be measured by their domestic and Sanitary appliances.'[69]

Had he lived until the close of the century, Jennings might well have been satisfied with progress made on the plumbing and sanitation front. British achievements in these fields were undeniable. The water closet had been thoroughly incorporated into the modern water system and, as a piece of technology and as an architectural space it had become central to plans for improving public health and morals. Rather than sanitary reform, it is more accurate to say that Britain led a sanitary revolution, one that profoundly shaped how the boundaries

of public and private life were drawn and the effects of which we continue to live with today. British sanitaryware, pipes and fittings had
monopolized the international market for well over four decades and
exports would continue to account for more than 50 per cent of many
companies' sales.[70] 'It is a common thing', remarked Joseph Hatton of
Twyford's, 'for orders to be received from remote towns in South
America for the rearrangement of the sanitary works of an entire
community.'[71] From the 1890s onwards, however, many countries
began to develop their own manufacturing capabilities: by the end of
the century, for instance, Indian producers were able to meet locally
the demand for supply piping and sanitary fittings.[72] And in the
increasingly competitive overseas market, the British would lose
ground to one country in particular: America.

2 The Iconic Bathroom

> The plumber . . . is the pioneer of cleanliness. He is the first artisan
> of the state, the billeting officer of culture, of today's prevailing
> culture. Every English washbowl with its faucet and casting is a sign
> of English progress.
> Adolf Loos, 'Plumbers' (1898)

Adolf Loos despaired. The architect, now recognized as one of the
fathers of modernism, believed that Germany and Austria had lost
their pre-eminence in design and in culture at large. This decline, for
Loos, had an obvious if surprisingly mundane cause: the British had
taken the lead in plumbing. Even more amazing from a European perspective, so too had the Americans. In his essay 'Plumbers' of 1898,
Loos identified one particular design variation as symptomatic of the
differing attitudes towards bathing and dirt in Anglo-America and his
own country. Instead of white tiles, Germans still preferred coloured
ones, supposedly on the grounds that these made dirt *less* visible. For
Loos this confirmed just how much they had to learn.

Loos was not alone in his appreciation of Anglo-American residential bathrooms. In the nineteenth century, as we have seen, the
British led the world in sanitary technology and infrastructural innovations. At the same time, however, they had also earned a reputation
for artistic and beautiful bathrooms, arranged like furnished rooms
with chairs, carpets, beautifully decorated tiles and ceramic ware
encased in fine woods. As the German architectural commentator
Hermann Muthesius stated, 'England has led all the continental countries in developing the bathroom.'[1] Yet, rather than the luxurious
bathrooms at the upper end of the market, Loos and Muthesius

Twyford's Unitas wash-out pedestal closet won Queen Victoria's approval in 1886.

reserved their highest praise for the functional and plain bathrooms of the lower middle classes, with their exposed pipes and fixtures. By the 1890s, the move towards 'open style' plumbing was beginning to affect all classes of bathrooms. It was becoming a mark of modernity.

But above all, as Loos's disparaging comments about coloured tiles highlight, it was the shift to white that became the truest and most reliable index of modernity. And not just of the bathroom's modernity but of the modernity of architecture itself. White fixtures and plain plumbing acted as guarantees that architecture was purging itself of the 'false taste' and 'scandalous' love of surface ornamentation that characterized Victorian design.[2] Both Le Corbusier and Sigfried Giedion saw it in this way, noting that the unadorned bathroom represented a more natural, honest and masculine aesthetic order than had previously existed. For these commentators, the exposed, white bathroom represented nothing less than the true spirit of modernism.

In reality, the stylistic and technological developments praised by Loos, Muthesius, Le Corbusier and Giedion were never inevitable. They happened in response to a host of social, technical and scientific changes. And they did not happen overnight. This chapter sets out to trace the development of the modern bathroom with its three standard fixtures: water closet, bath and sink. Why and how did it emerge? For that matter, why was it ever felt that a distinct 'bath room' was necessary at all? If this sounds like an absurd question, recall that a separate room was not thought essential by the Georgians, who rediscovered the habit of washing and bathing, mainly for curative purposes, after it fell out of favour in the Elizabethan era. Indeed, the bathroom's rationale was not obvious, for if you were a person of means – with staff to heat and carry dozens of gallons of hot water up and down the stairways of your home – you would likely have been quite content bathing in your bedroom. And if you were further down the social ladder it would have been quite logical to bathe in the kitchen, where hot water could easily be drawn from the boiler and the fire could warm you.

Like the Georgians, early Victorians did not see the need for a bathroom. Activities like bathing continued to take place in an ad hoc manner mostly in kitchens, bedrooms and dressing rooms. When bathrooms were provided, their fittings and arrangement were not fixed. This was often because people only added fittings to their homes incrementally, when money and space became available: they might have a water closet, for instance, but no washbasin or bath, or vice versa. But the diversity also reflected the fact that Victorians also had a wider repertoire of sanitary appliances to choose from than we do today. Consider baths. If a Victorian wanted to bathe with water instead of, say, vapour or steam (also popular until the end of the century), he or she might have chosen a free-standing slipper or boot bath, lounge bath, sitz bath – even a leg bath or foot tub. Full-length baths were not practical because of the amount of water they used, hence smaller models remained in widespread use late into the nineteenth century. Yet by the end of the century it was clear that the idea of a dedicated bathroom, with a more strictly delineated range of equipment, had carried the day. How and why did this come to pass?

Fixing the Victorian bathroom

The first answer to the question of why and how the modern bathroom emerged lies in the greater availability of plumbed-in water supplies. In the later decades of the nineteenth century, as water supplies were increasingly plumbed in to the home, movable fittings – baths and washbasins – could be fixed into place in a room of their own; in short, fittings became fixtures. Yet the use of portable bathroom equipment such as washstands, ewers, bowls and chamber pots persisted among the wealthier classes, who used them alongside rather

than in place of plumbed-in baths, showers, sinks and water closets. This was because they had servants to carry buckets of water and to empty chamber pots into dedicated 'slop sinks' or 'sloppers', which allowed older habits to persist. (As the social historian Alison Light observes, 'No lady would flit along a corridor to use a lavatory [that is, water closet] at night.'[3]) It also reflected the widespread fear of sewer gas, which stoked resistance to plumbed-in fittings for decades.[4] The lack of public facilities also meant that, when on the move, Victorians went out armed with an impressive array of portable appliances for their relief, such as bourdalous (slipper-like ceramic receptacles that could fit under women's long skirts) or collapsible travelling baths, made of new flexible materials like gutta-percha, a kind of natural latex.

But plumbed-in water supplies did not automatically make the kitchen or bedroom bath redundant for another simple reason.

Glass bottle-shaped female urinal, 1701–30.

Although it was technically possible to distribute cold water to any room in the house, and a quick cold shower formed part of many Victorians' morning routines, there was not yet an efficient way to heat this water. Many inventions were patented in the race to remedy this inconvenience. From the 1850s, self-heating baths and showers were sold with their own dedicated heat sources. Some came with their own coal-fired stoves and boilers and used existing chimney flues to draw away smoke.[5] Other baths were galvanized, fixed with metal plates heated from below by an open gas flame. Needless to say, the flames were extinguished before one got in.

Gas-heated bath made by G. Shrewsbury, London, c. 1885.

Suppliers of these early self-heating baths were not sanitaryware manufacturers like Jennings or Doulton. Rather they were 'kitcheners', iron founders who also manufactured boilers, kitchen stoves and ranges, such as Benham & Sons, who described themselves as *'Stove, Grate, Kitchen Range and Bath Manufacturers, General Smiths, Bell-Hangers, Hot Water and Gas Engineers, & etc.'* Founders like these were out in force at the Great Exhibition in 1851, promoting the virtues and pleasures of heated baths to the public. In his advertising prospectus the ironmonger James Barlow explained:

> The great difficulty that has hitherto existed in many houses, has been the want of a ready convenience for heating the water, and this has induced many persons to adopt the expensive and objectionable plan of resorting to public bathing establishments, where the good effects they might otherwise receive from their use, are often counteracted by the chance of taking cold in returning home. These objections are now most successfully obviated: this Bath with Fifty Gallons of Water, in summer, may be sufficiently heated (at the bed-side if required) in the short space of Twenty-five minutes, at the trifling cost of Three-pence.[6]

However great the potential advantages of self-heating gas baths, their disadvantages were equally apparent. They generated soot and unpleasant smells. Even more worrying, they had what one manufacturer delicately referred to as 'a liability to explode', though this problem was partially alleviated by the invention of safer and more efficient Bunsen burners from 1855 onwards.[7] And in the mid-1870s, even more effective new boilers called 'geysers' were invented that sped up the heating process to about five minutes.

The geysers' most serious drawback was the fact that they had to be directly attached to a particular appliance. By contrast, coal kitchen ranges could supply a whole house through a back boiler that circulated

hot water up to a storage tank and cold water from a cistern back down to the range. Further improvements to this basic circulation system, such as the replacement of a roof tank with a cylinder in the kitchen, meant that by the end of the century a single 'circulator' could supply a whole house with hot water.[8] But even if the rise of such fixed-pipe hot water systems made dedicated bathrooms more feasible, they did not immediately spell the end to kitchen baths. The sanitary engineer Samuel Stevens Hellyer continued to favour them for working-class houses to save on plumbing costs and space, and even suggested enclosing baths with lids so that they could double as

Geyser in A. C. Martin, *The Modern Practical Plumber* (1934).

a seat. (One bath-seat made a humorous appearance in 1920 in the brilliant Buster Keaton film *Scarecrow*, but was trumped by the cartoonist William Heath Robinson's even more absurd, space-saving 'combined bath-bedroom' of the 1930s.) Folding baths that could be simply tucked away into a cabinet or press after use were available throughout the nineteenth and twentieth centuries.

For those with the space, staff and money, however, a dedicated family bathroom with plumbed-in baths and washbasins was becoming an expected amenity in the home. The architect Calvert Vaux's

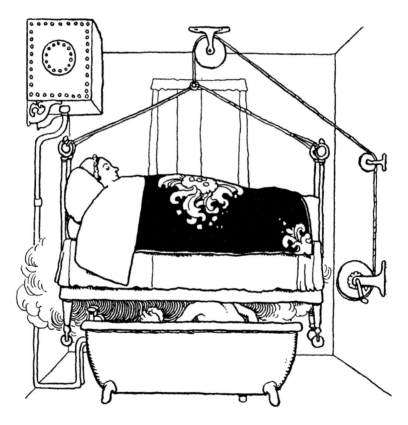

William Heath Robinson, 'A Combined Bath and Bedroom', in *How to Live in a Flat* (1936).

Villas and Cottages (1864) is a good index of when American houses were believed to merit their installation. Vaux's book provided plans for and commentary on villas and cottages that could be built for a cost ranging from $1,500 to about $20,000. While rural residences at the lower end of this scale were equipped with privies (for which Vaux included his own, picturesque designs), a bath and a water closet were introduced into plans for cottages costing $3,500 and up. This corresponded to Vaux's view that bathrooms were not necessities; rather, he still described them as 'special' features – luxurious add-ons, like servants' staircases.[9] But this view would change decisively in the coming two decades, and by the early 1900s bathrooms were common features of American middle-class houses.[10]

When supplied, Vaux's bathrooms were located on the bedroom or chamber floor, which was typical of the day. The primary advantages to having a bathroom on the same floor as one's bedroom were comfort ('a hot bath can be taken at night without having to shiver one's way through the cold air of a corridor') and privacy.[11] As bodily privacy was increasingly stressed, it became ever more important that the bathroom not be located in a thoroughfare room such as a kitchen. As well as the practical need to be near an external wall with a window for ventilation, the desire to make the bathroom a space through which others could not pass resulted in the tendency to fix it at the home's perimeter. Another popular option was the en-suite bathroom, located in the dressing room off the main bedroom but tucked discreetly in recesses or behind curtains or doors. This was true of Queen Victoria's shower and bath at Osborne House, the royal family's retreat on the Isle of Wight, which were each enclosed in a separate cupboard.

The contrasts between bourgeois and working-class bathrooms, of course, went beyond their location in the house. Differences were instantly discernible in the materials and workmanship of the various fixtures and fittings. Prior to the 1870s, as the historian Maureen Ogle notes, the appearance of American bathrooms would often have been highly idiosyncratic because it was typical to hire plumbers to custom-make lead fittings, from cisterns to showers to baths.[12] Architects and engineers often had their own designs made up rather than order ready-made ones, possibly because fine imported English fittings were very expensive, and cheap domestic ones were still crude. According to company lore, for instance, the American iron founders Kohler Co. only branched into the sanitaryware market in 1883 when John Michael Kohler realized that the cast-iron water troughs and hog scalders it already produced could serve humans as well. After enamelling his company's existing line, Kohler added a note to his catalogue informing readers that 'When furnished with Legs can be used as a bathing tub'.[13]

This story rings true in the sense that common household items such as iron skillets still often served as vessels for bathing for poor Americans.[14] And purpose-made baths were little more than containers made of sheet metal or wood, tinned or japanned inside. Early cast-iron baths were finished with enamel paint that required reapplication after several years. Only the most expensive residential models were made of marble or copper; while marble was the grander material, copper was the more effective in terms retaining heat. (Of marble baths Hellyer dryly remarked, 'they not only look cold, but strike so.') One luxurious copper bath was described in 1851 as: 'A COPPER WARM BATH Marbled and Polished inside, fitted in a polished Mahogany Case with steps, and a moveable cane back for altering the length of bath at pleasure.'[15] With lacquered stopcocks and a copper shower rose, this tub was clearly meant to be beautiful, but the inclusion of an adjustable back demonstrates a concern for comfort, too. While the adjustable back never caught on, full-length baths did often have curved ends for reclining.

As well as making concessions to bodily comfort, the appliances supplied to the wealthier classes were more mechanically sophisticated than their cheaper counterparts. As we will see, the wealthy had valve water closets; their servants made do with pan closets or plain hoppers. And in contrast to the sheet-metal bath of the working classes, the wealthy had extravagant 'combination' shower-baths that offered a vast array of shower and spray settings. New York firm Meyer-Sniffen offered one combination bathtub in 1887 that required eight handles to operate: two handles controlled the ordinary plunge bath (one handle for hot water, one for cold); two controlled the shower; two more controlled the needle spray; one controlled a cold douche; and one opened and shut the waste. The British humorist A. P. Herbert recalled the befuddlement these options could cause: 'the only two [settings] which were effective were WAVE and FLOOD', he reported after an encounter with one formidable combination. 'WAVE shot out a thin jet of boiling water which caught me in the chest, and FLOOD filled the bath with cold water long before it could be identified and turned off.'[16]

Increasingly, however, it was the level of decoration and craftsmanship that visually separated cheap from expensive bathroom fixtures. As they were fixed into place in dedicated rooms (mostly converted bedrooms) rather than being tucked discreetly away, homeowners began to take greater care in choosing them. While rubble or brick plinths with rough, wooden seats were deemed adequate for lower-class closets, valve closets were enclosed in fine mahogany cabinets. Giedion commented disapprovingly on the amount of money spent in the later decades of the nineteenth century on wooden 'hoods' for combination bath-showers: in 1888, one example cost £60, over £4,000 today – a price that did not include any plumbing or fittings.[17] Top-of-the-line cast-iron baths might have artistic decoration of cast bronze on the exterior. But the most elaborate decoration was reserved for ceramic bathroom fittings. Ceramic ware had long been beautifully decorated – there are many remarkable Georgian chamber pots and bourdalous – but toilet bowls, washbasins and baths became increasingly lavish.

A committed if critical modernist, Giedion surveyed the Victorian scene with palpable disgust, using the words 'grotesque' and 'feminine' to describe these decorative flourishes. But he was consoled by the fact that this stylistic trend was beginning to change, an 'evolution' he tracked through the washbasin, stating: 'Like a kernel emerging from its shell, the washbasin through the decades breaks loose from its envelope of furniture.' In Giedion's account, it was in the first decades of the twentieth century that the washbasin at last found its 'natural shape', thanks to the processes of mechanization.[18] But the story of how and why plumbing came to be exposed is perhaps better understood when one traces the developments of another sanitary fitting: the water closet.

'Unitas' and 'Simplicitas'

As established in chapter One, the water closet was the most truly revolutionary feature of the Victorian bathroom, in social as well as in technical terms. The general story of its rise is well known. Sir John Harington, godson of Queen Elizabeth I, built the first working model of a flush water closet in 1592. His invention then lay dormant until the horologist Alexander Cummings patented a version in 1775. Joseph Bramah, a locksmith, then patented an improved model in 1778. This model became an early best-seller, with 6,000 reportedly sold in the two decades after its patent. Once it was established that a market existed for water closets and improved water supplies made them more practical, the competition to produce the 'best' model kicked off. From the 1870s on, an astonishing array of patents and types of water closet emerged, each of which was proclaimed superior to the others.

It is easy to get lost in the details of these innovations, so it is important to remember that there are basically two things that an effective water closet is required to do. The first is to flush away human waste; the second is to seal off the smells and gases associated with that waste. And Bramah's water closet, which had a hinged valve rather than a sliding one, as did Cummings's model, did both reasonably well. Its intricate mechanism was set into motion when the user lifted the handle, simultaneously releasing water from an over-head tank through an inlet pipe at the top of the bowl and opening a hinged outlet valve at the bottom. Standing water and waste was flushed away through a soil pipe with a water-sealed trap. When one bought a valve closet from Bramah, then, one was actually buying a complex assembly of parts – overhead tank, bowl, spreader, inlet pipe, overflow outlet, valves, operating mechanism (handle, levers, counter-weights), valve box, soil pipe – all in an attractive wooden cabinet that hid the mechanism beneath.

But valve closets had a tendency to fail. This was in part because initially all of their components were made of metal, even the bowl, which rusted through contact with water. Pottery bowls were an obvi-ous and inexpensive solution to this particular problem. Already in the late eighteenth century, Josiah Wedgwood was manufacturing bowls for Bramah and others. It soon became apparent that pottery was well suited for another job as well: creating the all-important water-sealed traps that prevented odours from entering the home, thus bypassing the need for a valve altogether. Pottery makers also began making cottage pans, basic toilet models for the lower end of the mar-ket, which consisted simply of a bowl and trap. At this stage, however, they still required wood or brick structures to support them.

Pottery had some clear advantages over metalware: it was cheaper, lighter and easier to clean. And potters like Twyford and Doulton had a powerful financial incentive to break into the water closet market

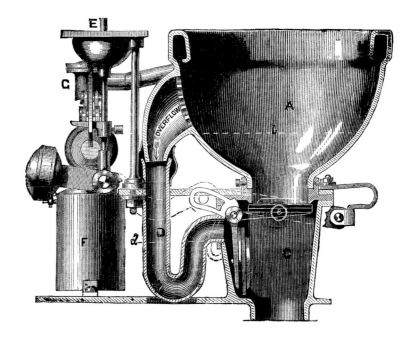

themselves. They received only about 2 shillings for their basins, while brass and iron founders got 20 to 50 shillings for their components.[19] But it was only in the 1870s and '80s that all-ceramic water closets at last came into their own, thanks to improvements in potting which made the manufacture of much larger pieces a possibility, and to the new zeal of the sanitarians. As we established in the previous chapter, sanitarians sought to combat sewer gas through ventilation, good plumbing and perfect joints and traps. For them, valve closets like Bramah's had a fatal flaw: the more intricate the mechanism, the greater the likelihood that one of its parts would rust, break or wear out, yet the closet's enclosure meant that it could not be easily inspected and repaired until it was too late.

Section of valve water closet in S. S. Hellyer, *The Plumber and Sanitary Houses* (1887). Note the flap-valve (e), separating the bowl from the valve-box. This valve would drop open to release the water once the handle (E) was raised.

In the 1870s, therefore, a powerful argument in favour of a simpler toilet emerged, preferably in a single piece to keep joints to a minimum. George Jennings had taken the first step in this direction with his one-piece ceramic 'monkey closets' at the Great Exhibition. These were the first 'wash-out' closets, so called because water hit the front of the bowl with enough force to wash waste backwards out over a weir into a trap. In most models of the 1870s, the flush swept across the bowl from the back, pushing contents out into a front trap and giving the wash-out a distinct frontal bulge. Jennings & Co. then upped the ante again, launching the Pedestal Vase closet at the International Health Exhibition in 1884, which enclosed the trap in a ceramic pedestal. The wooden seat was fixed to the wall and hinged, so the bowl could double as a slop sink and urinal. The Pedestal Vase also came with another innvative feature: a small siphonic cistern with a chain pull, containing enough water for a single 2-gallon (9-litre) flush.

The 2-gallon flush had been imposed in London as part of the Metropolis Water Act in 1871 in order to prevent water waste, which had reached extremely high levels: already in 1851, for instance, it was estimated that an incredible 29 million of the 44 million gallons pumped was wasted. This led to one of this era's most important inventions: the Water Waste Preventer designed by the plumber

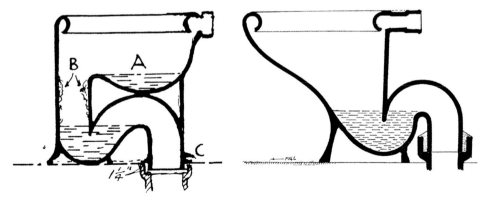

Sections of wash-out (left) and wash-down (right) water closets in A. C. Martin, *The Modern Practical Plumber* (1934).

Thomas Crapper, which ensured that only the right amount of water could leave the cistern with each flush and that it could no longer run continuously. (The fact that Crapper's cisterns all proudly bore his name is probably why toilets – which he did not manufacture directly himself – are still popularly associated with him today.[20] The 2-gallon limit was another important element of nineteenth-century efforts to control and manage water supply long term, and to establish clear definitions of what constituted 'normal' use. Like all issues to do with water, however, it was hotly contested, not least by the Sanitary Institute, who maintained that only 3 gallons would completely clear the toilet bowl and stop the spread of infectious disease. This was not mere conjecture: the Institute organized thirteen demonstrations between

An enclosed bathroom with 'Imperial' fixtures in *Catalogue 'G' Illustrating the Plumbing and Sanitary Department of the J. L. Mott Iron Works* (1888). Note the Combination Needle and Shower Bath, Foot Bath, and the Dolphin wash-out water closet.

1877 and 1893 across England and performed 800 experiments to prove that 2 gallons was inadequate.[21]

In spite of the Sanitary Institute's lobbying, the 2-gallon limit was widely adopted, a development that did not favour the wash-out, which required more water to be truly effective. The wash-down water closet then superseded the wash-out and became the preferred model in Britain. Wash-downs were very simple in construction, not unlike the funnel-style, short hoppers at the lower end of the market, but the trap was set higher so that it joined the bowl, raising the water level and reducing the amount of basin exposed. (It also meant that any waste dropped directly into water rather than lying exposed on a ledge

An aesthetic or 'open' bathroom in *Catalogue 'G' Illustrating the Plumbing and Sanitary Department of the J. L. Mott Iron Works* (1888).

as with the wash-out; for this reason, the wash-out remained the preferred model in countries such as Germany, where stools are inspected for signs of ill-health.[22]) The first all-ceramic one-piece wash-down, Frederick Humpherson's Beaufort, was debuted in 1885 at the meeting of the Sanitary Institute in Leicester.[23] It was soon followed by one of the most successful models, manufactured by Doulton: Simplicitas, whose name summed up its perceived attraction – its simple construction – perfectly.

Whether wash-out or wash-down, the ceramic pedestal closet's ascendance was assured by the Queen: after using Twyford's wash-out pedestal closet, the Unitas (pictured on p. 82), at the Angel Hotel in Doncaster in 1886, Victoria ordered several for Buckingham Palace. Regardless of its sanitary advantages, it is unlikely that Unitas would have won royal approval had its distinctive decoration not made it as elegant as a mahogany cabinet. Ceramic pedestals proved well suited to embossing, transfer decoration, hand painting and gilding – all the 'trimmings', as Giedion derisively called them. This meant that, initially at least, rather than having a stripped-down aesthetic, all-ceramic water closets were just as fantastical as their predecessors. In fact, during this period elaborate decorative schemes – 'Pompeiian', 'Elizabethan', 'Renaissance', 'Baronial' – began to extend across all of the bathroom's fittings, tiles and accessories: mirror frames, soap, sponge and brush trays, and toilet-paper holders. (The latter were still mostly designed to hold loose sheets of paper; perforated rolls would appear in the 1880s in Britain, shortly after their invention in America.[24])

Sanitarians were not troubled at first by decorative flourishes, because their priority had been to simplify water closet construction to prevent gases from escaping. Once they made progress on this front, however, they became more critical of decoration on the grounds that people spent too much money on it at the expense of good-quality plumbing. Harriette Plunkett, a sanitarian who wrote specifically for American women, summed up this view when she declared in 1885: 'Hand-painting is *not* essential to either health or happiness.' 'Of course,' she admitted, 'polished brass pipes have a certain elegance, but plain, well-made leaden ones have no occasion to be ashamed of themselves.'[25] Such sentiments chimed with those of the contemporary aesthetic movement, which advocated honesty in materials over 'sham' effects such as marbling; Plunkett herself referenced the American aesthetic bible *The House Beautiful* (1877), which championed simplicity and utility in home furnishings. Works like these increasingly attached moral significance to one's aesthetic choices.

For the most part, however, Plunkett's objections to decoration and covering up remained practical rather than aesthetic or moral. Encasing pipes or fittings made it more difficult to inspect them; air disinfectant, just hitting the market in the 1880s, was dangerous because it masked the telltale smell of blockages. Plunkett's belief in exposed plumbing led her to favour a more 'open' style of bathroom arrangement, noting approvingly:

> There is a growing fashion of arranging all fixtures in what is called the 'open' manner, i.e., with no wood casings about them at all. The bath-tubs stand up on feet, the lavatory-slabs [that is, the washbasin and marble surround] are supported on metallic brackets, and the whole arrangement leaves no dark corners to become filthy.[26]

In her concern for physical welfare and cleanliness, Plunkett prefigured the broader shift that would take place in the first two decades of the twentieth century when, as architectual historian Adrian Forty notes, the home was reshaped by the idea that 'the quality of the domestic environment had a major influence upon the physique and health of the nation.'[27] This new emphasis on functionality and health would have a major impact on the bathroom's status. Having become fixtures in the Victorian era, bathroom fittings were poised to become equipment in the modern one.

Marvels of constructive art

As evidence of the shift towards health as a priority in the early twentieth century, Forty notes that in domestic design the kitchen began to take on greater significance than the parlour, which had previously been the most symbolically important room in the home. It is certainly true that the kitchen became a focal point for domestic advisers and 'home engineers' for much of the twentieth century as they researched the home, its equipment and the labour of the housewife, all with an eye to creating a more efficient and hygienic domestic environment. By contrast, these same experts paid comparatively little attention to the design and arrangement of the bathroom, leaving these matters to manufacturers and plumbers or to the authors of architectural handbooks and building codes.

This, however, did not prevent the bathroom and its fittings from emerging as the modernist icon of choice. In fact, at the foundations of modernism we find not one but two toilets: Duchamp's *Fountain* (1917), widely considered the single most influential artwork of the twentieth century; and Edward Weston's *Excusado* (1925), a pathbreaking work of modernist photography whose subject was Weston's own toilet in his home in Mexico (*excusado*). And once we look to architecture, we find another iconic piece of lavatorial equipment, a pedestal sink, standing in the entrance of the key work of architectural modernism, Le Corbusier's Villa Savoye (1928–31).

The prominent role of the toilet in particular supports the artist Margaret Morgan's contention that it should be seen as the 'grand signifier of twentieth-century Modernism'.[28] But what exactly was it

Washbasin in entrance hall, Le Corbusier, Villa Savoye, Poissy, France, 1928–31.

believed to represent? Why did it – and bathroom fittings in general – become such a potent symbol of modernism? Very broadly speaking, from the opening decade of the twentieth century, bathroom fittings were used to help articulate modernist values, especially its central tenet, 'form follows function'. Perhaps the first to express this belief was Hermann Muthesius in the early 1900s when he identified the British bathroom as the place where 'Form . . . has evolved exclusively out of purpose.'[29] By the 1920s, this trope was so well established that it immediately sprang to Edward Weston's mind as he contemplated his Mexican toilet: '"Form follows function!" Who said this I don't know, but the writer spoke well!'[30] (The writer in question was the American architect Louis Sullivan, whose thoughts on the subject were to influence Adolf Loos and Le Corbusier.)

The modernist admirers of water closets had a very specific type in mind: the one-piece, all-ceramic model, now minus any extraneous decoration. Plain white water closets had been available since the 1880s, when they were sold as budget options and installed mainly in lower-middle-class homes. With their interest in social reform and workers' housing, it was perhaps inevitable that modernists were prepared to admire these basic models. But they also appreciated the fact that regardless of finish, upper- and middle-class bathrooms were all beginning to feature the same fittings (cast-iron baths) and technologies (wash-down water closets), in contrast to the earlier period, when fittings were sharply differentiated by class. As Le Corbusier observed, the fact that 'the objects of utility used by the rich and by the poor were not very different from one another' was a novel and socially radical feature of modernism.[31]

By this period, too, the 'open style' had decisively carried the day. Exposure was in; enclosure was out. In addition to its championing by sanitarians, the open style prevailed because it was now technically possible for most ceramic sanitaryware to be 'freed' from its envelope of furniture, just as the water closet had been. A great advance in potting came about in the 1850s with the introduction of a denser clay, known as fire clay, which enabled the manufacture of large, single pieces such as pantry sinks, slop hoppers, baths, urinals and, later, island wash fountains. These pieces were coated with porcelain enamel which, when fired at very high temperatures, produced 'a surface enamel polished as marble'.[32] These so-called 'porcelain baths' were ideally suited to use in institutions, hospitals and public baths, thanks to their impervious bodies and hard-wearing glazes. Moreover, lustrous fire-clay pieces were aesthetically pleasing enough that there was no longer a need to hide them beneath 'unsatisfactory and often insanitary wood tops, marble or slate'.[33] Fire clay's popularity only began to decline in the 1960s.

As a result of these innovations, Twyford biographer Joseph Hatton felt confident about declaring in 1897: 'it is now possible to produce lavatory ranges of any length, fitted together with joints so perfect and complete that they can scarcely be detected . . . *real marvels of constructive sanitary art*'.[34] Other advances further perfected the surfaces of bathroom fittings. One was the development of vitreous china, which steadily replaced earthenware between the 1920s and 1960s, at which point it dominated production. This was a fine, white clay that was far less porous (that is, far more vitreous) than earthenware; as a result it could be cast thicker than earthenware and its products were more resilient and did not crackle or craze.[35] In terms of metalware, a similar leap occurred with porcelain enamelling for cast-iron tubs, which was available by the 1870s in England and widespread by the turn of the century.[36] Porcelain enamelling gave cast-iron baths a durable finish that protected them from rusting or wear, offering a comparable product to fire-clay tubs at a fraction of the cost and weight (fire-clay tubs weighed about 800 kilograms). Lastly, improvements in metal casting methods changed the shape and appearance of bathroom fittings: they could now be produced in round, flowing shapes and be finished with chromium and nickel plating.

With these advances in 'sanitary art', the stage was set for the bathroom's transformation into modernist icon. Its ascendance was confirmed when in 1934 the architect Philip Johnson included several pieces of sanitaryware in his landmark 'Machine Art' exhibition at the Museum of Modern Art in New York. Johnson was interested in objects that exhibited a Platonic ideal of geometric beauty – 'straight lines and circles, and shapes, plane or solid' – and a 'perfection of surface' that, he said, could only be produced by materials such as porcelain, aluminium and celluloid, and the precision of machine manufacture.[37] The platonic beauty of these objects was convincingly captured in the accompanying catalogue, which was filled with artfully lit photographs. A mixer faucet and flush valve were featured, all swooping taps and gleaming surfaces, shot against blank backgrounds.

The photographs in 'Machine Art' make very clear one of the reasons sanitaryware was destined to play a starring role in modernism: its smooth, unadorned forms were perfectly suited to the medium of black-and-white photography. Weston's *Excusado* drives home the point. As framed by the camera, the sweeping lines of the humble *excusado* bring to mind the sculptures of Constantin Branscusi (Weston himself invoked the ancient *Winged Victory of Samothrace*). Weston claimed the photographs were revelatory for his own practice and they have since been hailed as masterpieces of formalism. There is a telling twist to the story, however. Weston felt it necessary to take more than one version of *Excusado*. While the first series showed the toilet's opening and the interior of its bowl, the second did not. Once the exhilaration over his first photographs had passed, Weston was beset by doubts. He noted that the toilet looked 'obscene' from certain angles; in particular, overt reminders of its use threatened its formal purity. Hence, in the second series, he excluded the seat, opening and basin interior from the frame.

No less than in 'Machine Art', where objects were deliberately presented outside of any functional context, Weston's selective framing was intended to suppress the signs of actual use. The same is true of Le Corbusier's washbasin at the Villa Savoye, of which the architecture historian Colin Rowe remarked, 'any details which one might associate with the act of washing (towels and soap) are conspicuously absent.'[38] A profound irony emerges: even as bathrooms were celebrated as rooms entirely 'dictated by need', the specific needs they served went unmentioned or were repressed.[39] This apparent lack of interest in delving into the specifics of use or of engaging with the technical challenges of bathroom design was to exasperate later commentators, from the visionary engineer Buckminster Fuller to the architect Alexander Kira who, as we will see in chapter Five, would

Niedecken mixer faucet, Hoffmann & Billings Mfg. Co., in Philip Johnson, *Machine Art* (1934).

direct the most comprehensive study of bathroom use ever undertaken. But if we accept that for most modernists the bathroom essentially served as an icon or was viewed as a planning problem (how could the space be most compactly arranged?), then we begin to understand why this type of total redesign was not a priority. Indeed, as Giedion's biological analogy of the kernel from its shell makes clear, bathroom equipment was valued precisely because it was viewed as the product of an internal evolutionary process through which a form 'naturally' emerged in response to human needs or to the anonymous processes of industrial production. The result was a pure form that embodied the epoch – the spirit of the age.

Again, it was Muthesius who first voiced this idea. Considering the British bathroom, he wrote:

> We have here an entirely new art that requires no propaganda to win it acceptance, an art based on actual modern conditions and modern achievements that perhaps one day, when all the fashions that parade as modern movements in art have passed away, will be regarded as the most eloquent expression of our age.[40]

Le Corbusier, the most important polemicist of the modern era, also took this line. A bidet featured alongside mass-produced objects like an aeroplane, automobile and typewriter in his seminal lectures on modernism in the 1920s; elsewhere, he proposed to include a bathroom ('its enamelled bath, its china bidet, its wash-basin, and its glittering taps of copper and nickel') in a museum of the modern period.[41] To Le Corbusier, such 'objets-types' ('type-objects') manifested an 'esprit nouveau' to which contemporary architects needed to respond. He was perfectly sincere in his admiration: he did not champion bathroom fittings to ironically subvert disciplinary values à la Duchamp. In fact, Le Corbusier was enraged when one critic suggested

that he held the bidet to be purer in form than the Parthenon. 'You don't confuse God with bidets . . .', he angrily shot back, 'do you really take me for a "noc fini" [complete ass]?'[42] Nonetheless, his own designs make evident that bathroom fittings were in some ways a curious and slippery choice of modernist icon.

Unlike his Bauhaus contemporaries, Le Corbusier did not impose a rigid functionalism in his bathrooms, though he would design his share of minimal ones (see chapter Three). Rather, he and his associate in charge of 'interior equipment', Charlotte Perriand, produced bathrooms with expressive curvy elements – think of the tiled chaise longue in the Villa Savoye – that linked to or even flowed into the adjoining bedrooms. This open treatment of the bathroom was a constant and occasionally notorious feature of Le Corbusier's projects

View from the master bedroom into the bathroom, Le Corbusier, Villa Savoye, Poissy, France, 1928–31.

throughout the 1920s and '30s: at his single-family villa at the Weissenhof Seidlung in 1927, the use of a mere half-height wall to separate the bedroom-bath area from the living room drew scandalized comments from German reporters.[43] Another half-height wall was deployed to separate bed from bath in Le Corbusier and Perriand's model flat, 'Equipment for a Dwelling', exhibited at the Salon D'Automne two years later (the interconnectedness of the bedroom and bathroom here cheekily emphasized by an integrated towel rail-bedframe).[44] And the master bedroom in Le Corbusier's Paris flat (1934) pushed openness to its limit: on one side was a sink and sitz bath and on the other a sink and cavelike shower. A bidet frankly greeted anyone entering the space – so frankly that Le Corbusier's wife, Yvonne, reportedly covered it with a tea cosy. Only the water closet was 'properly' enclosed.

It was not exceptional to find this level of sanitary excess in European bourgeois villas, which often had large numbers of bathrooms. And as we saw with Edward Weston, other modernists also found inspiration in the rounded lines, rolled rims and anthropomorphic shapes of bathroom equipment. Indeed, bidets, baths and water closets have all rightly been described as exemplary 'part objects', as they summon to mind the human bodies that use them – usually female bodies.[45] (In her defence of *Fountain*, poet Louise Norton suggested that the urinal evoked the shapely legs of a Cézanne nude; or, she teased, is it that the Cézanne nude really invokes the curves of a toilet?[46]) Even if they were not unique, however, Le Corbusier's sensuous and sculptural treatments highlight that bathroom fittings did not fit as neatly into the functionalist paradigm as did other examples of machine art.

One substantial difference was that, for all the innovations in materials and the rationalization of labour cited thus far, the production of sanitaryware was not actually mechanized. As one writer remarks, pottery making in this period remained 'an esoteric world of slip and slop, pugging and pressing, glosts and saggers, badgers and blungers'.[47] Earthenware was still made by skilled workers using traditional materials and methods: filling moulds, firing, fettling, glazing and firing again. Coal-powered bottle kilns and glost ovens were central to what was ultimately a labour-intensive manufacturing process with a high proportion of firing losses. This situation would only definitively change in the 1950s and '60s when partial mechanization was introduced to help with moving and lifting ware, along with oil-fired tunnel kilns to reduce rejection rates and devastating levels of pollution.[48] Automation was really only introduced in the 1960s with battery

Making fire clay baths, in Joseph Hatton, *Twyfords: A Chapter in the History of Pottery* (1897).

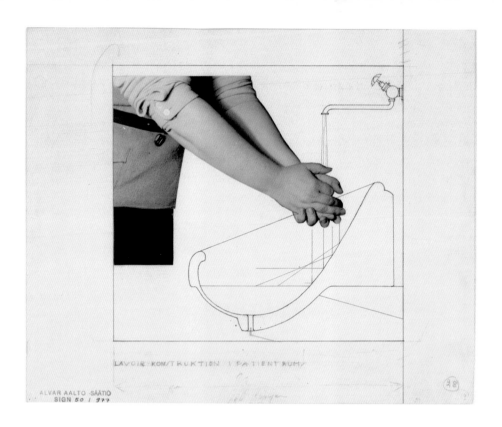

casting that allowed multiple moulds to be cast simultaneously. Metal-ware production was mechanized earlier on, which is probably why Giedion focused more on cast-iron examples: one innovation he mentions, for instance, is American Standard's introduction of the Reed Method, a turn-of-the-century process for mechanically enamelling tubs, toilets and sinks.[49] The very fact that this process was named after the man who invented it, however, challenges the notion that such developments simply happened. As Forty stresses, 'The design of manufactured goods is determined not by some internal genetic structure but by the people and the industries that make them.'[50]

This is undoubtedly true of bathroom equipment. That water closets, for instance, served their designated purpose reasonably well was

Section through washbasin in Alvar Aalto, Paimio Sanitorium, Finland, 1933.

the result of the efforts of many people across a range of industries, responding to particular technical, economic, legal and social requirements and constraints. The resulting forms can in no way said to be the most functional or 'natural'. Kira and Bernard Rudofsky would even argue that the water closet's form is profoundly unnatural, if judged from the point of view of human anatomy rather than flushing power.[51] For Le Corbusier, the fact that the basic design of the bidet had changed relatively little by virtue of being plumbed in or mass-produced showed that it had attained into a kind of formal purity or perfection; others (Kira again) believed that the persistence of certain forms only proved the inertia of the sanitaryware industry. At the very least, bathroom appliances could not said to be 'pure' in the sense that, however plain, they clearly bore the imprint of particular aesthetic preferences. Italian architect Gio Ponti observed that the design of washbasins remained fundamentally classical, their bases, stems and rims treated as columns.[52] Alvar Aalto's washbasins at Paimio Sanitorium (1933) were a departure. Seeking to eliminate any noise that might disturb patients' calm, Aalto designed a bulbous wall-hanging basin into which water would soundlessly fall and in the process demonstrated that there need not be anything 'columnar' about a washbasin at all. Despite his example, more radical experimentation with the bathroom's standard forms would only gather pace in the 1960s and '70s.

A scientific apparatus

Even if bathroom equipment was a relatively arbitrary icon of functionalism, it was more convincing as a symbol of other modern values. In Le Corbusier's case, the most plausible explanation for why he admired the lavatory, bidet and bath was that they reflected and celebrated hygiene. For Le Corbusier as for most of his contemporaries, a

GOOD HOUSING

GOOD SANITATION

GOOD ENVIRONMENT
IS THE BASIS OF HEALTH

FULL EMPLOYMENT

GOOD FACTORIES

GOOD SCHOOLS

BALANCED DIET

Ernö Goldfinger, exhibition display board with montage of photographs demonstrating how good sanitation, diet, living and working conditions form the basis of good health, Army Bureau of Current Affairs 'Health' exhibition, 1943.

modern lifestyle was implicitly a hygienic one. When Perriand listed the priorities for the 'NEW MAN', she neatly summed this up: 'Hygiene must be considered first: soap and water.'[53] Consider the washbasin in the Villa Savoye entrance hall. Although the washbasin had a function – it was meant for the chauffeur to wash his hands on entry – its placement was too pointed to be purely practical. Free-standing and isolated from its usual context, the washbasin most resembled a baptismal font. It functioned as a sort of sacred object, offering purification to those who entered the villa's precincts, cleansing them of the ways of the past and aligning them with progressive social goals: cleanliness and physical health.

The washbasin's resonance as a symbol was reinforced by contemporary theories of health and disease, which placed new emphasis on water purity. Following the research of Louis Pasteur and Robert Koch, germ theory had by this time decisively supplanted the miasma theory as the explanation for disease transmission. With Koch's microbiological research in the 1880s, for instance, the medical establishment finally accepted that cholera was waterborne, carried by the bacteria in faecal matter. Modern initiatives to improve public health were thus no longer concerned with preventing deadly miasmas but with the problem of keeping the water supply uncontaminated. To do so, they began to implement chemical and biological solutions alongside engineering ones, experimenting much more actively with forms of water filtration and treatment: chlorination was introduced during the First World War for water treatment in London, and biological methods of sewage treatment were tested from the 1890s onward.[54]

The acceptance of germ theory had an impact on everyday cleaning regimes too. Cleansing agents – soap, carbolic acid, chloride of lime and spirits of salt (hydrochloric acid) – were increasingly deployed to clean and disinfect foul surfaces or skin. Inspired by Pasteur, Dr Joseph Lister implemented a surgical cleansing routine at the Glasgow Royal Infirmary in the 1860s that included frequent hand washing and the sterilization of instruments with carbolic acid; this was also applied to wounds and their dressings. Disinfecting procedures significantly reduced infection rates and were carried into non-medical settings by sanitary commissions in times of war and sanitary inspectors in times of peace.[55] Disinfectants even began to be applied to the pulp of toilet paper: popular additives included pine oils, eucalyptus and aloe vera.[56] In the 1870s, Diamond Mills Paper Company in New York came out with Bromo toilet paper, infused with 'Bromo Chloralum' and carbolic acid. Bromo promised to ward off haemorrhoids while also disinfecting the water closet, and was awarded the highest prize at the Paris Exposition in 1878.

The faith in disinfection was also introduced to the home, in large part through cleaning and personal hygiene routines sited in the bathroom. The enforcers of these new regimes were the wives and mothers who now constituted a primary audience for literature on domestic economy and on sanitary plumbing, whether in books on home management or articles in ladies' magazines. Women were subjected to a barrage of advertisements selling cleaning products like Lysol or Listerine, an antiseptic named after Joseph Lister, that were said to keep the family clean and germ-free. While domestic cleaning products like these were not new, their advertisements now took on a highly charged, moralistic tone. Such emotive appeals had real force in the twentieth century because, even as the terror of cholera subsided, it was replaced by the terror of tuberculosis, which was known to spread via infected surfaces. Dark, inaccessible corners, long disliked by domestic reformers, became even more menacing once it was known that infectious *tubercle bacilli* could survive for decades in household dust. Only direct sunlight was thought to kill them.

It is in this context that we can make sense of Le Corbusier's denouncement of the average home as an 'old coach full of tuberculosis'

and his constant championing of sunlight and fresh air.[57] Such views had been common among sanitarians for upwards of five decades, but Le Corbusier went further by making the bathroom central to a regime of health designed to strengthen the body. For instance, in his book *Towards a New Architecture* (1927), readers were instructed to

> Demand a bathroom looking south, one of the largest rooms in the house or flat, the old drawing-room for instance. One wall to be entirely glazed, opening if possible on to a balcony for sun baths; the most up-to-date fittings with a shower-bath and gymnastic appliances.[58]

Here, Le Corbusier inserted various therapeutic devices into the home: showers, originally used for hydrotherapy (see chapter Four), and sun baths, part of the preferred treatment for tubercular patients in sanatoria. The built-in chaise longue in the Villa Savoye, of course, strongly evokes sanatoria cure chairs (though it can equally be said to evoke the chaises longues found in many luxurious French *cabinets de toilette* and the one Le Corbusier and Perriand designed in 1928). In

Leaflet advertising Bromo paper toilet tissue, manufactured by the Diamond Mills Paper Company, New York, c. 1878.

emphasizing sun, exercise and relaxation, Le Corbusier viewed the bathroom as a place devoted to the care of the body in the broadest sense – 'an instrument of health' – not unlike the contemporary modernist health centres devoted to disease prevention.[59] The idea of the bathroom as a 'health room' did gain some traction. In the Standard Sanitary Manufacturing Company's 'Better Bathroom Design' competition of 1930, the jury stated that treating the space as a 'sanitorium' with solarium, lounge rooms or gymnasium was a logical step in the home's 'social evolution'.[60] And in one of the first Corbusian designs to cross the Atlantic to America, A. Lawrence Kocher and Albert Frey's Aluminaire House (1932), the master bedroom did in fact feature an exercise room and bathroom that could be closed off by a folding partition.[61] The idea of a bathroom as a home gymnasium, however, would not truly take off until the 1980s fitness craze.

While these schemes pushed the idea of the bathroom as a health room further than most, they were not alone in trying to treat it more clinically. Already in 1904, Muthesius had articulated the idea that a 'truly modern' bathroom was a 'piece of scientific apparatus'.[62] Underlying this statement was a rejection of the Victorian principle of decorating the bathroom with upholstered chairs and sofas, carpets and wallpaper as if it were a room like any other. The modern bathroom took on a laboratory aesthetic as it was filled with what Le Corbusier approvingly termed 'household equipment', including mirrored medicine cabinets and diagnostic items like bath scales, then still box-like mechanisms of cast-iron standing nine inches high (their now familiar flat form with clockface dials was only popularized in the 1940s). The clinical function of the bathroom was conveyed in the prevalence of non-porous, sealed and easily wiped surfaces: sanitaryware was enamelled, metal components were plated in chrome and nickel, and walls and floors were covered with marble, glazed tiles or embossed zinc sheets.

But the definitive sign of the modern bathroom's scientific aesthetic was the use of white. The association with white and health was a well-established one. For instance, limewash, long known for its disinfecting properties, was applied to the walls of privies, cesspools and public urinals through much of the nineteenth century and was particularly valued as a defence against cholera and typhoid. But, even without lime's disinfecting properties, white surfaces on their own began to denote cleanliness. In her hugely influential 1863 edition of *Notes on Nursing*, Florence Nightingale was unequivocal. 'The only way to ensure dryness and cleanliness in the compartments where the water-closets and lavatory [washbasin] accommodation are placed', she said, 'is to cover the walls with white glazed tile.'[63] Even though she did not subscribe to germ theory, Nightingale still believed that it was only against white surfaces that cleanliness became tangible and visible. They were guarantors of purity.

White took on a similar signifying role in modern domestic settings. As Mary Douglas, Adrian Forty, Mark Wigley and others have observed, the objective in deploying white was not so much to practically effect cleanliness but rather to create the look of cleanliness – to project 'the imagery of hygiene'.[64] And in the porcelain-enamelled surfaces of sanitaryware (so much more enduring than whitewash), Le Corbusier found perhaps the ultimate embodiment of the aesthetic of purity. But it is important to recall that he, along with other modernist admirers of the bathroom, never intended to leave it at that. The bathroom's aesthetic was always a means to a wider end. In valorizing the bathroom and its fittings, they were trying identify a modern style and spirit that could lead a transformation of the house and of home life. And it did, as its shiny equipment, white surfaces and smooth forms spilled out into the domestic environment at large, at the avant-garde of the modernist revolution.

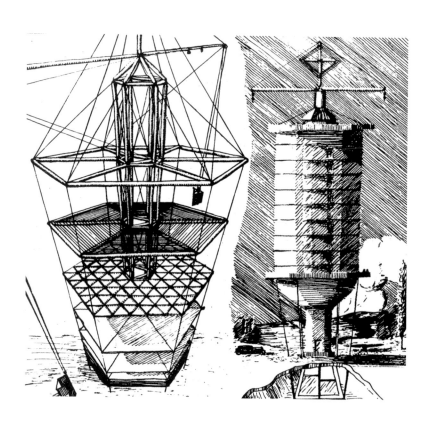

3 The Rational Bathroom

Let Architects dream of glass boxes with steam
And rich clients in hordes at their knees
Just give me a home in a great circle dome
Where the birds and the bees are at ease.

Roam home to a dome
Where Georgian and Gothic once stood
Now chemical bonds alone guard our blondes
And even the plumbing looks good.
Buckminster Fuller (to the tune of 'Home on the Range'), from
'The Cardboard House' (1953)

In the above ditty, the engineer and architect Buckminster Fuller adopted an unusually playful tone as he skewered architects for failing to move with the times. It is no coincidence that Fuller chose to focus on domestic architecture or that his refrain ended with a reference to plumbing, as these had been among his chief preoccupations since the late 1920s. Throughout his career, Fuller would rail against architects' failure to subject the house to the same kind of rigorous rethinking as had been applied to the aeroplane and automobile and to ask the question, 'What is a house?'[1] Fuller's answer to this would evolve over the decades, until the conventional house disappeared, replaced by a dome.[2]

For Fuller, the bathroom was crucial to solving the problem of the house. As it had evolved over the last century, the bathroom had become an integral part of the home's physiology. But, in Fuller's eyes, it had also become the way in which the house was effectively 'immobilized',

Buckminster Fuller, multistorey mast house, 1927–8. Note the prefabricated bathroom pod being hoisted up the structure by a crane.

as architects settled on 'real estaters' sewers like hens on glass eggs'.[3] In order to free the house, Fuller believed it had to carry its own waste treatment system with it. Fuller's first significant dwelling unit, the 4-D multistorey mast house (1927–8), came equipped with its own septic tank, located in a lightweight, central supporting staff. It was, Mark Wigley observes, 'a polemically independent building', less house than ship.[4]

Fuller's work also made a strong case for the benefits of rationalizing bathrooms, and his efforts to do so had radical architectural implications. The first lesson of the 4-D dwelling unit (soon renamed Dymaxion) was that all pipework, including that in the bathroom, could effectively be concentrated into a services core that would act as the home's heart. This opened the door to prefabrication, because it meant that this core could arrive on-site and, with minimal labour, be plugged in and begin giving life to the domestic organism. The second and perhaps more important lesson was that it was not enough for architects to make use of standardized bathroom fittings and fixtures. To really reconceive the home – to realize Le Corbusier's call for a 'machine for living' – they would have to go beyond the wall. They would have to get their hands on the plumbing.

Setting standards, democratizing comfort

To fully appreciate why Fuller's insistence on a hands-on approach was so ground-breaking, it must be understood that, by the early twentieth century, architects typically had little to say on the subject of bathroom fixture design or plumbing. Whereas an architect like Calvert Vaux in the 1860s might still have custom-designed a privy and its plumbing, within a few decades the widespread availability of high-quality bathroom fittings and manufacturers' recommendations about how they should be installed meant that architects became less involved in these details. Indeed, part of the appeal of bathroom fittings was that their forms were believed to have emerged from an anonymous industrial process. They were standard products that could be plucked from a catalogue. The sense that bathrooms were somehow 'other' to (and inferior to) architecture would only grow stronger in the first decades of the twentieth century, thanks to the adoption of national standards and building codes, which imposed greater uniformity in bathroom fittings and restricted the architect's scope for creative input or control.

At this time, it was sanitaryware manufacturers who shaped bathroom fixture design and production most directly. Although their wares were the result of a design process, they generally did not use named designers for product development. New products were created in-house and were the result of a collaboration between managers, mechanical engineers, pottery modellers and the occasional consultant industrial designer; these teams, in turn, relied on sales figures and various middlemen – sales representatives at branch offices, jobbers, agents and plumbers – to gauge public response. Sometimes manufacturers consulted with independent bodies such as women's organizations, home economists or colour experts in order to better accommodate popular tastes, but they mostly kept the design process close to home.[5] As later critics would argue, this market-driven and unscientific mode of research created a limited feedback loop that stymied any serious rethinking of bathroom appliances. Some efforts were made to introduce a more objective approach, as when American Standard set up a Bureau of Design Development in 1934, headed by the well-known industrial designer and artist George Sakier. A dedicated facility like this one, however, was not the norm within the industry.

In their efforts to improve standards and drive down costs, builders and developers also played a significant role in shaping bathroom design, especially in America. Sigfried Giedion noted the rise of the 'bath cell' in American hotels which, as he noted, had sweeping technological and social implications. While luxury American hotels had featured advanced plumbing since the 1820s, patrons of mid-level hotels could still expect to share bathrooms at the end of the century. The Buffalo Statler Hotel's introduction of compact, three-fixture bathrooms in all rooms in 1905, however, meant that even ordinary guests began to enjoy an upper-class standard of privacy, a significant step towards what Giedion called the 'democratization of comfort'.[6] The hotel's founder, Ellsworth M. Statler, banked on the en suite's appeal, advertised through the slogan 'A Room and a Bath for a Dollar and a Half'. Statler was able to deliver en suites because he standardized the plumbing: all the fixtures were lined up along one wall, and the bathrooms were built back-to-back with a shared plumbing shaft, saving space and making pipes more accessible for repairs. While many American hotels would adopt this arrangement between 1910 and 1920, it would take decades before it was regularly deployed in Europe.[7]

Recognizing the appeal of the bathroom as Statler had done, mass builders began installing them in tract housing developments throughout the United States from 1905 onwards.[8] Sales of bath fittings directly corresponded to housing starts: when housing starts rose, surpassing 400,000 in 1927, so too did the sales of sanitary appliances.[9] On the back of this vast domestic market, manufacturers like American Standard and Crane Plumbing overtook their British competitors to become the largest suppliers of plumbing goods in the world. The bathrooms favoured by builders were not unlike hotel bath cells: they were compact, with three fixtures only – bath, toilet and sink. The 'loose' arrangement of fixtures preferred by the British had disappeared.[10] So too had some of the quirkier fittings of the Victorian era – the sitz bath, for instance, along with the stand-alone shower and a separately enclosed water closet (a convention that, in any case, had never been as dominant in America as it was in Europe).

Rather than following European precedents, then, American three-fixture bathrooms were something new, domestic counterparts to the Ford Model T. The architectural critic Lewis Mumford made this link explicitly when he noted in 1929: 'None of our [i.e. American] decorations . . . can approach for sheer beauty of line and color a modern automobile or a simple tiled bathroom or the fixtures of a modern kitchen.'[11] And like American automobiles, American bathrooms would also be aggressively streamlined. This was the era of the 'suite', when a trio of matching fixtures and accessories was installed at once to create a visually integrated and coordinated space. Instead of having an obvious decorative theme ('Elizabethan', 'Baronial' and so on), the space was unified by simple, usually classical lines, created through what the design historians Ellen Lupton and J. Abbott Miller have called a 'process of elimination': bathroom fittings were rounded, pipework was enclosed in pedestals, cisterns were 'close coupled' with the toilet and claw feet gave way to integrated bases.

The impact of such innovations was not only stylistic: they saved space and were believed to deliver improved cleanliness and comfort. Prior to the rise of 'close coupling', for instance, water closet cisterns were located high up on the wall because a powerful rush of water had been necessary to flush wash-down bowls. The invention of the siphonic water closet, which operated by suction and was the preferred model in America, meant that cisterns could be lowered, becoming more compact (they could fit under windows, for instance) and quieter – gone was the tumbling roar of the old flushes. The rise of one-piece baths with integrated ceramic aprons in the 1910s had an equally dramatic effect. These seamless baths alleviated the perennial difficulty of how to clean the joints between the tub and its enclosure. Installed flush with the wall in their own recessed bays, the bathtub's

dimensions became the determining factor in the average bathroom's size and shape: 5 by 7 feet (1.5 by 2 metres). Despite further stylistic changes, the 5-by-7 bathroom would remain the standard in America for decades to come.[12]

By the 1920s the compact, standardized bathroom was gaining ground in Europe as well, though in this case it was tied to the question of how to deliver high-quality social housing at a reasonable cost. Though the majority of social housing projects still relied on communal bathing facilities, some began to introduce private indoor toilets and bathrooms. This was revolutionary at a time when most working-class people were living in flats with few services. The historian of architecture Susan Henderson notes that in 1930, 'only half of the households in Frankfurt had private toilets . . . a mere one in five had a bath, more than 10 percent had no running water'.[13] In this situation, a bathroom represented a real advance in living standards, but it also presented a challenge that architects could not afford to ignore. Kitchens and bathrooms were proportionately more expensive to build and install than other parts of the house, so there

Streamlined bathroom (right): a bathroom 'Before and After', in *Architectural Forum* (January 1933).

was an urgent need to standardize fittings, wiring and connections for reasons of cost.

An important effort to supply bathrooms at a mass scale was made in the new housing estates built in Frankfurt in the late 1920s and '30s under its director of city planning, Ernst May. Interestingly, the case for private bathrooms was made on the grounds that public ones were so unpopular that people did not make use of them. But, to be economically feasible, private baths had to use a minimal amount of space; they were thus subjected to the same space-saving analyses as their more famous prefabricated counterpart, the Frankfurt Kitchen. Bathrooms were made smaller thanks to the use of a sitz bath instead of a full-size one. Henderson notes: '[The architect Ferdinand] Kramer's bathroom was dubbed the "cella" bath, and sold as a prefabricated component that included the bath, sink and toilet within a tiled niche. At 2.55 square meters [about 27.5 square feet], it was advertised as the "smallest bath in the smallest space."'[14] Known as the Frankfurt Bath, this design was likely first introduced at the Westhausen public housing project, and it was also listed for sale in the Frankfurt Register, an early directory that helped consumers select modern, functional furnishings.[15]

In this same period, too, some manufacturers began to develop products that were better suited to personal cleansing in small spaces: for instance, in 1928 the German company Hans Grohe introduced what it claims was the world's first hand-held shower. It was in France, however, that flexibility was most encouraged and embraced; for instance, the French used mobile furnishings, such as bidets that could be rolled out from a corner when needed and pushed back again after use. They also experimented with many ingenious space-saving forms of bathroom equipment. The standout example of this period was Le Corbusier, Pierre Jeanneret and Charlotte Perriand's 'sanitary cabin', designed for the sanitaryware manufacturer Jacob Delafon for display at the Exposition

Internationale in Paris in 1937. This cabin was a prototype for a pre-fabricated bathroom unit for use in Alpine hotels: the intention was that Atelier Jean Prouvé would manufacture it of sheet metal.

With dimensions derived from Le Corbusier's Modulor, his system of measurements based on the golden section, the cabin was an incredibly compact space of just over 4 feet by 4 feet (1.25 by 1.25 metres). Fitted with a sink, toilet-bidet and shower, the whole room was designed to get wet: water from the shower would simply drain away through slats into an enamelled cast-iron pan beneath. The cabin's most memorable feature, however, was its toilet assemblage consisting of a normal-height seat which could be raised for those who preferred to squat over the low bowl. (Squat toilets, known as *sièges à la turque*,

Le Corbusier, Pierre Jeanneret and Charlotte Perriand, 'sanitary cabin', Exposition Internationale, Paris, 1937.

were commonly found in the public conveniences in French cafés or in train stations and one can understand why they appealed to Le Corbusier, Jeanneret and Perriand.[16] All devotees of the cult of hygiene, they would likely have shared the view that squat toilets were cleaner than throne-style *sièges à l'anglaise*, not to mention healthier and more authentic in permitting '*défécation naturelle*'.[17]) To complete the toilet assemblage, a bidet could be lowered to fit neatly inside the seat. All faucets and taps were located on wall panels above the ceramic fixtures; one nozzle next to the toilet pivoted out to fill the bidet. The cabin was never mass produced but Perriand would carry on her experiments in compact bathroom planning and eventually installed prefabricated units in her Les Arcs winter resort in the French Alps (1975).[18] In the meantime, the 'sanitary cabin' served as a provocation: how small and multipurpose could a bathroom be?

Even when they were not the result of specific experiments like these, bathrooms everywhere became more uniform as external bodies began to exert more influence over their dimensions, arrangements and fittings. As noted earlier, from the second half of the nineteenth century, American and European governments steadily became more interventionist about sanitary arrangements, establishing rules about building, housing, drainage and plumbing in the name of public health and safety. Regulations mandated, for instance, that all new dwellings be connected to the sewer system and that factories or tenements provide a certain number of water closets. From the turn of the twentieth century, too, standards organizations were created with the aim of encouraging standardization in manufacturing and construction and of improving health and safety. The British Standards Institute was established in 1901, and similar German, French and American institutions followed during the First World War. Even though standards on plumbing and sanitary appliances were – and are – advisory they are often linked to building regulations, which are legally enforced.[19]

Standards have long periods of gestation as research and consultation is carried out and they are subject to constant revision; furthermore, real variation exists in standards between different nations. Even if we cannot track the history and effect of each set of standards, locally and internationally their ascendance generally is an important part of the story of how certain plumbing arrangements were established and 'locked in' over the course of the twentieth century.[20] And their influence today is undeniable. Many of the design features that most frustrate toilet campaigners and mystify average users have their origins in standards, which may prescribe everything from a facility's minimum dimensions to that most contested of issues, the appropriate ratio of male-to-female toilets in public buildings.

Further examples of efforts to standardize will be mentioned in chapter Five, but the key point here is that standards created a paradoxical situation. By the 1920s, the bathroom was becoming accessible to a broader cross-section of the Western populace, bringing higher levels of cleanliness and privacy to those even lower down the social scale. Yet even as the bathroom helped to promote individual privacy, it became less personalized as a space, subject to more external forces and to tighter regulation. And even as architects adopted the bathroom as a modernist icon, they became increasingly marginal to its design, giving over influence to many external groups, from manufacturers to standards organizations. A self-fulfilling cycle was set into motion: the more external forces shaped bathrooms, the less actively architects tended to engage with them, relying instead on building regulations or the recommendations of manufacturers, plumbers or handbooks. Without being fully aware of it, they had gradually ceded control over one of the most potentially significant aspects of the built environment.

At least, this was how Buckminster Fuller saw it. And this was the situation he set out to change.

From icon to Dymaxion

As touched on in the introduction, Fuller had many complaints about conventional plumbing: it immobilized architecture, it was inefficient and so on. But he reserved particular ire for architects who, in his view, simply went through the motions as far as plumbing was concerned and in the process made themselves as 'marginal as journeymen, tinkers, and drivers of hansom cabs'.[21] It is worth reading his lengthy condemnation of the Bauhaus, the German design school most strongly associated with the drive to bring industrial methods and modes of production into architecture:

> What convinced me that the Bauhaus international designing was of secondary rank . . . was the fact that their designing consciously limited itself to formulated employment of the component items manufactured by the going old-line building materials world. The Bauhaus international school used standard plumbing fixtures and only ventured so far as to persuade the manufacturers to modify the surface of the valve handles and spigots and the color, size, and arrangements of the tiles. The . . . school never went back of the wall surface to look at the plumbing, never dared to venture into printed circuits of manifoldly stamped plumbings. They never inquired into the over-all problem of sanitary functions themselves . . . In short, they only looked at problems of modification of the surface of end products, which end products were inherently subfunctions of a technically obsolete world.[22]

It was, perhaps, an excessively harsh indictment. Elsewhere, Fuller took a more forgiving, though hardly more flattering, view of architects, whom he portrayed as hamstrung by clients, community codes, building laws and bank mortgage biases.[23] Standards were a factor in poor bathroom design because they were set without sufficient research, entrenching obsolete technologies. (Fuller referred to sewerage as a 'three-thousand-year-old invention'.[24]) Though most uncompromisingly expressed by Fuller, most twentieth-century critics of bathroom design would make similar observations about how antiquated standards and poor designs were locked in through a combination of regulations and the inertia of sanitaryware manufacturers, architects and the building industry.[25] They further complained that mechanical equipment was dealt with in an ad hoc fashion: 'We have added plumbing, heating and other equipment to a structure designed before such utilities were in use', lamented *Architectural Forum* in 1943.[26] In Fuller's opinion, the only solution to these problems was to research the structural conditions that governed production and distribution from the ground up: rationalization, not standardization.

One of the most celebrated results of Fuller's research was the Dymaxion Bathroom. As its name suggests, the idea emerged directly from Fuller's Dymaxion House project of the late 1920s. The Dymaxion Bathroom's fixtures (shower, bath, toilet and sink) were all integrated into a single die-stamped metal body. Interestingly, Fuller built a prototype of the room as early as 1930, but this version was never publicly shown because, he claimed, 'The manufacturer [American Radiator Company] was convinced that the plumbers' union would refuse to install the bathrooms.'[27] Though Fuller's own discussions with plumbers convinced him that they were not hostile, the assertion that labour unions would never accept prefabrication proved to be a consistent roadblock to his work's development.

In 1936, Fuller produced the Dymaxion Bathroom with another manufacturer, the Phelps Dodge Corporation, this time with more success. The Dymaxion consisted of a tub-shower compartment and a sink-toilet compartment that together covered a floor area of 5 feet squared (1.5 metres squared) – somewhat smaller than an average bathroom, though the tub was larger than average. The whole unit

THE NEWEST
prefabricated bathroom
IS ALSO NEAREST

1.
THUD

2.

CLICK

4.
PRESTO!

SNAP
3.

On the 29th floor of 40 Wall St. there sits the finished model of a new plumbing fixture that might well bug the eyes of any bystanding master plumber, a fixture that to all intents and purposes constitutes a one-piece bathroom. Designed by Architect Buckminster Fuller (Dymaxion House, Dymaxion Car) it accomplishes, by the simple connection of four basic parts, a complete bathroom weighing 404 pounds, with integral lavatory, toilet and bath. First known as the "Five by Five" (because that's the space it takes up), the official designation is now "The Integrated Bath".

In the research department of the Phelps Dodge Corporation it sits, ready for moderate production (100 units) in 1937. Architect Fuller has assigned his patents to the PD organization, and rumor discerns a new manufacturing and marketing subsidiary in the immediate offing. The range of uses for the unit is broad: pullmans, planes, trailers, trains, but mainly small homes. In fact, Mr. Fuller hopes this light, compact, complete bathroom will even inspire renters to install copies in their apartments, and remove them when they move. All of which lies in the realm of speculation. For the immediate future the device will probably induce fewer orders than conversations. None the less the fact remains that this prefabricated bathroom comes closer to commercial reality than any of its predecessors.

The Integrated Bathroom consists roughly of two oblong sections that form a partition where they join, which conceals the piping and other mechanical appurtenances. The sections (each a monometal stamping) are each split in the middle, the top being aluminum and the bottom 272 pounds of sheet copper unmetallized and tinted by a coating of silver, tin and antimony alloy. The bottom of one section is the lavatory and toilet, of the other a flat-bottomed tub.

The toilet, though reminiscent of the old backyard one-holer, is fully sanitary. The seat lifts and remains upright by compression against the walls. Underneath is a standard form of bowl (though chrome nickel bowls are also available).

Two men can handle an installation in three hours, for all piping except a minimum amount of connection material is integral with the unit. So are electric connections, ventilation equipment, etc. Fresh air is drawn by a motor under the lavatory from the nearest room, and exhausted—wherever circumstances permit.

Miscellaneous features: A composition Venetian blind gives privacy to the bather, and, while permitting the escape of steam, prevents the escape of water. The door-frame between the two sections is six inches thick, permitting use as seat. Complete cleansing of tub is easily attained. The plumbing layout was devised in collaboration with a local master plumber, copper tubing being used for water lines. Particular care was used to avoid back-siphonage possibilities. Sliding doors conserve space. The metallic finish has a "hammered" appearance while at the same time being thoroughly sanitary, the inventor claims. Under surfaces of the base metal are covered with Dum-dum, a sound deadening material. An electric heating system between the two units warms the metal itself, radiating heat to occupant of bathroom. Removable panels permit access to plumbing traps and connections under toilet and lavatory.

Reprinted from the April, 1937, issue of THE LADLE official publication of the New York State Association of Master Plumbers

'The newest prefabricated bathroom is also nearest.' Advertisement for Buckminster Fuller's Dymaxion Bathroom in *The Ladle* (1937).

consisted of four pieces of sheet metal that were light and small enough to be easily carried. Once in place on-site, these pieces were bolted together to form a whole. The process was summed up as 'Thud-Click-Snap-Presto!' Within minutes, so the theory went, users would have a fully operational bathroom.

Despite its compact size, the Dymaxion was not austere: not only did it have all the expected fixtures and services (ventilation, heat, lighting) of a conventional bathroom, but it had new technologies such as air conditioning. It also featured many designed-in details that were intended to add to user safety and convenience, from cork-lined steps up to the bathtub to a raised floor in the tub-shower compartment to make it easier to clean. The U-shaped doorway between the two compartments served to conceal the plumbing and heating equipment while also providing a 'seat saddle' for those in the tub-shower. The tub had built-in alcoves for soap and sponges; even built-in armrests were provided. And, for the washbasin, Fuller dispensed with traditional knobs and spigots in favour of an orifice out of which hot and cold water flowed from front to back in order to prevent splash-back. A knob, pushed to the right by the knee, activated the drain.

The Dymaxion Bathroom cost just a little more than it would cost to produce an automobile sedan body. In theory, given how easily it could be moved and installed, the bathroom was to be transformed into something more like an appliance, like a refrigerator or washing machine. Patented in 1938, nine prototypes of the Dymaxion were produced, and in 1973 it was reported that over half were still in use. Some found their way into domestic settings: architect Richard Neutra installed two in his Windshield house on Fishers Island, New York.[28] Others were exhibited: one at the Bureau of Standards laboratory in Washington, DC (it reportedly satisfied the requirements of all American building codes), and another at the New York Museum of Modern Art in 1939. However, the bathroom failed to find a larger market.

Again, the unions were blamed. And again, Fuller disputed this account, arguing that the bathroom appealed to the Plumbers Union, who hoped to benefit from a repeat market in the same way that electricians did, generating fees for connecting the bathroom with each move.[29]

In spite of the small scale of its realization, the Dymaxion Bathroom, along with Fuller's later design of 1943 for a mobile mechanical unit, ended up casting a very long shadow over post-war design, as we will see. Discussing these inventions exclusively through the post-war avant-garde, however, can lead to a distorted sense of their uniqueness: Fuller was not alone in his desire to rationalize bathroom production. Many other types of prefab bathroom were in circulation between the 1920s and 1950s. One of the most celebrated was Sakier's ARCO system for American Standard. Made of enamelled steel, these prefabricated panel units for sink, bath and toilet came complete with all the 'logical accessories, integral chassis and plumbing casings'.[30] 'Logical accessories' included curtain rails for baths, mirrored medicine cabinets and lighting and storage for sinks. ARCO panels were praised in the architectual press for their versatility: they could be used in new constructions or joined with existing plumbing for bathroom renovations.[31] ARCO was probably the most commercially successful of the prefab modular systems of the time. While others went into production – including one sectional bathroom whose six 'fixturepanels' were based on Le Corbusier's Modulor – most never left the drawing board.[32]

Moreover, modular bathroom systems never electrified the later architectural avant-garde in the way that Fuller's complete facility did, probably because they did not enable conventional notions of housing to be completely rethought, as did the Dymaxion. Yet, again, the Dymaxion Bathroom was but one of many proposals made for prefab mechanical cores in this period.[33] One successful example was the

British Ministry of Works Unit, a back-to-back kitchen and bathroom, fireplace with back boiler, airing cupboard and water closet, which was installed in thousands of prefab houses erected as part of the Temporary Housing Programme (1945–51). But the unit was likely too inflexible and conventional to have fully satisfied Fuller or his followers, who preferred to seek inspiration from bathrooms that freed users entirely from the shackles of infrastructure. For this, they turned to facilities designed for trains, ships, buses, recreational vehicles, aircraft and, later, manned spacecraft.

While Victorian passengers had made do with a variety of portable vessels to relieve themselves privately in transit, this began to change from the 1840s onwards, with the development of a public rail network. People began to travel in greater numbers, average journey times became longer and the unfortunately termed 'bladder leash' was stretched to its limit. The short-term solution was to allow travellers to take rest breaks at regular intervals and to provide facilities at stations and terminals. Many of the cast-iron urinals produced by Walter Macfarlane & Co., for instance, were installed in railway stations or along tram lines. Some first-class passengers also began to enjoy valve water closets on board: they appeared on the first sleeping car in Britain which ran on the North British Railway from 1873, and were standard on all luxury Pullman cars imported from America. For those further down the social ladder, simple hoppers were provided and passengers were requested not to flush at stations. Later closets had tanks to hold waste, which was deodorized by a combination of chemicals such as bleach and formaldehyde before being emptied at the nearest station. All of these methods of waste disposal were crude and few were odourless as advertised. Vacuum flush toilets were a considerable advance in this regard. Since NASA's *Skylab* launched in 1973, they have been a feature of all manned spacecraft and space stations. In a zero-gravity environment, the suction of the vacuum is essential

George Sakier, ARCO panel system, *Architectural Forum* (May 1933). Note that the metal wall comes with an integrated wash bowl (on adjustable chromium-plated legs), mirror, electric lights, shelving and cupboard. The piping is behind the wall.

Toilet facility on a train, in a London & North Western corridor coach, 1906, with toilet, washbasin, hot and cold water and electric lighting.

to collecting urine and faeces; the vacuum is also used to dry solid waste for storage until it can be returned to earth for analysis and disposal.[34] More prosaically, vacuum flush toilets have also been installed on passenger aircraft since the mid-1970s.

Whatever the technology, Fuller admired one aspect of mobile facilities especially: they achieved great economy of space. In Fuller's Dymaxion Chronofile, his monumental logbook of his life's interests and activities, we find an advertisement from 1928 for the Pickwick Nite Coach, the world's first overnight bus. Designed by engineer Dwight E. Austin, the Nite Coach was a bi-level vehicle that contained all the necessary facilities for its passengers on board, including a compact sink and flush toilet. This coach, like Fuller's own Dymaxion, was in general a marvel of space-saving design, with folding card tables and luggage racks. It made use of technologically advanced systems, from ventilators to steam tables for cooking. And, significantly, it deployed new materials for its construction: Bakelite plastic and the aluminium alloy Duralumin, from which contemporary aircraft bodies were also being constructed. It was on these modern materials that the future development of the rational bathroom now seemed to depend.

Plastic fantastic

When Fuller originally designed his Dymaxion, he knew that it would not be realized anytime soon, largely because the materials did not yet exist at the standards he required. As he stated, 'it would be a minimum of 25 years before the gamut of industrial capabilities and evolutionary education of man . . . would permit the emergence of the necessary physical paraphernalia.'[35] The Dymaxion Bathroom was made of copper, thus making it far heavier than Fuller desired. He believed that the refinement of lightweight metal alloys would eventually halve its weight.

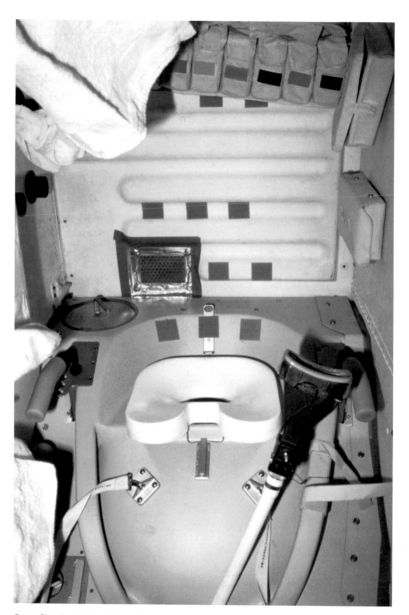

Space Shuttle vacuum toilet, 1980s.

Up to the 1950s, most prefabricated houses were of wood, copper, steel, aluminium, asbestos or reinforced concrete. Then, a new, light-weight material burst on to the scene: plastic. The commercial exploitation of Bakelite had begun in the first decade of the twentieth century in the United States and had proved the value of synthetic materials for building and industrial design. While plastic components such as cladding or window frames were in use in the 1930s, it was only after the Second World War that all-plastic houses appeared. Three post-war exhibition house projects in particular brought the heady possibilities of plastics to the fore: Ionel Schein's Maison tout en Plastique (1955), Alison and Peter Smithson's House of the Future (1956) and the Monsanto House of the Future (1957) at Disneyland. The English architect and plastics enthusiast Arthur Quarmby viewed the Maison tout en Plastique particularly as a 'great landmark', but observed that its finished shells of glass-reinforced polyester (GRP, fibreglass) 'needed a tremendous amount of hand-finishing and final trimming with a hacksaw', rendering mass production difficult.[36]

In Quarmby's judgement, the most inspiring and successful feature of the Maison tout en Plastique was its moulded bathroom unit. Such a statement was not unusual for the time. Following in Fuller's foot-steps, many avant-garde architects regarded prefabricated bathroom units or heart units as the foundations around which truly flexible housing enclosures could be built. In 1963 the avant-garde architec-ture group Archigram dedicated the third issue of their magazine to the theme of 'expendable architecture'. In it, they highlighted how core units were vital to realizing prefab structures, as the concentration of services significantly reduced the need for complicated, on-site pipe connections. Accompanied by images of Fuller, Schein and Monsanto's bathroom units, page three of the issue graphically depicted a progression from 'bathrooms' (cores) to 'bubbles' (prefabri-cated houses) to 'systems' (industrialized processes for fabricating houses). The message was clear: from bathroom units, houses would follow – but not houses as typically conceived. Rather, as envisioned in countless visionary schemes, they were to be highly serviced 'volumes of habitation', with sprayed-on plastic or pneumatic walls.[37] Archigram member David Greene's Spray Plastic House Project (1961), for instance, proposed to create a dwelling in three phases: first, rooms were excavated out of a polystyrene block, second, the carved-out walls were sprayed with fibreglass, and finally the polystyrene was dissolved to reveal a free-standing structure. The only 'pre-formed' element was a 'Fuller-type' bathroom unit.[38]

Spurred on by these radical visions, a flurry of experimentation ensued, with bathroom and heart units being designed in America, France and Italy, among others, and made of PVC (polyvinyl chloride), fibreglass and acrylic.[39] It was not just the avant-garde whose imaginations were captured: mass-market science magazines like *Popular Mechanics* and *Mechanix Illustrated* became positively giddy when reporting on the new generation of plastic bathroom fittings (inhabited, invariably, by voluptuous, bikini-clad models). It was this cocktail of technological innovation and fanciful glamour that defined the Smithsons' House of the Future for the Daily Mail Ideal Home Exhibition in 1956, a domestic fantasia of plastic products and attractive models in space-age costumes. Living areas flowed around an interior courtyard; an ovoid unit containing the water closet was the only fully enclosed room. This unit was an obvious homage to the Dymaxion – indeed, the whole project reflected Fuller's dream of a self-cleaning, temperature-controlled environment with great storage – but the architects departed from Fuller's treatment of the bath itself. Their bathing area was large and theatrical, located off the dressing room and equipped with a sculptural washbasin looking out on to a rainwater cistern, a self-cleansing, thermostatically controlled red tub, a shower that blew users dry, and a sun lamp.[40]

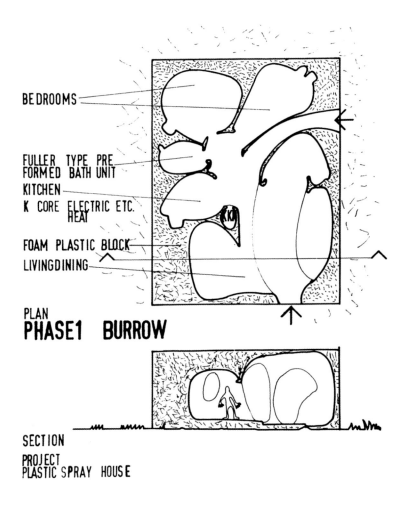

BEDROOMS

FULLER TYPE PRE FORMED BATH UNIT

KITCHEN

K CORE ELECTRIC ETC. HEAT

FOAM PLASTIC BLOCK

LIVINGDINING

PLAN
PHASE1 BURROW

SECTION
PROJECT
PLASTIC SPRAY HOUSE

One can still see why the House of the Future attracted attention: it evoked the aesthetics of the space age with its moulded forms, seamless lines and consoles complete with infrared remote controls and operating panels. But there was a more fundamental reason for the interest it drew: it was only in the post-war period that private bathrooms were

David Greene, 'Spray Plastic House', Phase 1 Burrow, 1962.

becoming more widely available in Europe, as they had been in the United States since the 1920s. Americanization was a phenomenon that not only included cars, kitchens and vacuum cleaners but bathtubs and indoor flush toilets as well, leading at least one critic to complain bitterly: 'Everyone is hypnotized by production and conveniences – sewage systems, elevators, bathrooms, washing machines.'[41] Bathroom provision became a popular measure of national progress, a clear index of the improved quality of life that post-war reconstruction was meant to bring. Conversely, the lack of a private bathroom or an indoor toilet was increasingly treated as a sign of deprivation or blight. In 1952, a chart in the influential home decorating manual *L'Art Ménager Français* showed Switzerland and the United States leading the world, with 75 and 69 per cent of their inhabitants enjoying a bathroom versus only 13 per cent in Britain and 6 per cent in France.[42]

Plastic bath in *Mechanix Illustrated* (December 1947).

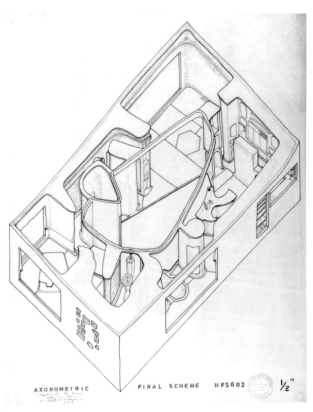

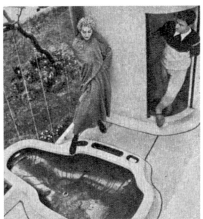

Bird's-eye Axonometric of the final scheme for Alison and Peter Smithson, 'House of the Future', at the *Daily Mail* Ideal Homes Exhibition, London, 1956.

A contemporary photo of the Smithsons' 'House of the Future' in *Mechanix Illustrated* (September 1956).

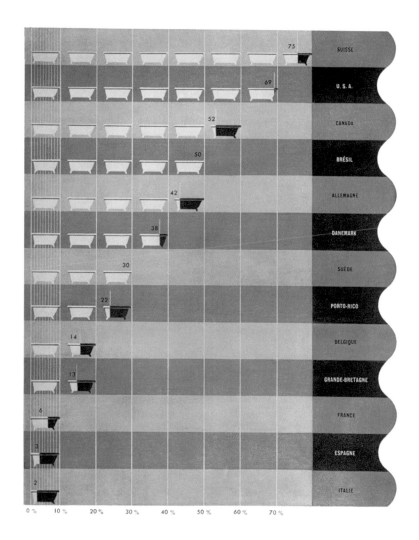

Chart of Bathrooms, *L'Art Ménager Français* (1952).

While these figures seem low or out of date – the 1952 census found that the proportion of homes with baths in Britain was actually around 63 per cent – the mere inclusion of bathrooms on such comparative charts speaks to their cultural significance.[43] When people were asked what they most wanted in their homes after the war, a domestic bathroom regularly topped the list.[44] And growing numbers

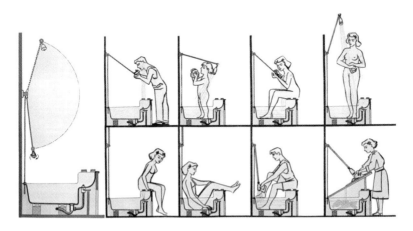

Bloc Poliban, *L'Art Ménager Français* (1952).

of Europeans were able to join the ranks of bath owners in the immediate post-war decades, as existing homes were upgraded and new housing was built. In fact, sanitaryware manufacturers could barely meet demand and most embarked on ambitious modernization programmes to expand production. Much of the new provision, however, remained as minimalist as it had been before the war, especially that installed in state-funded housing. In France, for instance, fixtures were combined into 'blocs': one might have a *bloc-douche* (with shower, sink and bidet) or a *bloc-bain* (with bath, sink and bidet). The *Poliban* was an all-in-one cleansing station – at once a sink, bath, shower, bidet and laundry tub.[45] And finally there were the *salles d'eau* (literally, water rooms), single rooms adjoining the kitchen that consolidated most of the home's 'wet' activities, from bathing to laundry.[46]

Turning its back on such compact, multipurpose spaces, the House of the Future confidently anticipated a time when bathrooms and their users would be less utilitarian. In this sense the Smithsons were prescient, and their conviction that plastics would transform the appearance of the average domestic bathroom was soon proved right. Their belief that society would move towards technologically assisted personal cleansing also came a step closer at Expo '70, the World's Fair in Osaka, when Sanyo sensationally unveiled the Ultrasonic Bath and Human Washing Machine: in this device the user was soaked, washed with ultrasonic waves, rinsed, massaged with rubber balls and then dried using heat lamps.[47] While this design may seem impossibly utopian, it is in fact in use today: Sanyo's latest version of the human washing machine, the Harmony in Roll-lo Bathing (HIRB), can be found in Japanese nursing homes. Elderly users are rolled into the HIRB, which closes like a clam, leaving only the head exposed, and the machine releases soap, washes and massages the body. When viewing publicity photographs of cheerful Japanese senior citizens

Sanyo's Ultrasonic Bath and Washing Machine, Osaka World's Fair, Japan, 1970.

undergoing the ministrations of HIRB, one feels the Smithsons' predictions were fulfilled here too.

Yet avant-garde architects largely rejected the Smithsons' consumerist, feel-good vision, and hung instead on to the belief that the bathroom unit could be the catalyst for architectural *and* social reform. For technological rationalists firmly believed that ways of life should be radically redesigned alongside technologies. Given that most prefabricated prototypes from the 1950s and 1960s assumed very conventional bathroom uses, for instance, Arthur Quarmby viewed them as failures. They were, he said, 'the same old units in a box . . .

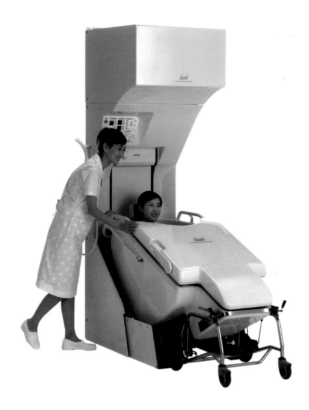

Sanyo's Harmony in Roll-Lo Bathing (HIRB), Japan, 2012.

work to date has accepted too much of the traditional way of life'.[48] Considering the failure of prefabricated houses or bathrooms to win public acceptance, however, most technological rationalists, including Fuller, accepted that they were far more likely to be adopted first in collective settings where there was less resistance to change.

Pods go public

Collective environments, of course, were also precisely where the necessary economies of scale could be achieved to justify mass production, and social housing and hostels would provide the most fertile testing ground for prefabrication. Among the most iconic prefabricated projects of this era were Moshe Safdie's Habitat 67 in Montreal (1967), the Nakagin Capsule Tower in Tokyo by Kisho Kurokawa (1972) and Charlotte Perriand's Les Arcs in the French Alps (1975), all of which had prefabricated bathroom units at their heart. More prosaically, from the 1970s, compact bathrooms (now 3.3 square metres, approximately 35 square feet) were included in East Germany's prefabricated Plattenbau concrete-slab housing units, of the WBS 70 type. And at the 1972 Olympics in Munich, acrylic prefab bathroom units were used in the Olympic Village.

The real monument to prefabricated bathroom units, however, was Terry Farrell and Nicholas Grimshaw's Bathroom Tower in London of 1967–8, often cited as the first example of a British High-Tech building.[49] It responded to a very specific problem: how to provide modern bathroom facilities for a student hostel in an old honeycomb of Victorian terraced houses. Rather than trying to retrofit the terraces, Farrell and Grimshaw instead connected them to a six-storey freestanding column of bathrooms, which could be accessed from each floor via ramps. The tower's steel mast was built in three weeks and, once erected, became a temporary crane from which the lightweight,

Terry Farrell and Nicholas Grimshaw, 'Bathroom Tower', London, 1967–8.

fibreglass bathroom pods could be winched into position. The whole structure was then enclosed within glazed panels. The bathroom units, designed by the architects and Integral Plastic Services, were assembled off-site; four moulded pieces were combined to produce either a bathroom or a divided shower/water closet unit. The pods required a rethinking of cleaning methods, too: eventually it was decided that they should be scrubbed with soft brushes attached to a hose, as in a carwash. Even if Bathroom Tower ended up having a short life (the toilets were quickly damaged and could not be easily repaired), it was significant enough to be visited by Buckminster Fuller himself in 1968.[50]

Given the emphasis on social reform, it is perhaps surprising that one of the great masterpieces of technological rationalism turned out to be a corporate headquarters: the Lloyd's Building in the City of London (1977–86) by Richard Rogers Partnership. Rogers was committed to the idea that mechanical services deserved their own architectural expression. Hence the Lloyd's service core is not placed at the building's heart but in six towers at the building's perimeter, marked out by glass-walled elevators that rise and descend theatrically. The facade also features clearly expressed bathroom pods. In their individual articulation, Lloyd's went beyond Grimshaw and Farrell's Bathroom Tower, where bathroom units were subsumed within a singular column. Instead, the visitor to Lloyd's is meant to read the bathroom pods as *components* that have been plugged into the infrastructural frame of the building and can be replaced – in theory at least. It is a real live Plug-In City, a message symbolically reinforced by the bright-blue cranes permanently perched above.

While there are many obvious precedents for the Lloyd's Building's bathroom pods, including the Portakabin, which had recently been introduced, they were actually inspired by Airstream trailer homes. The pods were manufactured in a factory, trucked on to site and hoisted into

place by crane. According to one tale, however, the Rogers Partnership's proposal to have the pods fitted out with laminate-topped basins and rubber flooring was rejected out of hand as 'not Lloyd's'. Lloyd's insistence on marble vanity units and ceramic tiles increased the risk of breakages during the installation process and undermined the intended impression of functionality and impermanence.[51] The company's desire

Rogers Partnership, Lloyd's of London, 1985. Note the 12 bathroom pods running up the facade (left).

for gravitas set other limits, too: the lively colour-coding of services, as at Rogers and Renzo Piano's Pompidou Centre, was never an option at Lloyd's. The whole was clad in stainless steel to evoke a sense of ruggedness and durability. Inevitably, wags maintained that the use of stainless steel only served to evoke a giant appliance, and the building was jokingly referred to as 'the espresso machine'.

Lloyd's marked a turning point. With the very notable exception of Kisho Kurokawa's Sony Tower in Osaka (1976), it is hard to think of another piece of avant-garde architecture that makes such a feature of bathroom pods. As Kenneth Powell remarks, ready-made modules would never again be 'as blatantly expressed' as at Lloyd's.[52] Yet at the very moment that the avant-garde's interest in the expressive potential of pods waned, they became commercial successes, thanks to the rise of fast-track construction and to companies like RB Farquhar and Armitage Shanks (now Venesta), based in Britain, and the now-defunct Danish company EJ Badekabiner. Today's pods are more prosaic than poetic. Manufactures produce them in factories, deliver them to site, lift or crane them into position and plumb and wire them in. Or they install pre-plumbed panels into a frame on site: Armitage Venesta reports that thanks to so-called 'click-fix assembly', unskilled and part-skilled workers can install a facility in 70 minutes.[53]

Due to the ease of their construction and installation, pods are now everywhere: in office buildings, hotels, rest stops, shopping centres, sport stadiums, airports, student residences, schools, barracks and hospitals. RB Farquhar alone turns out about 10,000 a year – one pod every fifteen minutes – and boasts of the superior quality of its products, which are fabricated in highly controlled conditions. This is likely one reason contemporary pods are more acceptable to the public: they cannot be distinguished from conventionally built bathrooms. (Farquhar boasts, 'Once installed, only a practised eye could differentiate between a factory-fabricated and a traditional bathroom'.[54])

Farquhar continues to use components such as ceramic tiles that require skilled labour to install (this is done, however, in the factory) and to offer clients a choice of sanitaryware from established manufacturers. In short, this is prefab, but not as Fuller saw it – as the rationalization of an obsolete system. Rather, most of these bathroom pods are an efficient, pre-installed assemblage of the usual 'end products', which do not affect overall construction methods (other than to speed them up) or shape architectural expression or social mores. Indeed, it is quite the opposite. Pods today are accepted because they look and function exactly like traditional bathrooms.

Superloos

One place where bathroom pods continue to be 'blatantly expressed', however, is on the city streets. As discussed in chapter One, prefabricated facilities have always had a highly visible presence in the public realm, either in the form of urinals or in conveniences offered by cast-iron manufacturers like Macfarlane. Today's version is the Automated Public Convenience (APC), colloquially known in Britain as the Superloo. First appearing in Beaubourg, Paris, in 1981 (possibly to blend in with the Centre Pompidou nearby), APCs made their UK debut in Leicester Square, London, two years later. In some ways, APCs realize the dream of creating a self-contained, self-cleansing bathroom unit: they are totally free-standing structures, automated and hands-free. Customers insert a coin into a slot to gain admission, use the water closet and sink (which are activated by sensors), and the facility is automatically cleansed, disinfected, air-dried and deodorized after each use.

On paper, APCs are a reasonably progressive piece of urban design, providing clean facilities to the public 24 hours a day. European governments turned to them as part of campaigns to modernize city

streets and to eliminate old pissoirs, which were increasingly seen as embarrassing eyesores. In fact, according to popular myth, APCs were invented after Jacques Chirac, then mayor of Paris, asked his friend Jean-Claude Decaux to come up with a replacement for pissoirs that could also be used by women. This inclusive originary myth has since been entrenched, albeit provocatively, by artist Lars Ramberg in *Liberté*, installed at the National Museum of Art in Oslo in 2005 and at the Nordic Pavilion at the Venice Biennale in 2007. Ramberg repainted three original concrete Decaux APCs, one red, one white and one blue, and replaced the 'toilette' sign on each with 'Liberté', 'Egalité' or 'Fraternité' to symbolize French democratic ideals – a modern-day Statue of Liberty. In the Oslo installation, the APCs were actually plumbed in: when visitors went inside and shut the door to

Lars Ramberg, *Liberté*, National Museum of Art, Oslo, Norway, 2005.

use the facility, they were treated to historical speeches from great world leaders (Charles de Gaulle, King Haakon VII, Franklin Roosevelt) accompanied by national anthems.

Without wishing to undermine Ramberg's choice of symbol (I would argue that a public convenience is a very apt symbol of democratic ideals), the true story of how the APC came about seems to be more mundane.[55] Rather than responding to a personal request by Chirac, Decaux himself identified a gap in the market after Paris City Council banned pissoirs. Importantly, Decaux was not a sanitary engineer like Jennings; his line was in what is now called 'out-of-home' advertising. He saw the surfaces of street furniture, from bus shelters to phone boxes to public toilets, as largely untapped sources of advertising revenue. He also saw that this revenue might be a way of meeting one of the main demands of government authorities: that public conveniences be financially self-supporting. Not unlike Jennings, who 100 years earlier had offered to run conveniences in exchange for user fees, Decaux proposed to supply and maintain conveniences in exchange for rights to advertising revenue.

It might seem hard to argue against such a hassle-free and economical solution to the problem of providing public conveniences, now commonly regarded by local governments as an expensive headache and the loci of antisocial behaviour of all kinds. Many are only too happy to close their own facilities and sign long-term contracts for APCs to lower maintenance and labour costs, or at least to use them to supplement attended facilities, which have more limited opening hours. And even though many may in theory dislike the idea of yet more of the urban streetscape being taken over by advertising, there is a long tradition of street furnishings being used in this way, the most oft-cited example being Paris's green cast-iron Morris columns. It is therefore not surprising to find that APCs have proliferated: there are at least 2,678 of JCDecaux's around the world, from

Belgium to Portugal to the US. This figure does not include APCs provided by other outdoor advertisers such as Wall, Cemusa, Clear Channel, Viacom or CBS Outdoor, usually as part of larger street furnishing contracts worth millions of dollars.[56]

Even though APCs are increasingly common in Western metropolitan centres, they are regarded with considerable ambivalence. The automation of APCs means that there is no longer any need for an attendant, which removes one of the most expensive elements of a typical public convenience but also the most effective guarantor of accountability and safety. APCs are consequently built like fortresses to minimize damage from vandalism, leading to the charge that they are 'space invaders', cluttering pavements and disfiguring public spaces. And many users mistrust them: in a recent survey of over 500 people, 67 per cent said they would not use them.[57] With their anti-vandal features and wet surfaces, many find APCs unpleasant at best and scary at worst, with the fear of having the door open automatically – as it does after a set number of minutes – only superseded by the fear of not being able to get out at all. Urban myths of the trapped-user-drowned-in-automated-cleansing-cycle variety are fuelled by the occasional real disaster: in one memorably ironic incident, one Superloo exploded in Stoke-on-Trent, the historic heart of Britain's ceramics industry.[58]

Incidents like these draw a latent fear of automated environments, and of building services more generally, to the surface. Considering the enduring appeal of the 'building gone bad' plot in disaster movies, the architect David Bass connects the dislike of exposed plumbing to a wariness of the sophisticated, artificial 'life' of the support systems contained in building walls today:

The naked pipe's capacity to offend is only the surface effect of a deeper threat . . . it contains things that move, unseen. A leaking pipe gives cause for anxiety. The breaking or removal of a pipe frees its contents, revealing a low-grade form of life. This 'life', normally restrained but occasionally bursting forth insolently and extravagantly, is at the root of the feelings of disquiet, fear and fascination which are provoked by building services.[59]

The original APCs were about as close to naked pipes as one could get: they looked, quite simply, like extruded bits of infrastructure. Today, their Brutalist exteriors have been tempered with colour and historicist detailing, so that they evoke the Victorian cast-iron facilities they were designed to replace. They have become more environmentally friendly and user-friendly. After some high-profile clashes between manufacturers and disability activists, inclusive APCs are now available: the streets of Paris, for instance, are now graced by Patrick Jouin's elegant, universal design models, which are free of charge.[60] Other notable architects and designers have been involved in restyling APCs as well, including Nicholas Grimshaw, whose firm was commissioned by Cemusa to design its facilities for New York City, the first new public conveniences there for many decades.[61] As one of the architects of the Bathroom Tower, Grimshaw's involvement in APC design seems inevitable, a kind of closing of the circle, as APCs and their kin (for instance, the Urilift pop-up street urinal) can be seen as the purest manifestation of technological rationalism on city streets today.

It seems unlikely, however, that hardcore technological rationalists of the 1960s would admire APCs or indeed any structure that remained so firmly anchored to the ground by infrastructure. Fuller, as ever, was uncompromising about the need to eliminate fixed sewerage. Speaking of the Dymaxion Bathroom in 1955, he claimed to have no interest in pursuing its design further because it had only ever been an interim solution. 'Today we have learned from industry that when we clean a watch or a gyroscope we do not have to dunk it in a bath tub', he observed. 'We found that it was possible to get along without a piped-in water supply by using atomized water under air pressure.'[62] This was not simply speculation: Fuller did, in fact, invent a Fog Gun for bathing in the 1940s. It worked by combining compressed air and atomized water with triggered-in solvents; high-pressure air, Fuller claimed, was far better for human skin than high-pressure water. He also anticipated a time when 'the other functions of the bathroom' could be met by 'odorless, dry-packaging machinery, employing modern plastics, electronic sealing, dry-conveying systems' – in short, a system that would shrink-wrap excrement, allowing it to be collected and reused.[63] This technology was actually incorporated into his design of 1943 for a mobile mechanical unit, which came with its own air compressor and tank.

By the 1970s, too, the awakening ecological movement made water conservation a priority. Arthur Quarmby, for instance, condemned waterborne sewage as 'ridiculously extravagant in an age of exploding demand on our water resources'. In Fulleresque mode, he went on to wonder whether human bodily functions could themselves be redesigned with the use of food pellets. He mooted the possibility of ultrasonic bathing. And he drew attention to domestic water recycling systems where waste water was purified, re-circulated and topped up with rainwater, asking: 'Can we now doubt that eventually the dwelling will be as self-contained as the transistor radio, and that the umbilical cords which tie buildings to the ground – water, gas, electricity, drainage, will one day be cut?'[64] That day has not yet come – nor has there been a widespread turn to food pellets – but we have recently entered a great phase of experimentation in pursuit of a self-contained toilet. We return to these and other experiments in chapter Six.

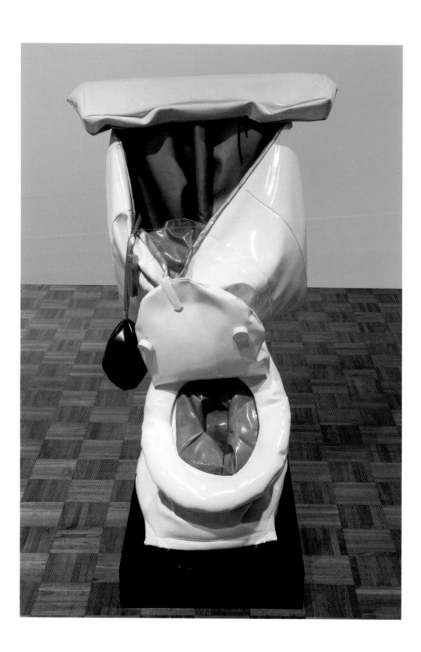

4 | The Soft Bathroom

In 1966, the sculptor Claes Oldenburg produced *Soft Toilet*, one of a group of 'soft' pieces that also included a washbasin, bathtub, engine, fan and typewriter. With this series, Oldenburg effectively reproduced a Corbusian catalogue of industrial type-objects, with an important difference: his works were all made of sheet vinyl. They sagged. They yielded. Their seams stretched. Their innards spilled out. In short, they were anything but the purist heroes of modernist lore. *Soft Toilet* did not seek a radical break or a head-on collision with this lineage of iconic mythmaking; rather, it was about its gentle deflation.

Oldenburg's piece was timely, for the bathroom was changing. Instead of being dominated by a utilitarian and hygienic aesthetic, bathrooms softened and warmed up. This was a literal process as plastics and other materials entered bathroom design, replacing hard, cold materials with soft, warm ones. And as central heating became more common, bathrooms became far more enjoyable during the winter months, spaces in which one might conceivably linger.[1] Even toilet paper became softer as the British began to abandon their hard, non-absorbent tissues, known as 'shinies', in favour of the creped toilet papers that Americans had long preferred. These material changes, along with the reintroduction of colour, meant that bathrooms lost their clinical aesthetic and began to be more closely integrated into

Claes Oldenburg, *Soft Toilet*, 1966. Wood, kapok, vinyl, wire, Plexiglas: on metal stand and painted wooden base, 144.9 x 70.2 x 71.3 cm.

the rest of the home. In 1970 the designer David Hicks summed up this shift when he insisted: 'A bathroom is a *room*, not just a plain tiled cubicle.'[2]

The softening was also manifest in the way in which people spoke about bathrooms. With the move towards more casual, sexually liberated lifestyles, bathrooms began to be more widely treated as places of leisure, sociality and sensuality – places for 'regeneration' as well as for 'ablutions'.[3] The basic, standardized bathroom no longer seemed sufficient for the various activities and functions the room might serve. The 1970s thus saw the emergence of a different kind of bathroom space: the 'living bath', a highly personalized, multi-purpose space for the whole family.

The film star in her bath

For the wealthy, of course, the bathroom had been a soft space for many decades. In this sense, the upper-class bathroom had a very different trajectory than the mostly middle- or working-class bathrooms covered so far in this book. While there is not space for a full exposé of this type, it is worth expanding on some of their features, as they were to strongly influence bathroom aesthetics between the 1950s and the 1980s.[4] Three features were of particular importance to the twentieth-century luxury bathroom: the bath, the treatment of surfaces, and the use of colour, which was never banished as thoroughly as modernists liked to claim.

Even today, there are few more recognizable, if clichéd, symbols of luxury than a woman immersed in bubbles in an oversize bath (preferably pink). But this visual trope would have bemused, say, the Georgians, who seriously revived the habit of bathing and 'taking the waters' in the eighteenth century. Those in the higher echelons of eighteenth-century society installed oversize baths in their homes, but these were plunge baths, more like small swimming pools. Plunge baths were prescribed by doctors as part of a medical regime and were to be taken cold. Even if these baths were very elegant, plunging into them was unlikely to have been relaxing in the modern sense, any more than were the popular water cure treatments of the time.

Following the German practice established by Vincenz Priessnitz, hydropathic cures used cold water in all its forms: one showered, bathed and ingested it with the aim of improving circulation. Catharine Beecher, one of the most influential household experts in nineteenth-century America, approvingly chronicled her treatment at Brattleboro Hydropathic Establishment in Vermont in 1850. At four in the morning, she was packed in a wet sheet for several hours before being immersed in a cold plunge bath and then sent on a long walk. She was then subjected to a ten-minute douche of cold water falling from a height of eighteen feet (5.5 metres). More walking followed, until it was time for a sitting bath, again in cold water, for half an hour. Throughout the various phases of packing, plunging, douching and marching, she consumed glasses of cold water.[5]

How did bathing move from being part of a curative regime to being a pleasurable part of daily life? How did the bath shift from medical aid to status symbol? The change in attitudes towards bathing did not happen overnight. Even once the habit of body cleansing became more common (around the mid-1800s, though this varied con-siderably among different classes), adherents of both sexes were instructed to rub themselves vigorously with a coarse towel or brush 'to promote a healthful excitement' that would leave the skin glow-ing.[6] The availability of mass-produced bathroom fittings and plumbed-in hot water made bathing more habitual – and surely more relaxing – but the notion that water could be used to stimulate the skin, aid circulation and combat lethargy persisted. Combined shower-baths of the nineteenth century were faithful to the water cure in offering settings like 'plunge bath', 'needle spray' and 'douche', which doused users with a powerful stream of cold water from overhead. Even today, with the popularity of powerful 'rainfall' and 'monsoon' shower heads, we continue to embrace the bracing, naturalistic use of water.

This lingering association of 'the cure' with water might help explain why, even among the very wealthy, the first dedicated bathrooms tended to be plain or modest affairs. The early bathroom was to be a place of rectitude – of perfunctory self-cleansing. From the 1870s on, however, a combination of expensive materials, elaborate decor, fine workmanship and more technologically advanced fittings began to transform many upper-class bathrooms into showpieces. This could result in rooms of astonishing lushness, such as the extraordinary bathrooms designed by architect William Burges for his patron, the Marquis of Bute, at Cardiff Castle in 1873. Demonstrating the shared antiquarian tastes of architect and client, the Marquis's own Gothick bathroom, with rich marble panels set in mahogany, was separated from the bedroom by a screen of two gilded Islamic arches.[7]

To contemporary readers, the fact that this early showpiece bath was designed for a male patron might seem surprising. This pinpoints the major shift that occurred between the 1870s and the 1920s which was key to the bathroom's softening: the luxury bath became feminized. This process required that the upright pummellings of hydropathy be rejected and that more exotic traditions of recumbent, warm bathing be evoked instead, for instance Turkish baths or hammams, which were strongly associated with female sensuality. This association was exploited in endless nineteenth-century paintings, from Ingres to Gérôme, of harem baths inhabited by languid, semi-clothed odalisques. These paintings were in no way an accurate

description of the mostly respectable Turkish baths found in British hydropathic resorts from the mid-1850s onwards. Rather, they represented a fantasy of bathing women as languorous and sexually available, an image that was to become a stock-in-trade of later, Orient-themed Hollywood films. Baths anchored a seductive, if largely imaginary, empire of the senses.

The actual inhabitation of the luxury bathroom by women did not happen consistently or all at once. Even with the rise of fixed plumbing, daily cleansing operations did not move straight away to the bathroom. Many activities, from sponge baths to face washing, still

The Marquis of Bute's bathroom, Cardiff Castle, Wales, 1873.

took place in bedrooms or in the commodious dressing rooms in which late Victorians were groomed and clothed. When baths were installed, they still tended to be tucked away, out of sight: recall Queen Victoria's dressing room at Osborne House on the Isle of Wight, in which the bath and shower were hidden behind closet doors. As the discreet nature of her bathing equipment underlines, the Queen belonged to an age when bathing was not yet entirely respectable. As one aristocrat memorably sniffed: 'There is in the taste for sitting down in a bathtub a certain indolence and softness that ill suits a woman.'[8] To help ward off even the hint of impropriety, women often wore linen chemises when they bathed.

The French sociologist Monique Éleb, however, identifies both prudery and coquetry in the dressing room: while the ideal of femininity demanded that women cleanse themselves modestly, it also valorized the art of the *toilette*.[9] The distinction between equipment dedicated to hygiene and that to beauty meant that, even as bath fittings (those 'indiscreet items which reveal too personal an aspect of life') were kept out of sight, ladies' dressing rooms became increasingly luxurious.[10] Nowhere was this more evident than in French *cabinets de toilette*. These were the softest of all possible spaces. Furnishings included dressing tables with mirrors and the ultimate symbol of repose and female horizontality, the chaise longue. Expensive materials from marble to onyx, silk draperies, carpets and poufs were layered to create sensual, colourful and fantastical settings.[11] Émile Zola described one elaborate French *cabinet* in the 1870s featuring a muslin tent descending from a silver dome and a black, bearskin carpet. The link between the *cabinets* and the art of female beauty was so strong that the arrival of the 'open' Anglo-American bathroom in France was seen to threaten femininity itself. On viewing an example at the Exposition d'Hygiène de 1900, one journalist decried its exposure of water closet, bath and bidet. The bathroom, he despaired, had been transformed into a 'factory of washing' with 'no place for refinement, elegance, and for the thousand little things that contribute to a woman's charm'.[12]

It was only in the 1910s and '20s that baths moved into the spotlight: surrounded by mirrors, they became starring features of the most decadent European Art Deco bathrooms. This did not mean, however, that the distinction between hygiene and *toilette* disappeared. Rather, the luxury bath itself became more closely associated with rituals of female beauty; in turn, free-standing needle showers, with their stark pipework exoskeletons, became associated more with 'masculine' cleansing functions. As beautifying and cleansing activities were remapped on to bath and shower respectively, the sharp distinction between bathroom and dressing room also eroded. Activities that had formerly been sited in the dressing room, such as the application of make-up, shifted to the bathroom, along with related furnishings like dressing stands and vanity tables. Whereas Victorian bathrooms had only small, framed mirrors, these now escaped their frames and multiplied; their appearance on walls, doors and even ceilings announced that the luxury bathroom was now as important a space for female self-invention and display as the dressing room had been before it.

Art Deco rapidly developed a highly reflective and interiorized bathroom aesthetic. As we have seen, it was not unusual for upper-class Victorian bathrooms to make use of opulent materials to create strong effects: over 60 different marble panels and alabaster windows were used in the Marquis of Bute's bathroom at Cardiff Castle.[13] Art Deco deployed an equally wide palette of materials to accentuate spatial effects, but this now included industrially made ones such as aluminium, stainless steel, Lucite, Bakelite, Formica and plate glass. The milky, alabaster windows in the Marquis's bathroom might be rendered instead in a pigmented, structural glass like Vitrolite; his marble panels in the vitreous Carrara or Sani Onyx faux-marble. The

tortoiseshell, horn or ivory vanity sets of the Victorian era were now produced in celluloid. New kinds of lighting such as neon tubing were introduced (most houses would only recently have been equipped with electricity), as well as metal reflectors to cast indirect light. Bold, geometric tile patterns predominated – hexagons, octagons and lozenges – and were echoed in angular, 'cut-corner' bathroom appliances.[14] Mirrors, polished floors and shiny, metallic wall surfaces emitted a glow not unlike that created by Josef von Sternberg when he dusted aluminium powder on to the face of Marlene Dietrich.

Not coincidentally, the most famous Art Deco bathrooms were created for female stars of film and stage. One of the most sensational was the concoction dreamed up in 1932 by the arts patron Edward James and the artist Paul Nash for James's wife, the dancer and actress Tilly Losch. Its bathroom fittings were jet black but its 'accent' colours were peach and deep, metallic purple, selected by James to complement his wife's hair and eyes. The walls were lined with plate glass and stippled cathedral glass, an industrially made glass that was rippled

Oliver Hill, bathroom for Lady Mount Temple, Gayfere House, London, 1931.

to look as if rain was falling against it. For lighting, Nash used crescent-shaped neon tubing on the walls and a combined mirror/light fixture on the ceiling. A chromium-plated dancer's barre completed the scene.[15]

Rich with textures and atmosphere, and tailor-made to set off Losch's looks and physique, the bathroom seemed both to celebrate and to cocoon her. In its sensual showcasing of the female body, Tilly Losch's bathroom evokes Adolf Loos's earlier, unrealized house for Josephine Baker (1927), and it is pertinent here to recall the architectural historian Beatriz Colomina's discussion of that project. The Baker

Paul Nash, bathroom for the dancer Tilly Losch, London, 1932.

House was designed around a double-height swimming pool and wrapped with windows to allow visitors underwater views of the dancer. On one level, it is hard to conceive of a more voyeuristic project. But rather than seeing it as one-way viewing device that simply objectifies Baker, Colomina points out that it is equally possible that Baker would have derived pleasure from the sight of her own body reflected in the pool windows.[16]

The intermingling of exhibitionism, narcissism and voyeurism is a defining feature of luxury bathing spaces. In particular, we find that

Carlo Scarpa, bathroom, Villa Ottolenghi, Bardolino, Italy, 1978.

a teasing game of display and concealment is often played out in them, one usually set in motion by the partial or total exposure of the body through a screen or transparent or translucent fittings. Consider the glass bathtub designed by Otto Wagner for his own Viennese apartment in 1898.[17] Or the bathroom pod fitted with one-way glass, standing at the threshold of the master bedroom in Carlo Scarpa's Villa Ottolenghi, on Lake Garda (1978), like a sort of voyeuristic sentry box.[18] Today such games are commonplace in the bathrooms of boutique hotels and restaurants, as well as in the dressing rooms of stores like Prada in New York City, which use high-tech materials such as Priva-Lite glass to allow customers to modulate the degree of transparency themselves. Like the pool in Loos's Baker House, these spaces confuse any clear-cut distinction between performer and audience; in fact, performer and audience are often one and the same.

Bursting into colour throughout

Following the Second World War, the bathroom continued to be a female-focused space, though it stepped back from the overt sensuality of Art Deco. Instead, the post-war period saw the 're-energised domestification of women', as women were urged on all sides to be 'nurturants, beautifiers and consumers', roles many had set aside during the war years.[19] Manufacturers of sanitaryware identified colour as a means of attracting female customers because it would allow women to personalize their bathroom spaces. Indeed, since the 1920s colour had been central to the industry's concerted efforts to transform bathroom fixtures into consumer goods, which would be more frequently renewed than staple wares. Home decorators signalled their readiness to embrace alternatives to the standard white bathroom. As the American expert on etiquette Emily Post exclaimed in 1930: 'I would like very much indeed to rip all white [fixtures] out and burst into colour throughout.'[20]

The example of Kohler demonstrates how sanitaryware manufacturers used colour to stimulate consumer demand. In the 1920s, Walter Kohler identified colour and styling as the means by which to address the problems of under-consumption and the slow turnover of products. Using mass advertising, innovative designs and new forms of monetary credit, Kohler rolled out a campaign to introduce 'Beauty in the Bathroom', with the aim of increasing average spends and of encouraging homeowners to remodel. In 1927, in a full-page colour advertisement in the American magazine *Saturday Evening Post*, Kohler announced the centrepiece of its campaign: the Colorware range, in six shades – Autumn Brown, Lavender, Spring Green, Old Ivory, West Point Grey and Horizon Blue. Following a consultation with the Taylor System of Color Harmony (the same firm that advised Henry Ford on colours for the Model A), Old Ivory was replaced by the Tuscan line, which became a best-seller. Jet Black was introduced in 1928.[21] Other companies, including the American industry giants Crane and Standard, launched their own coloured lines soon afterwards, with extravagantly Europeanized titles (Rose du Barry, Orchid of Vincennes, Ivoire de Medici) to add to their allure – and to justify their higher prices.

The implications of the introduction of colour were dramatic. As the same colour could now be applied to a cast-iron enamel finish *and* a vitreous china glaze, it became possible for customers to buy a set of fittings matched in a single colour other than white. Any chance that customers might mix-and-match fixtures from different companies, however, was limited by the fact that American firms would not cooperate to produce standard colours, as the National Bureau of Standards urged them to do and as British companies did.[22] Despite some initially encouraging signs, efforts to take colour mainstream faltered in the 1930s, chiefly because there were far cheaper ways for home renovators to freshen up their bathrooms. Why pay for new fixtures

when a coat of paint or matching towels would do the job?[23] It was only in the 1950s, in the post-war consumer boom, that coloured fixtures truly took off. In keeping with the age of 'frilly femininity', the taste was for perky, Doris Day hues – pink, turquoise, peach – carried through in 'ensembles' of towels, bath mats and toilet seat covers. When in 1957 the London-based company Andrex introduced pink toilet paper, the possibilities for colour coordination grew even further.[24]

By now, most middle-class women could afford certain luxury features in their homes, or at least sample them on their holidays, as

Advertisement for Kohler's Colorware range, 1928.

baths became tourist attractions in their own right. American honey-moon resort owners, most famously those in the Poconos in Pennsylvania, gambled on women not being able to resist the lure of fancy bathrooms and transformed theirs into the stuff of populuxe dreams. In one advertisement of the mid-1960s for the Royal Suite at Pocono Gardens Lodge, readers were treated to the view of a 20 by 20 foot bathroom (6 by 6 metres) complete with a round, elevated, pink-and-white tiled bathtub surrounded by Roman statuary, mirrors and potted plants. In a resort dedicated to newlywed love and together-ness, the groom was conspicuously absent; instead, the advert focused exclusively on the decorous bride, who enjoyed her big bath alone. Devoted to bodily pampering and to 'delicious' self-indulgence, the bathroom was a hyper-feminine *mise en scène* in which the bride could temporarily inhabit the role of film star in her bath.[25]

It was an image that most women would have known well. This was the great age of the film-star-in-her-bath publicity shot. On 30 September 1946, *Life* magazine's cover image featured actress Jeanne Crain in a foamy bath, a single, delicate bubble balanced on her fin-ger. The image was perfect for the post-war period: playful, light, hopeful. The bubble bath augured a time when domestic life would be less weighty – an especially appealing message for young war brides setting up house for the first time. Roland Barthes observed a compar-able use of bubbles in French post-war commercials for laundry detergent, noting the way their sheer uselessness and airiness sum-moned up the idea of luxury in housewives' minds. Bubble bath, like laundry detergent, was a mundane product, available in any super-market; the real thing being sold, the magic promise of the bubbles, was liberation from the elbow grease and labour of housework. As Barthes said, 'it gratifies in the consumer a tendency to imagine matter as something airy, with which contact is effected in a mode both light and vertical.'[26] It was frictionless, effortless.

The image of the Royal Suite also makes clear how plastics were changing the appearance of bathrooms. Due to its malleability and almost unlimited range of colours and effects (metallic, marbled, china-like), fibreglass enabled the creation of oversize or unusually shaped 'feature' baths.[27] For the most part, however, plastics were used more prosaically. Low-cost and lightweight bathroom fittings were ubiquitous by the mid-1960s, from Plexiglas shower enclosures to polypropylene toilet seats to vinyl flooring. By the 1970s, over a third of new baths were of vacuum-formed acrylic.[28] Beauty products and cleansers began to be packaged in polyethylene squeeze bottles. The proliferation of plastic containers and also of disposable paper products, from Kleenex to tampons, helps explain why long countertops and built-in storage units became an essential feature of the post-war bathroom.[29] Built-in vanities and cabinets, faced in colour laminates such as Formica, once again enclosed sinks. Continuous surface was in; exposed pipes were out. One design handbook declared: 'There is nothing more important to achieving a visually satisfactory bathroom than concealing the pipework.'[30]

Advertisement for Pocono Gardens Lodge's Royal Suite in *Bride's Magazine* (1965).

Lastly, the Royal Suite drives home the point that technology was now a much bigger presence in post-war bathrooms, speeding up and easing the job of caring for the body. A salon hairdryer is visible in the Suite's mirrors: such dryers, along with Florida sunlamps for tanning, were the latest must-have items. Though few women would have been able to afford a salon hairdryer or sunbed in their homes, a battery of appliances was just at this time becoming part of daily beauty routines, from hand-held hairdryers to electric toothbrushes – and the associated need to store these items further explains the new emphasis on storage.[31] In keeping with other post-war domestic technologies, careful attention was paid to the styling of these products, resulting in design classics such as Raymond Loewy's streamlined 'Flight' bathroom scales to Braun's 'Sixtant' men's electric shaver. Technology's presence in the bathroom would only increase in the coming decades, eventually leading to innovations like the Jacuzzi, which produced bubbles mechanically and seemed to render plain bubble baths obsolete.

Even a quick glance at the Royal Suite reveals why the compact, prefabricated bathrooms discussed in chapter Three proved to be such a hard sell among homeowners. Bathrooms were becoming spaces of aspiration, replete with associations of pampering and leisure. In *The House and the Art of Its Design* (1953) the architect R. W. Kennedy noted a growing schism between the fantasy bathroom and its more pedestrian reality: 'Obviously the sybaritic atmosphere, designed for pleasure in warmth, steam, nudity, sex, flowers and alcohol, cannot appropriately combine with the bathinette, the toidy seat, and the diaper pail.' But he saw a way out of the impasse, noting that 'the well-designed family bath, large, commodious, practical, somewhat ascetic, can be a magnificent thing.'[32] Kennedy's words would be prophetic as the 1970s would see the introduction of a new type of bathroom space: the living bath, which held out the possibility that dream and reality might be knit together at last.

The living bath

The living bath would not have been possible without the shifting attitudes to the body and bathing ushered in by the sexual revolution of the 1960s and '70s. The sexual revolution had an immediate impact on bathroom design. American society generally in this period has been described as becoming 'progressively prosthetic' in terms of sex, relying increasingly on technology, gadgets and devices of various kinds to mediate experience, sensation and bodily pleasure.[33] This was the age of the motorized bed and the bachelor pad, the oversize bath and Jacuzzi. The oversize bath had long been a popular status symbol because it managed to convey wealth and (inevitably Roman) decadence through its excessive size – it was much bigger than it ever practically needed it to be. But the oversize bath now began to serve a real purpose: it was designed for two or more and signalled a freer, more liberated attitude to the body and to sex.

The sexualization of the bathtub was detectable already in the late 1950s. One of the most memorable images of this period must be that of the pin-up Jayne Mansfield in the bathroom at her Hollywood mansion, the Pink Palace. Mansfield and her husband Mickey Hargitay were involved in designing every last detail of the Pink Palace, from the bathroom to the overlarge bed to its most notorious feature, the heart-shaped swimming pool. (Hargitay had been a plumber before he won fame as Mr Universe.) It is almost impossible to know where to begin to describe the bathroom space they created, so overwhelming is the profusion of textures that greets the viewer. The gold-coloured, heart-shaped bath is fitted with gold-plated taps and gold knick-knacks of various kinds. Deep-pink shag carpet gobbles up every surface: floor, walls and ceiling. Pink pendant lights dangle down. And, in the centre, Mansfield herself, in a bubble bath, serenely brushing her signature platinum-blonde hair.

Mansfield's *mise en scène* obviously drew on the Hollywood film tradition of using bathing scenes to highlight the sexual desirability

of its female lead as well as her sensual and moral decadence. Cecil B. DeMille set the trend with *Male and Female* (1919), in which a spoiled English aristocrat, played by Gloria Swanson, enjoys a provocative splash in a sunken tub. In *The Sign of the Cross* thirteen years later, DeMille upped the ante yet again, depicting the corrupt Roman empress Poppaea, played by Claudette Colbert, bathing in asses' milk. The Pink Palace also recalled Tilly Losch's bathroom in the way it cocooned its famous occupant. But here the cocooning reached a whole new level: padded in pink shag, the bathroom resembled nothing so much as a cell in a lunatic asylum conceived by Liberace. Why would one need – or want – carpets on the wall? Or the ceiling? Or a bathtub shaped as a heart? It is as total a rejection of functionalist doctrine and its hygienic vision as one could devise. The pneumatic

Jayne Mansfield takes a bubble bath at the Pink Palace, Hollywood, California, 1960.

Mansfield herself is more decorously posed than was her wont, perhaps because the space itself said it all. Bursting with texture and colour, the bathroom's surfaces were transformed into 'a medium for visceral and tactile fulfilment'.[34] The Pink Palace bathroom was a profoundly infantile space that appealed not to the mind but to the body. Its softness was meant as an invitation.

The invitation was made explicit in the honeymoon resorts in the Poconos. In the mid-1960s, Cove Haven resort announced an alternative to its 'frilly feminine' pink baths: scarlet, heart-shaped ones. The heart-shaped tub now became *the* focal point of the newlywed experience and set off a national craze. Cove Haven's owner, plumber-turned-hotelier Morris Wilkins, noted: 'each [bath] costs over 3,000 dollars to build, but it's worth it. Couples call us for reservations and don't even care what kind of accommodation they get, as long as they get the big bath.' A photo in an issue of *Life* in 1971 showed newlyweds kissing in Cove Haven's heart-shaped tub, surveyed by a camera on a tripod; the bride held a shutter-release cord, judging the perfect moment to CLICK. For *Life*, this detail confirmed that America had entered an era of affluent vulgarity. 'Apparently,' the editorial intoned, 'just being with each other doesn't seem to be enough. We need, or think we need, some affirmation.' At the very least, the suite made clear that the bath was no longer about the performance of femininity but of sex – the self-conscious and 'prosthetic' kind popularized by *Playboy*.[35] (Hugh Hefner, naturally, had a massive Roman-style bath in his own private 'porntopia', the Playboy Mansion.[36])

Developments in Hollywood, holiday resorts and the Playboy Mansion were not necessarily typical. But even if few people had such overtly pornotopic spaces in their homes, the hedonistic mood affected the average residential bathroom too. A kind of humid sensuality took hold. Many bathrooms began to boast carpets, artwork, plush seating, skylights and 'a veritable jungle' of potted plants.[37] Pastels were replaced by bold shades: deep reds, oranges, browns and the era's best-seller, avocado. Bathrooms became more spacious to accommodate a greater number of users and activities and in 1968 a survey of 951 British housewives confirmed that a bathroom's size was the single most important determinant of user satisfaction.[38] These larger bathrooms were separated into zones and the most decadent were multi-level, with elevated or sunken features. Baths also inflated in size: some were up to 7 by 5 feet (2 by 1.5 metres) – formerly the size of an entire compact bathroom. And at least some featured whirlpool baths or Jacuzzis, which had previously been reserved for hydrotherapeutic use in public institutions. More than any other innovation, the Jacuzzi's appearance in the home announced that the era of relaxation had arrived.

Bathroom expert Alexander Kira welcomed this new focus, confidently predicting in 1975, 'Whereas the '50s and the '60s were the era of the kitchen and the family room, the '70s will be the era of the bathroom and body care.'[39] Even those who could not afford built-in whirlpools might still enjoy new gadgets, from portable spas to hot-mist facial machines. The toilet was affected too. In 1975 the Detroit-based Olsonite Company introduced the AD 2000 Comfort Control Center. The AD 2000 was a water closet seat with a tilting, vibrating back, reading light, television, radio and ashtray (smoking was such a common bathroom activity in this period that the vulnerability of plastic to cigarette burns was considered its major drawback). Even more radical than any of these features, however, was the AD 2000's built-in bidet. Americans generally disliked bidets, reportedly because they were associated with 'loose' (read: French) sexuality. Perhaps Olsonite Company thought that the spirit of sexual liberation would overturn this prejudice, but in this they were mistaken, and the Comfort Control Center soon joined the long list of failed bathroom experiments.

The new emphasis on bodily care, however, meant that other taboos were relaxed. Bathrooms in this era became more couple- and family-oriented. Most bathrooms had always served multiple family members at busy times and some already had features that acknowledged simultaneous use, such as zoned areas to create privacy. But now the potential for familial socializing began to be fully embraced. His-and-Hers bathtubs joined His-and-Hers sinks. In 1966 the upmarket American department store Neiman-Marcus featured His-and-Hers baths in their glamorous Christmas catalogue, and sanitaryware manufacturers began to offer baths for two.[40] Prominent design gurus welcomed this development, arguing that bathrooms should take over some of the functions of more conventional living spaces. In *The Bed and Bath Book* (1978) the British designer Terence Conran, founder of the iconic home furnishings store Habitat, proposed installing couches, writing desks and telephones in bathrooms to enable 'more energetic pursuits'. He then reproduced an image of his own, commodious bathroom, which was a converted reception room with an open fire, worktable and couch, and praised its convenience. 'From your couch', he noted, 'you can also supervise the children's first exploratory water play . . .'.[41]

The most ambitious version of the family bathroom could be found in Germany. The Wohnbad, or 'living bath', manufactured by Röhm, debuted at the IDZ Berlin exhibition in 1973. It had all of the elements expected of a bathroom along with some more unusual ones, including a bar and a coffee maker. Röhm's display also included that most quintessential of 1970s design features, a carpeted conversation pit, thus aligning the 'living bath' with more informal social regimes. The whole set-up, in fact, reflected more relaxed social mores, especially the easing of prohibitions around nudity. In one telling publicity photo, for instance, a family is shown in the Wohnbad, the naked mother in the tub and the bathrobe-clad father and child on the floor beside her.[42] In response to the efforts of sexologists and feminists to challenge the secrecy and shame that surrounded certain bodily functions (Judy Chicago's art installation *Menstruation Bathroom*, 1972, is the standout example), the naked adult body began to be celebrated as a natural element of human existence. Baths were even built with internal ledges so that adults and children could bathe together. This taboo-breaking spirit would reach its zenith with the publication of Kira's *The Bathroom* (first published in 1966 and substantially revised in 1976), which sought to do for the bathroom what Masters and Johnson did for sex.

The living bath concept was also inspired by the contemporary fascination with traditional bathing practices, particularly communal and naturist ones. Kira remarked that in treating the bathroom as 'a natural part of human living' the Wohnbad came close in spirit to Scandinavian saunas and Japanese baths, but these were only two of the bathing traditions that were being widely studied.[43] The bible of the alternate bathing movement was *Sweat*, published in 1978 by the photographer Mikkel Aaland, which explored everything from

Wohnbad, in Alexander Kira, *The Bathroom* (revised edition, 1976).

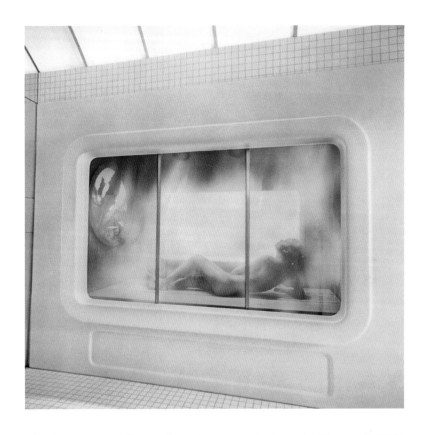

Finnish saunas to Native American sweat lodges. And between 1976 and 1981, the California-based magazine *Wet: The Magazine of Gourmet Bathing* covered similar ground, seamlessly mixing its celebration of bathing and nudism with ecological awareness and avant-garde typography. One result was that Nordic-style dry-heat saunas and Japanese-style baths were introduced in many American and European homes in this period. By 1966 the *New York Times* claimed there were 20,000 saunas in America and listed Philip Johnson, Paul Newman and Robert F. Kennedy as devotees.[44] Foreign

Kohler, 'The Environment', 1977.

baths, another article noted simply, were teaching Anglo-Americans how 'to make bathtime therapeutic'.[45]

Another effect of the interest in traditional bathing habits was that bathing moved outdoors, as hot tubs and al fresco showers were installed on patios, and nature moved indoors via high-tech inventions like Kohler's 'Environment'. The Environment was a vitrine-like enclosure, brought to the market in 1977. Trumping that old standby, the Florida sunlamp, both in terms of climatic range and exoticism, the unit could reproduce anything 'from tropical rain to Baja sun [and] from jungle steam to warm chinook winds' courtesy of four heat lamps, four sunlamps, six 24-carat-gold electroplated spray heads, a steam generator and two warm-air circulating systems.[46] While the Kohler Environment seems profoundly of its time – and technologically speaking was very much of the moment – it also relates to the 'back to nature' movement of two centuries before in its effort to produce a perfect simulation of nature with the mere push of a button.

A place to linger

In the 1970s, the bathroom also softened in the sense that it became more personalized. There were many reasons why this was so. As manufacturers of sanitaryware introduced new technologies and automated artisanal fabrication techniques, they were able to increase production significantly, offering good-quality sanitaryware at lower prices.[47] With this shift, ownership of domestic bathrooms finally became almost universal except for among the very poorest in America and Europe. As the bathroom became more ubiquitous and more devoted to relaxation, it was finally released from utilitarianism. After noting the past tendency to treat the bathroom as 'an efficient people-cleaning machine', Conran commented: 'this attitude is on the decline and the bathroom is . . . where you will want to linger and enjoy yourself.'[48] As the idea that bathrooms should be a place for enjoyment caught hold, so too did the idea that they should express their owner's personality. This was not a question of buying the latest bathroom suite from the showroom but about creating a space that responded to one's particular lifestyle and had an 'individual' look.

Conran's monumental *Bed and Bath Book* served as a manifesto for the personalized bathroom. Declaring that the bathroom 'can be anything you want it to be', Conran demonstrated his point by taking readers through an astonishing smorgasbord of bathroom options: Victorian, Scandinavian, Modern, Pop, in every conceivable size, shape, colour and material. Walls were covered with smoked glass, traditional hand-painted tiles and tongue-and-groove panelling. Floors were stone, terrazzo, vinyl and cork. Sinks were antique, gold-plated, mosaic-lined and marbled. Conran's examples were bursting with every manner of furnishing, carpeting and accessory. Exercise equipment appeared, anticipating the boom in bath-gyms and the fitness craze, in the 1980s.[49] Significantly, the only type of bathroom that wasn't included was a standard one. Conran did not believe such a thing should exist, insisting: 'If you are a Spartan health fanatic or a hedonistic sensualist, the bathroom should demonstrate these proclivities.'[50]

By emphasizing 'proclivities', Conran introduced a rather watered-down tenet of the 'counter-design' movement to the middle classes. Counter-design had emerged from 1960s counterculture, spurred by the desire to free the home from both commercial design and the earnestness of high modernism, neither of which, its proponents believed, left enough room for 'the emotional outpouring of creative personalities'.[51] Some alternative interiors were whimsical and bizarre as their designers resisted usual conventions and behaviour. Others were highly aestheticized and reflected contemporary art movements like Pop. Still others were anti-object, such as the mobile furnishing units proposed in 1972 by Ettore Sottsass for an exhibition on Italian design at MoMA, New York. Sottsass explained that his goal was to cure users of the 'self-indulgence of possession' by creating containers equipped with all the tools to meet human needs – cooking, bathing and going to the toilet. He predicted that users would feel 'so detached, so disinterested, and so uninvolved' within these moving containers that they would fade into insignificance.[52] Their amorphousness would set users free.

The eclectic, rebellious and adaptable spirit of the 1970s continued into the 1980s. No style was out of bounds, and new ones came to the fore. At the same time as it was becoming a symbol of corporate London (via the Lloyd's Building), 'high-tech' also entered the home as a style. In its domestic form, High-Tech fetishized the machine and the industrial while cheerfully eschewing the reformist agenda of technological rationalism. The calling card of the High-Tech style was the incorporation of 'off-the-peg' or industrial building features into the home. As the authors of *High-Tech: The Industrial Style and Source Book for the Home* put it in 1978, 'In the bathroom, where gold-plated swans or chrome nuggets once reigned supreme, hospital faucets are adding a new cachet.'[53] Bathrooms were to be filled with lab sinks, locker-room cabinets, rear-view mirrors, naked light bulbs, tampon dispensers and motel towel racks. *High-Tech* even recommended that, for extra authenticity, readers stock up on disposable hospital toothbrushes and towels from the Holiday Inn or YMCA.

Rather than Buckminster Fuller, domestic High-Tech style at home was actually inspired far more by a rediscovered, earlier modernist icon, the Maison de Verre (1928–32) in Paris, designed by Pierre Chareau.[54] The Maison de Verre's bathrooms were particularly influential: indeed, the Maison de Verre had an incredible surfeit of spaces for washing – five in total in the residential space, plus two separate water closets and a further two in the doctor's surgery on the ground floor. Apart from the master and guest bathrooms, bidets, sinks and baths were located directly inside bedrooms behind sliding perforated metal screens, an arrangement that was typical in France but risqué elsewhere. The house's master bathroom was a model of flexibility, from its pivoting Duralumin storage units to its rolling bidet and adjustable shaving mirrors, all illuminated by naked light bulbs. And it almost goes without saying that, in the Maison de Verre, bathroom plumbing was proudly exposed.

The Maison de Verre's spirit can be detected in architect Eva Jiřičná's London flat (1982). Created while she was working on the interiors for Richard Rogers's Lloyd's Building, Jiřičná paid indirect homage to Chareau (via Norman Foster) through the motif of studded rubber flooring. In 1975 the architect Norman Foster had used this flooring – a bright green version of the white one used in the Maison de Verre – in the pool area of his High-Tech Willis Faber & Dumas building in

Pierre Chareau, bathroom in guest bedroom, Maison de Verre, Paris, 1932.

Ipswich, Suffolk. Eva Jiřičná then used Willis Faber & Dumas's cast-offs to adorn her own apartment's conversation pit (or 'pool'), kitchen and bathroom, though here it covered walls and counters rather than floors. The bathroom itself was accessorized with bright yellow Vola fixtures, neon lights and industrial doors with portholes. To complete the aquatic look, buoys were hung on the walls.[55] Her bathroom later played a starring role in film-maker Peter Greenaway's documentary *Inside Rooms: 26 Bathrooms* (1984), essentially a tribute to

Eva Jiřičná, bathroom in own flat, London, 1982. Note Arne Jacobsen's Vola taps in the background.

the personalized bathroom (and in which David Hockney's bathroom also makes an appearance).[56]

Surveying these exemplars, it is obvious that bathroom fittings alone did not set the mood of these spaces; instead, scenographic effects were created through colour, flooring, accessories and witty decorative flourishes (hence, the importance of disposable hospital toothbrushes). Terence Conran was dismissive of modern bathroom fixtures, which he felt were too 'small and mean' to support pleasure, and advocated the refurbishment of old fixtures instead.[57] And, as we have seen, High-Tech decorators mostly preferred the use of industrial fixtures rather than those made for the domestic market.[58] That designers rejected the typical products of the sanitaryware industry is not surprising given their desire to break free from convention and commercialization, but it should be stressed that the industry itself was changing in this period. For the first time, it was also starting to embrace fully the potential of design.

An infrastructure of stylish fittings

Historically, as we have established, sanitaryware manufacturers had preferred to keep design in-house and anonymous, although from the 1930s there were some exceptions to this rule. The most notable were Crane's three-decade collaboration with the industrial designer Henry Dreyfuss; American Standard's long association with the industrial designer George Sakier; Società Ceramica Italiana di Laveno's with the architect Guido Andlovitz; and Richard-Ginori's with the architect Gio Ponti.[59] Emerging from the Second World War, however, sanitaryware manufacturers were more determined than ever to transform bathroom fittings into consumer goods. Some, like American Standard, chose to invest heavily in research and development and focused on bringing new products to the market. In Europe, the preferred strategy was to bring in well-known designers to act as consultants; the rationale for producing more design-conscious products was to appeal to architects, who with their ability to specify products for large-scale building projects represented a very important – if not the most important – block of consumers.

The pioneer of these post-war collaborations was Ideal-Standard SpA, the Italian arm of American Standard. The company's first partnership was with Gio Ponti, who created the Zeta series in 1953–4 with a diamond-shaped rimless toilet, trapezoidal sink and three-point 'star' faucets (the latter were manufactured separately by another company). Encouraged by Zeta's healthy sales – 400,000 appliances were sold annually – in 1966 Ideal-Standard again secured Ponti's services for its Oneline series.[60] Ponti, however, turned down the job of designing the company's cheapest range, Roma, which went instead to the English industrial designer Douglas Scott, best known for the design of London's Routemaster buses. For the Roma series, Scott created a vitreous china washbasin that took both the methods of its production and its use into account: it had a shallow, scalloped shape that Scott determined would to be less expensive for the manufacturers to fire, while also being better suited for baby bathing.[61] Thanks to its pared-down, modernist aesthetic, the Roma washbasin won high praise in design circles and was selected for display at MoMA in New York.

Ideal-Standard SpA continued to push the design envelope with collaborations with cutting-edge Italian designers Achille Castiglioni, Mario Bellini and Gae Aulenti. But perhaps the company's most successful collaboration was in 1977 with the architect Paolo Tilche: his Michelangelo line (pictured on p. 220), with its resolutely straight edges, was a best-seller. It also represented one of the first collaborations between the various European arms of Ideal-Standard (Italy, Germany, Belgium, France and the UK). Up until that point, most products had been country-specific: it was not believed that Ponti's

designs would appeal to British tastes, for instance, and even though the Zeta range was exhibited briefly in the show windows of Liberty's department store, it was not sold by Ideal-Standard UK. Michelangelo, however, broke the mould and showed that bathroom design could cross national borders successfully.[62]

Other design-conscious Italian bathroom companies in this period were Richard-Ginori, S.C.I. and Pozzi (the three companies have since merged to form Pozzi-Ginori, owned by Sanitec). These companies worked with many well-known consultant designer-architects, including Ponti, Le Corbusier and Tilche, but also nurtured their own, talented in-house designers such as Antonia Campi. Campi in particular became associated with the return to coloured, figurative bathroom fittings inspired by the forms of nature: for instance Torena, whose basin was inspired by the structure of a mushroom, and Conchiglia,

Gio Ponti, Zeta series, Ideal-Standard SpA, 1953–4.

which was inspired by seashells.[63] The rather astonishing plasticity of Campi's work was generally avoided in the UK. The British sanitary-ware producer Adamsez best exemplified this more restrained sensibility: it launched its Meridian One range in 1964, designed by Knud Holscher and Alan Tye, in which sink, toilet and bidet bowls were mounted flush with the wall, neatly concealing any supply pipes; the sink had an 'elegant' bottle trap rather than an 'unsightly' U-bend.[64] Ideal-Standard UK also scored a hit with the trim lines of Brasilia, launched in 1968, which designer Norman Westwater created after working on Brazil's new capital city.[65]

Mixer taps with hand wheels or levers and pop-up wastes were now preferred over traditional pillar taps with crosshead handles and plugs. Danish architect Arne Jacobsen's Vola line for I. P. Lunds, introduced in 1968, most influenced this trend. Like Meridian One, the most strik-ing thing about Vola was what it concealed: the mixing mechanism was hidden behind the wall, leaving only tap and faucet exposed. Though initially available in chrome, when Vola was produced for export it came in a brightly coloured (grey or orange) epoxy finish that perfectly captured the vibrant Pop sensibility of the times. Simi-larly, in association with Frog design in 1974, the German company Hansgrohe, which remains among the most design-friendly of all com-panies, produced the Tribel hand-held shower, its distinctly curved plastic head available in a startling candy-box of colours. Customers might complete a Pop-inspired look with Conran's Crayonne acces-sories in polished ABS plastic, a coordinated system for one's wall-mounted soap dish, hand towel ring, towel rail and so on.

Inevitably, the new desire of sanitaryware manufacturers to align themselves with the worlds of fashion and art led them to reshape their advertising campaigns, too. In the 1980s, Kohler launched its Surrealist-inspired 'Edge of the Imagination' campaign, in which fix-tures were photographed in super-saturated colours as far from their

ON THE WAY TO SAN RAPHAEL...

You never thought you'd see a toilet quite like this. But there it is.

San Raphael™ Not a mirage. But a one-piece toilet of ingenious design.

The sleek, low-profile styling conserves space.

The efficient design uses less water than most conventional one-piece toilets—only three and one-half gallons.

Shown in Swiss Chocolate, it's available in a variety of decorator colors.

San Raphael has an oval-shaped bowl. A similar toilet Kohler calls the Rialto™ offers a bowl in the round.

San Raphael, by Kohler. It's really hard to pass up.

For many more kitchen, bath and powder room products see the Yellow Pages for a Kohler showroom or send $2 for a 48-page catalog to Kohler Co., Department HC9, Kohler, WI 53044.

THE BOLD LOOK
OF **KOHLER**

Advertisement for Kohler, 1983.

usual domestic settings as possible – the company's new water-conserving toilet, the San Raphael, for instance, was photographed on the yellow dividing line of a US highway in a parched, cracked desert. And in 1985 Villeroy & Boch commissioned the renowned fashion photographer Helmut Newton to shoot its wares in a series of fourteen highly staged black-and-white images. These were filled with Newton's trademark glamorous women, but with a twist: they now heroically hefted toilets, sinks and bidets above their heads – perfectly made-up female Atlases.

Not everyone was overjoyed by these changes. While acknowledging the emergence of 'a whole infrastructure . . . of stylistic fittings', one rather jaded historian of 1970s house design sighs that the same ones were 'used again and again by architects everywhere'.[66] And the reforms only went so far. Bathroom production overall remained piecemeal. Makers of sanitaryware were still very much focused on the production of individual objects: pottery companies continued to produce basins, toilets, baths and bidets; metalware companies made basins and baths, faucets and taps; and yet other companies produced storage units and bathroom accessories. Some manufacturers were attempting to create more comprehensive bathroom systems: for example, the German firm Poggenpohl began to offer customers the possibility of combining different ready-made fixtures and storage units, down to 'fruit segment'-style moulded plastic trays.[67] But for the most part bathrooms lacked the kind of coordinated, modular solutions commonly available for domestic kitchens. And though the dream of producing totally prefabricated bathroom units lived on in the prototypes of avant-garde architects from Joe Columbo to Max Clendinning, only single-unit moulded plastic showers and tub-showers were being mass-produced for the home market at this time.

Yet there is no denying that residential bathrooms had experienced some real and dramatic transformations over the preceding decades.

While those at the luxury end were still considerably more opulent and expensive than those at the bottom, they were all now tied more closely to the cycles of fashion. As we have seen, the conscious reshaping of bathroom fixtures into consumer goods had been many decades in the making. Social changes since the 1960s supported manufacturers' efforts in the sense that they had opened the bathroom up to new kinds of appliances, configurations and uses. The bathroom was transformed from a utilitarian, backstage space into a more expressive, front-stage one; from a symbol of anonymous production in the 1920s, to a symbol of personal taste and consumption in the 1970s and '80s. With this shift, too, the bathroom and its fittings became an acceptable showcase for progressive design and avant-garde designers. Companies did not yet brand these lines as consciously as they do today, but the benefits of being aligned with 'good' design were increasingly clear. By 1992, Ideal-Standard's 'Bathroom Impressions' catalogue would list not only the designer of each of its different lines but also the designer's city of origin (London, Brussels, Milan, Frankfurt) to emphasize the company's cosmopolitan sophistication. At the same time as we consider how the residential bathroom changed, however, we should not lose sight of the way in which public facilities were also undergoing their own process of 'softening' during this period, thanks not to the influence of fashion but to a growing awareness of people with disabilities and the elderly. We now turn to these issues.

Sanitärkeramik
Modell-Übersicht

VILLEROY & BOCH

5 | The Inclusive Bathroom

In 1966, the same year of Claes Oldenburg's *Soft Toilet*, another notable bathroom-themed work appeared: the architect Alexander Kira's book *The Bathroom*. The result of seven years of research at Cornell University, this landmark study combined cultural analysis, fieldwork and laboratory testing, and culminated in a series of proposed new fittings. In terms of bathroom design, this publication remains almost unique, because it tries to grapple seriously with the design problems posed by the bathroom not only from the perspective of production but also from the perspective of use.

This user-centred approach would be immensely important for bathroom design: it not only brought the user into the picture for the first time but it also acknowledged the needs of different kinds of users – people of different ages, sexes and physical abilities. In this body-conscious era, it is not surprising that discussions about health, safety and ageing began to be researched more seriously by sanitaryware manufacturers and certain members of the design profession. But the 1960s was also the age of civil rights, and this new awareness of the user cannot not be separated from disenfranchised groups' demands for equality: women, black people and people with disabilities.

In terms of public space, the demand for equality meant equal access to public buildings and facilities, especially bathrooms – and

Luigi Colani, bathroom series for Villeroy & Boch, 1975.

this proved to be an important issue for campaigners on both practical and symbolic grounds. The question of equal access is in part a design issue since it requires the removal of physical barriers and the addition of safety features, and this chapter will consider how the needs of different users have been addressed through bathroom design and planning. But it is also a legal, political and civil rights issue. On this front, a major step was taken in 1961 when the American National Standards Institute (ANSI) issued A117.1, the world's first access standard, which established the principle that public buildings and facilities should be made accessible to people with physical disabilities.[1] Over the coming decades, other countries would follow the American example.

The A117.1 standard took an important step towards enabling people with disabilities to live independently. It is bitterly ironic (and often unremarked) that it was formulated when America was still a racially segregated country. Thanks to Jim Crow laws, African Americans in the southern states were not allowed to use whites-only public facilities. These included drinking fountains and restrooms, even in the officially desegregated train stations and bus stations of the Interstate Highway System. When provided at all, facilities for 'coloreds' were inferior, dirty and often outdoors. Segregation was thus both a practical barrier, as the lack of facilities limited African Americans' mobility in public, and a symbolic one, as it aggressively reminded them of their unequal status. The African American legal scholar Taunya Lovell Banks, who experienced segregation as a child in Washington, DC, in the 1950s and as a lawyer in Mississippi in the 1960s, comments: 'Perhaps only people who have been denied access by law to bathrooms can fully understand the impact both on body and dignity of this form of discrimination.'[2]

Creating a truly inclusive bathroom, then, is not only about installing ramps, grab bars and non-slip surfaces, though these are important. An inclusive bathroom is a space that does not exclude particular user groups either by design or by law: rather, it positively promotes mobility and well-being. An inclusive bathroom is a necessary component of a socially just society. Historian Judith Plaskow puts it simply but effectively: inclusive bathrooms enable 'a maximum number of persons to participate fully in public life'.[3] As well as looking at some historic campaigns for equal bathroom access and tracing the move towards inclusive or universal design, this chapter considers what kinds of facilities might be in our public spaces and in our homes in future. It engages with research into user needs and with design projects that suggest ways forward in the quest for inclusivity.

A not-so-public convenience

Earlier chapters have addressed the rise of public facilities of various kinds from the mid-nineteenth century onwards, from bathhouses to conveniences. They have traced some of the reasons they were provided, for example to improve the cleanliness of city streets, public health and working-class morality. They have also traced the major factors that shaped their provision and design and locked them into place: cost, location and, again, morality. In theory, many thought public facilities admirable or at least accepted them as a necessary part of modern city life. In reality, however, they were often the subject of fierce disputes because of the way they upset dominant ideals of gender, class or race and promoted what some viewed as 'promiscuous' social mixing. As a result of such anxieties and the need for them to be self-financing, when provided, conveniences often adopted discriminatory practices such as charging a user's fee, which meant they were rarely inclusive in practice.

The reason so much is known about discriminatory practices is that campaigns were almost immediately mounted to challenge these inequities. Among the first to take place were those that sought to improve provision for women. One skirmish took place in 1879 in London, when the *Women's Gazette* and the Ladies' Sanitary Association joined forces to lobby local governments in London for more female public conveniences. The historian Erika Rappaport observes: 'Their arguments [in favour of conveniences] were tied to broader feminist demands for work, education, and political rights', but also stemmed from a dislike of the fact that women were required to buy things from shops in order to use their amenities.[4] Separately, the Union of Women's Liberal and Radical Associations of the Metropolitan Counties lobbied London's local authorities to make one free water closet available to working-class women in every public facility on the grounds that they could not afford the penny fee. Despite the persistence of these campaigns, one contemporary described the authorities' responses as 'weak' and 'halting'.[5]

Campaigns for women's conveniences continued into the twentieth century. While it is impossible to do them all justice here, certain themes consistently emerged. Campaigners questioned why men had more public facilities than women. They chronicled the negative impact the lack of conveniences had on women, from urinary tract infections to lost productivity at work.[6] They challenged the fact that women often had to pay to use facilities while men did not. And they critiqued the poor or inadequate design of women's facilities, but used noticeably different criteria to assess them when compared to men's. In 1933 the Women's Bureau of the United States Department of Labor produced a bulletin chronicling the many failings of factory toilets in different states. While they cited many problems that no doubt affected male workers too (lack of ventilation, lighting or cleanliness), the Bureau stressed female workers' greater need for privacy – an argument shaped by the belief that women were at once more vulnerable and more inherently modest than men. On this basis, employers were advised to ensure that female workers had separate facilities, with screened or discreet entrances and fully enclosed cubicles, measures that were not deemed necessary for male workers.[7]

In a lighter vein, in the 1960s the architect Denise Scott Brown produced a very funny but no less damning critique of the inadequacies of female 'powder rooms', pointing to their obscure locations and their lack of suitable storage. Rather than blame such problems on weak regulations, as did the Women's Bureau, Scott Brown suggested that they occurred because most of the key decisions about fittings and facilities were made by men, who often had no understanding of how 'powder rooms' were actually used. She wryly remarked:

> As I have used these facilities in office buildings, theaters, academic buildings and drive-ins throughout the land, I have become convinced that the architect's lack of personal experience and involvement in what he is planning constitutes a real problem here – the more so as I imagine he is unaware of it.[8]

Just as in the Victorian era, the veil of modesty surrounding women's bodies exacerbated the situation, inhibiting frank discussion of female behaviours and requirements. In an article of 1953, *Architects Journal* commented that at least some of the 'men who produce and sell lavatory equipment were embarrassed, and, even worse, not aware the reasons for the variations in the designs of the equipment they made'.[9] Although surveys occasionally asked housewives about their preferences for domestic bathrooms, women were almost never consulted about how workplace or public ones might be improved.[10]

While these problems are often attributed to ignorance on the part of male politicians and designers rather than to deliberate prejudice against women, the problem is more endemic. It is a result of

349

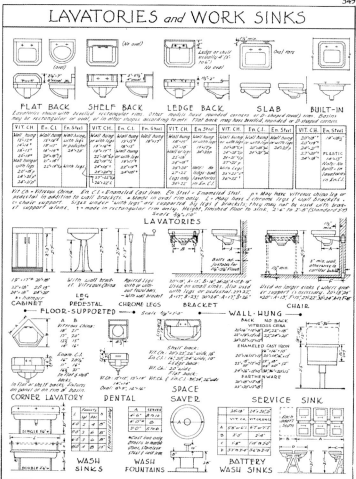

Lavatories and work sinks from *Architectural Graphic Standards* (1955).

the discrimination that women have historically faced in the built environment, the consequence of their under-representation in government and in the design professions, and of their lack of influence in decision-making processes. The reasons for the discrimination against women in the built environment have been explored extensively in feminist literature.[11] Rather than re-summarize those arguments here, this chapter will explore more specifically how a particular system of production contributed to the problem. It will demonstrate how the drive to standardize bathroom production and design, and the hands-off attitude of designers, resulted in facilities that were inadequate for many user groups – not only women.

Standardizing users

With characteristic perceptiveness, Scott Brown diagnosed a basic problem with convenience design: 'I have an uneasy feeling', she said, 'that perhaps [the public convenience] is not a problem handled by architects at all. They merely supply a certain amount of space based on a rule-of-thumb allowance per person, or possibly per sales-foot', and the facility was then supplied ready-made.[12] Scott Brown's 'uneasy feeling' was on the mark. From the 1850s, manufacturers had been actively advising clients about planning facilities and providing them with designs to meet their needs, as well as the requirements of public health legislation and local building regulations. Already in 1863, Walter Macfarlane & Co. assured readers that, on receiving a rough site plan and an estimate of user numbers, the company would 'be glad to furnish (free of charge) a ground plan of the arrangements we would suggest for adoption'.[13] Ranging from prefabricated cubicles to full structures, these facilities were delivered and assembled on site. Additionally they were often managed by specialist firms, from the Châlet Company or Wilhelm Beetz in the late 1800s to JCDecaux or CityLoos today.

In this way, manufacturers and entrepreneurs had a hand in designing many – if not the majority of – public and institutional facilities. And it was not only the manufacturers of sanitaryware that declared their expertise in the field. Scott Paper Company, one of America's first and largest toilet paper suppliers, set up a Washroom Advisory Service in the 1950s which helped employers plan easy-to-clean and functional spaces with 'proper traffic flow from washbowls to towels to exit doors'.[14] Scott Paper claimed that their bathroom-lounge facilities increased employee happiness, yet the constricted, metal-locker-lined spaces they supplied do not appear terribly comfortable. In fact, aside from the opulent 'executive' washrooms of the time (those in Mies van der Rohe's Seagram Building in New York City being the ultimate example), there was little room for aesthetics in employee or public washrooms. Rather, advisers sought to make them cost-effective, space-efficient, easy to clean and hard-wearing. To do this they turned to prefabricated metal partitions, wall-hung sinks and urinals, stainless-steel fixtures and hard, black rubber toilet seats. It is not surprising that the resulting facilities often looked unappealing: they had, quite literally, been user-proofed.

Noting the increasing reliance of architects on such advisers, the architect Alexander Pike concluded glumly, 'As buildings become more complex, new contingents of specialists emerge . . . whose recommendations the architect, with dwindling perception of the subject, is frequently forced to accept.'[15] While both Pike and Scott Brown lamented architects' disengagement from bathroom design, it does not follow that architects would automatically have produced more user-centred spaces, given that many of them also subscribed to the principle of standardization or relied on tools that did. And a necessary part of the standardization process was to standardize users as well as fixtures and connections. As Le Corbusier declared in 1930: 'Our needs are the needs of men. We all have the same limbs, in number, form, and size; if on this last point there are differences, an average dimension is easy to find.' He concluded with a classic piece of modernist sloganeering:

Standard functions,
standard needs,
standard objects,
standard dimensions.[16]

While it is easy to criticize such sentiments today, we should recall that the drive to standardize was closely connected to the real need to alleviate the critical social problems of the day: to improve standards of hygiene and to provide good-quality housing for the working class on a mass scale. These aims drove the experiments in prefabrication covered in chapter Three. They also drove efforts to collect and make available large quantities of data on building materials, construction methods and human dimensions so that building professionals could eliminate wastefulness, reduce costs and improve housing quality. Creating a normative user – an average or 'normal' figure constructed out of the best available statistics about human dimensions, reach and movement – was essential to meeting these goals. Architects' 'bibles', such as *Architectural Graphic Standards* in the US and *Architects' Data* in Europe, used these figures to establish minimum space requirements for bathrooms, design standard layouts and set installation heights for all fittings, from towel rails to toilet paper holders.

This approach had a major weakness. Working to average dimensions and assuming everyone has 'the same limbs' essentially ensured that certain groups would be excluded. It was never the case that, in providing for an average user (that is to say, the fiftieth percentile), a *majority* of users would be comfortably accommodated. In addition, average dimensions were calculated in such a way as to guarantee blind spots; for instance, the upper and lower percentiles of the population (the top 5 and bottom 5 per cent) were typically not included in calculations, so that 10 per cent of the population – the very short and very tall – was not represented at all.[17] And then there was the question: from where was all this data on human dimensions derived? The standard source of information on human dimensions for the most popular anthropometric texts, like Henry Dreyfuss's *The Measure of Man* (1960), was US military studies, meaning that the data was always inherently biased towards young, white, fully able, male bodies. Those who did not match the criteria found themselves stigmatized as not 'normal'.[18]

There was a further problem. Even though they provided some limited technical information on fixtures and plumbing, handbooks did not consider actual bathroom behaviour in any systematic way. (This is why Scott Brown remarked that information about what women actually did in bathrooms was 'not found in the *Graphic Standards*'.[19]) Instead of making recommendations about the height or placement of fixtures with reference to use, handbooks simply followed manufacturers' recommendations or trade practice. A perfect circle was created as the books ended up simply reinforcing existing practices, however obsolete. Still in the 1970s, the architects Julius Panero and Martin Zelnik observed that design was too often 'still based on unchallenged and outdated standards, rules of thumb, intuitive judgments, antiquated trade practices, and manufacturer's recommendations, many of which are insensitive to human factors'.[20]

While many culprits were blamed, one was insufficiently acknowledged. Questions of human anatomy and use had never been prioritized by manufacturers because other criteria – notably the demands of public health and hygiene – were deemed more important: water closets, for instance, had historically been judged on the basis of their ability to flush away waste effectively, not to accommodate users in the physiologically optimum way. A strong case would have to be made to upend these powerful, deeply embedded priorities. And this is where Alexander Kira and the Center for Housing and Environmental Studies at Cornell entered the scene.

Alexander Kira's *The Bathroom*

Before working on *The Bathroom*, Cornell University's Center for Housing and Environmental Studies had produced a research bulletin that comprehensively reorganized the design of the kitchen along rational lines. *The Cornell Kitchen* (1952) was well received and, on its heels, it seemed logical that the Center would turn its reforming attention to the home's other 'functional' space, the bathroom. For *The Bathroom*, the centre used the same successful formula as in *Cornell Kitchen*, setting up an interdisciplinary research team made up of home economists, social psychologists, engineers and architects. However, when the bathroom study was launched, the scale of the challenge ahead must have been apparent to all. The researchers found themselves in a terrain of psychological complexity completely unlike that of the kitchen. A yawning gap existed between the popular fantasy of the bathroom (what people wanted) and its compact reality (what most people had or were provided with), not to mention the host of taboos with which they had to contend.

The stated ambition of *The Bathroom* was to establish a fresh set of design criteria for bathroom facilities that, for the first time, would focus on human anatomy and behaviour. Hence the team's first priority was to get a realistic picture of what people did in their bathrooms. How were they thought about, used and experienced? A landmark survey of 1,000 middle-class American households was conducted to identify 'current attitudes, practices, and problems' associated with bathrooms.[21] This was followed by laboratory tests that studied people carrying out personal hygiene activities, in order to pinpoint any practical design issues associated with them. In response to the survey and to the laboratory studies, Cornell's team then set basic design parameters for each hygiene activity, developed hypotheses about how best to meet them, and produced working models based on these hypotheses.

The Bathroom's empirically based and iterative mode of working reflected the credo of 'human engineering' or ergonomics, which assessed the suitability of tools, objects, systems or environments for human use. Kira succinctly described this ethos as 'fitting the activity, or the equipment, to the man, rather than vice versa', a mode of working that opposed top-down and standardized modes of design. Kira, however, did not completely reject the modernists' approach. He shared their belief in the need to rationalize production: he championed a fundamental reorganization of the bathroom industry and the creation of modular bathroom units like Sakier's ARCO system.[22] But Kira also recognized that, no matter how sophisticated anthropometric data became, standardized products would always have limitations. Unless people bought highly specialized fittings for every stage of their life, there would never be a single facility that would perfectly meet the needs of all: a child under five would never be well served by fittings designed for full-grown adults.

Kira thus advocated a more pragmatic and adaptive approach. Bearing in mind the changes that anyone might expect to experience over the course of a normal lifetime (weight gain, pregnancy, ageing and illness, for example), he advised that safety features be installed even in standard facilities, noting:

> while in some instances these incapacities may be quite critical they represent, for the most part, not new problems but only more severe degrees of those encountered by the 'normal' population . . . What might other-

wise be regarded as refinement now becomes a necessity: adequate support, seats, hand-sprays, proper fitting design and location and other considerations.[23]

He also sought to make his bathroom fittings more flexible. Consider the changes Kira proposed for sinks. The survey of daily hygiene practices had revealed that the majority of people washed their hands under a stream of running water rather than in a pool at the bottom of the sink. Because the form of conventional sinks was basically that of the old-fashioned washbowl, the faucet was not suited for this mode of hand washing: it was set too close to the back of the sink, forcing users to stoop to reach the water stream. While *Architectural Graphic Standards* recommended a basin rim be 31 inches (80 centimetres) high, Kira's laboratory studies established that the optimal height for hand washing was between 36 and 38 inches (91 to 97 centimetres), though it was lower for face washing and higher for hair washing. To serve this range of washing activities, Kira proposed a fountain-type water source that sent the water stream arcing upwards, and he altered and enlarged the shape of the basin.

This pattern was then repeated as Kira tested the design of the bathroom's three other major fittings and concluded that bathtubs were too low, showers too small and water closets too high. Supported by the evidence of the hygiene survey, laboratory studies and anthropometric data (he considered small, medium and large human dimensions), his findings and redesigns seem unobjectionable at first glance. But as Kira understood only too well, certain activities – especially urination, defecation and perineal cleansing – were highly charged and any substantial changes were likely to meet with resistance. Unlike sanitary engineers or technological rationalists who dismissed 'subjective' factors as irrational, Kira tried to make sense of such factors with reference to anthropologists, sexologists,

Height of Subject = 48 3/4"

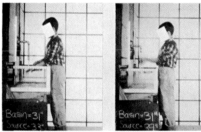
Height of Subject = 54"

Height of Subject = 64"

Height of Subject = 74"

'Comparison between postures assumed by persons of varying sizes', in Alexander Kira, *The Bathroom* (1966).

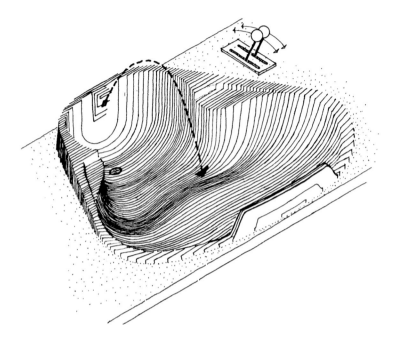

developmental psychologists and psychoanalysts. He knew that cultural beliefs and taboos were among the greatest obstacles to change, stating, 'It may almost be said that *the* problems to be solved are the psychological and cultural ones.'[24] Subjective factors could ultimately override any health or hygiene argument – Kira cited the American rejection of the bidet and the urinal in the home as two examples.

Nevertheless, the time seemed ripe to confront bathroom taboos. It was the great age of consciousness raising and taboo smashing. With human sexuality no longer off-limits, it was not unreasonable to hope that bathroom functions would be next in line. And, as we saw in the previous chapter, dramatic shifts in the way domestic bathrooms were perceived had produced equally dramatic stylistic and aesthetic changes. But rethinking the bathroom was still mostly bound up with

'Experimental lavatory [sink] incorporating suggested criteria', in Alexander Kira, *The Bathroom* (1966).

the choice of decor, colours and accessories, not with safety features and ergonomically appropriate design. Despite wide and enthusiastic reviews, in the wake of *The Bathroom*'s publication there was no immediate rush on the part of manufacturers to put Kira's designs into production or to apply his principles. In 1967 Ideal-Standard UK did commission Douglas Scott to create a three-piece bathroom suite using *The Bathroom*'s criteria for the Ideal Home Exhibition in London but the company was not confident that it would sell – and apparently it did not.[25]

Kira thus found himself in a chicken-and-egg situation. Many of his designs and recommendations would not be accepted given existing social and cultural attitudes, but how could social and cultural attitudes be shifted in advance of new designs? The battle clearly had to be won in hearts and minds: for real change to occur, producers and consumers alike had to be persuaded to want human-engineered bathrooms. It is hard to imagine that Kira's vision could ever really compete with the luxury bathroom's promise of glamour and beauty or that he would ever persuade manufacturers and builders to spend extra money developing his designs. By 1966, when the results of the Cornell study were published, however, Kira was no longer a lone voice in the wilderness. Other important voices were making themselves heard, strengthening the case for safe, human-centred bathrooms.

Designing for people with disabilities

Of all the campaigns for equal bathroom access since the Victorian era, those mounted by or for people with disabilities have had the greatest impact on public bathroom facilities. This certainly does not mean that the battle for equal access has been won (far from it) or even that there is consensus among disability campaigners on key design issues. However, the rapidity with which accessibility has become part of the design agenda is striking. Disability standards, codes and regulations, particularly those that mandate equal access to public buildings, have been vital in terms of ushering in a sea change in social attitudes towards people with disabilities and in destabilizing the default assumption of able-bodied personhood.

As mentioned earlier, the world's first standard for disabled accessibility was only issued in 1961. Prior to this, people with disabilities had to adapt to the environment, rather than the other way around. The architect and disability expert Selwyn Goldsmith recalled his brief spell as a hospital architect in the early 1960s: 'It simply had not occurred to anyone in the hospital-building business that access for wheelchair users into and around hospitals . . . should be a paramount planning and design consideration.'[26] The same was true of home bathrooms, where users with disabilities had to make do 'somehow', negotiating narrow doorways and poorly laid out equipment, often at the expense of personal dignity.[27] While some specialized bathroom equipment did exist, domestic modifications were often of the do-it-yourself variety. The British guide *Equipment for the Disabled* (1960) was thus part product index, part builder's manual: not only did it list items that were commercially available, but it also gave instructions for how to rig up suitable equipment at home, such as benches and ropes for entering and exiting baths.[28]

Over the course of the 1960s, however, the relationship between disability and the built environment began to be studied more seriously, with special attention paid to housing and community planning. Sweden and Denmark led in the former field; America led in the latter, thanks in large part to Tim Nugent. Nugent was director of the University of Illinois at Urbana-Champaign's rehabilitation education programme, an experimental regime part-funded by the United States Veterans' Administration, which trained people with disabilities to live

'Bath rope', from *Equipment for the Disabled* (1960).

independently. Nugent believed the best way to accomplish this was by promoting self-reliance and teaching students with disabilities to get by in the same environment as able-bodied students – the 'treat as normal' philosophy. So that they could reach classrooms, Nugent campaigned to have all of the buildings on the Urbana-Champaign campus made wheelchair accessible; when the university agreed, Nugent wrote an architectural brief that specified the width of doors, the gradient of ramps and dimensions of public toilets. This planted the seed for A117.1, which was to extend barrier-free environments across the United States.

In 1959, after the American National Standards Institute decided to issue a standard on the topic of accessibility, Nugent drafted its specifications, testing them out at the university among 400 men and women with disabilities. 'A117.1 Accessible and Usable Buildings and Facilities' was slowly given teeth by various state governments, the federal Architectural Barriers Act of 1968 and the Rehabilitation Act of 1973. More broadly, A117.1 encouraged the creation of disability standards in other countries and inspired later civil rights initiatives, notably the independent living movement that emerged in the 1970s in Berkeley, California. Yet the standard is not above criticism. Shaped by an emphasis on self-reliance and physical fitness, Nugent's specifications perpetuated their own exclusions. Take, for instance, Nugent's specifications for public toilets for wheelchair users. The resulting facility was small (3 by 4 feet 8 inches, 0.91 by 1.4 metres) and required a wheelchair user to wheel straight into the space, manoeuvre on to the toilet with the aid of handrails, fold their wheelchair and push it to the side before closing the door. Goldsmith noted that this extremely challenging set of actions reflected the physical abilities of the students whom Nugent had trained, all of whom were under 45 and in peak physical condition.

By contrast, Goldsmith, who was severely disabled, initially went down the so-called 'treat as different' path, which insisted that people

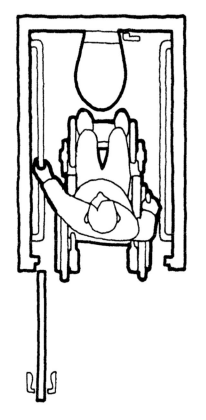

with disabilities required dedicated accommodation that was designed for them specifically. Goldsmith's views were very significant because he drafted the British version of A117.1, CP96 Access for the Disabled to Buildings (1967), and he wrote the most influential design manual for architects, *Designing for the Disabled*, which appeared in three editions in 1963, 1967 and 1976. In advance of the second edition, Goldsmith, with the guidance of a sociologist, prepared detailed questionnaires for wheelchair users, a survey of disabled drivers and a study of blind people. With this, he stated pointedly, 'I had a unique resource of solid information and data, not a medley of suppositions drawn from impressions, surmises, legend and mythology.' Preparing for the third edition, he worked with the UK Department of Health's consultant ergonomist, Dr Glyn Stanton, to test aspects of public convenience design, thus producing the nearest equivalent to Kira's work on bathroom use for people with disabilities.[29]

From Goldsmith's interviews with 284 wheelchair users, public toilets emerged as a major concern: 64 per cent of interviewees named it the public building they most wanted to see made wheelchair accessible. Goldsmith noted: 'The inaccessibilities of public lavatories, and the frustrations, embarrassments and calamities that occurred in consequence was the dominant theme of my conversations.'[30] In particular he realized that the sex segregation of toilets meant that personal assistants

Water closet for disabled people as set out by the 1961 American Standard in Selwyn Goldsmith, *Designing for the Disabled: The New Paradigm* (1997). The dimensions of this facility are 3 by 4 feet 8 inches, 0.91 by 1.42 metres.

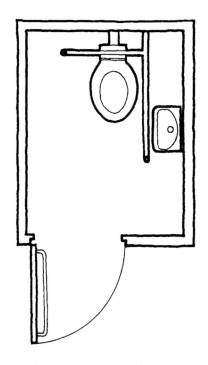

of the opposite sex, usually spouses, were not able to accompany wheelchair users into cubicles to help them. For this reason, Goldsmith recommended unisex toilet provision when he drafted the first British Standard for the disabled in 1967 and when he redrafted it in 1979.[31] Providing one separate disabled-only unisex toilet became the model for provision across Britain. The 1970 Chronically Sick and Disabled Persons Act then mandated that people with disabilities have access to sanitary conveniences ('if any') in public buildings 'in so far as it is in the circumstances both practicable and reasonable'. Enforcement regulations for the Act, however, only appeared in 1992.[32]

There is insufficient space here to precisely track all the developments in standards and enforcement regulations between the 1970s and 1990s, when comprehensive civil rights legislation was finally passed (the Americans with Disabilities Act of 1990 and its Amendment in 2010; and the UK Disability Discrimination Act of 1995 and the Equality Act 2010).[33] But this brief survey confirms that, by the 1970s, the needs of people with disabilities had gained increased recognition from design professionals; for instance, sections on the requirements of such groups were now regularly integrated into architectural handbooks, and exhibitions were mounted on the topic of designing for disability. People with disabilities now had far more

CP96 unisex toilet as set out by 1967 British Standard in Goldsmith, *Designing for the Disabled*. The dimensions of this facility are 4 feet 6 inches by 5 feet 8 inches, 1.37 by 1.75 metres.

choice in terms of bathroom equipment, whether specialized shower units or lifting chairs for bathtub access. A 1978 catalogue of equipment for people with disabilities observed that '92% of all aids issued in one year were designed to assist activities related to personal care.'[34] Non-standard users were becoming part of the design agenda for bathrooms at last.

From disabled to universal design

In parallel with the rise of access laws, at least some in the design world also began to accept Kira's view that even normal bathrooms should be designed with present and *potential* medical issues in mind, and incorporate safety features when possible.[35] This job was made easier as sanitaryware makers began to develop a wider range of suitable products: in 1965, for instance, with a great whirl of publicity, American Standard released the Stan-sure 'skid-resistant' bathtub,

Bathroom display from the 'Design and Disability' show at the Design Centre, London, 1981. Note use of Paolo Tilche's Michelangelo wall-mounted toilet and bidet by Ideal Standard SpA and Arne Jacobsen's Vola taps.

possibly to capitalize on Kira's recommendation that all bathtubs have non-slip bottoms.[36] American Standard's sudden concern for user safety is significant as it reminds us of another activist movement that was making itself felt at this time: consumer activism.

It was not coincidence that Ralph Nader, the leader of the consumer activist movement in America, endorsed Kira's revised edition of *The Bathroom* in 1976, describing it somewhat dryly as an exposé of the 'inadequate safety, hygiene and convenience features in bathrooms'.[37] In fact, there were strong parallels between *The Bathroom* and Nader's revolutionary *Unsafe at Any Speed: The Designed-in Dangers of the American Automobile* (1965), which triggered national legislation to improve auto safety. While not as sensationally dangerous as automobiles, Kira's safety concerns about bathrooms were supported by some impressive numbers: in his new edition, he cited the US Department of Housing's estimate that 275,000 people were injured each year in baths, a figure then breathlessly repeated in most reviews of his book.[38] And, quite apart from injuries, Kira claimed that several aspects of bathroom design had a variety of negative long-term effects, causing conditions from haemorrhoids to scabies.

Kira's most publicized comments, however, related to water closets. Noting the agreed medical view that the optimal posture for defecation was a squat, he asserted that ideally water closets should permit the assumption of a 'squat-like posture'. By gradually strengthening abdominal and upper-leg muscles, Kira hoped this design would bring an end to many medical problems among the aged, particularly constipation. This was not as eccentric a proposition as it might at first sound. Since the late nineteenth century, constipation or 'autointoxication' was regarded as one of the great evils of urban life: another vocal squat advocate, the physiotherapist F. A. Hornibrook, described it as 'the greatest physical vice of the white race'.[39] To combat this 'vice', semi-squat closets known as 'health closets' had been available

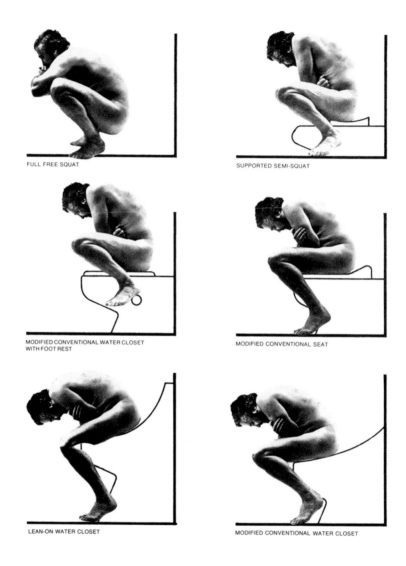

FULL FREE SQUAT

SUPPORTED SEMI-SQUAT

MODIFIED CONVENTIONAL WATER CLOSET
WITH FOOT REST

MODIFIED CONVENTIONAL SEAT

LEAN-ON WATER CLOSET

MODIFIED CONVENTIONAL WATER CLOSET

'Possible approaches to a modified squat posture', in Alexander Kira, *The Bathroom* (revised edition, 1976).

in Britain since at least the 1920s, as had posture footstools, which brought the knees above seat level. In France, Le Corbusier continued to explore the possibilities of squatting when he designed a water closet for the sanitaryware firm Pozzi in 1960 that had peg-like footrests to draw the feet back and lift the legs. While this design was widely publicized (and was reproduced in Kira's revised edition of *The Bathroom*), it never went into production, perhaps because this was the moment when French consumers were actually turning away from squats and towards throne-style toilets on the grounds that they were more comfortable.[40] In arguing for semi-squat toilets as standard, then, Kira was putting health needs on a collision course with contemporary tastes and fashion.

Kira knew only too well what an uphill battle this would be. Although Nader mainly accused manufacturers and industry 'stylists' of actively ignoring safety concerns, Kira placed equal blame on

'Lanrick' Washdown Closet, Shanks catalogue, 1938. A low-inclined 'health' closet.

builders, architects and consumers for consistently privileging fashion over health. Kira's more conciliatory note towards manufacturers was probably to be expected, given that American Standard had sponsored his research and that he hoped some of his experimental designs would be mass produced by the company. American Standard did eventually put one of Kira's designs into production, a posture-mould toilet seat, and he was also consulted about the design of other products such as the fully loaded, prefab Spectra 70 bath and enclosure, with built-in lumbar support and a fold-out tray.[41] And Kira claimed to see progress more generally. In the revised edition of *The Bathroom* he included photographs of contemporary bathroom fixtures (none

Gio Ponti, drawing for Zeta series, Ideal-Standard SpA, 1953–4.

had been included in the first edition) to acknowledge 'the response the industry has begun to make' to ergonomic research.[42]

Kira had reason to be optimistic. In the decade following *The Bathroom*'s publication, his work had begun to inspire mostly European designers who were more receptive to his criteria than Americans. This was likely because they already had some interest in designing more 'natural' bath fittings: Gio Ponti had created his trapezoidal Zeta sink in the 1950s, for instance, to better accommodate the washing movements of forearms.[43] Post-Kira, these efforts became bolder. At the hands of Antonia Campi at Pozzi-Ginori, Kira's ergonomic functionalism grew into an exuberant biomorphism. The sink in Campi's 1970 Ipsilon series had an ellipsoidal shape, a fountain-type spout with lever, a horizontal drain, integrated soap dishes that allowed water to drain away and a plum-and-avocado colour scheme.[44] The toilet of her even more dramatically contoured Metha, designed in 1978, encouraged squatting by means of an integrated footrest as Le Corbusier had done.[45] Bathroom biomorphism, however, was to reach its most sensational heights with designer Luigi Colani's melting designs for the German company Villeroy & Boch in 1975 (pictured on p. 198). Kira's plea for modular designs was not forgotten either and another German manufacturer, Röhm, launched Plexmobil, a modular bathroom system made of Plexiglas, complete with low-level water closet.[46]

Such virtuoso designs aside, more ordinary bath fittings were quietly incorporating safety and convenience features, from non-slip surfaces to flexible hand sprays. But the semi-squat water closet proved again that there were limits to how far bathroom reforms could go. Kira's discussion of the subject continues to inspire 'modern-day squat evangelists', who attach plates to convert their toilets to squats, but generally the *siège à l'anglaise* still reigns supreme.[47] Other more surprising points of resistance to *The Bathroom*'s criteria emerged, too: safety bars were widely rejected by the able-bodied, Kira complained, because they were seen to be 'geriatric'.[48] And industry conventions and standards proved stubborn. Published over three decades after *The Bathroom*, the tenth edition of *Architectural Graphic Standards* (2000) states that, though sinks are typically mounted at a height of 30 to 32 inches, the height of 34 to 38 inches is more 'comfortable' – a decidedly non-committal nod to Kira's findings.

The resistance to the incorporation of safety features hugely frustrated Kira, who continued to insist that sensitively designed bathrooms would benefit all users, not only people with disabilities. At the same time, other design gurus, most notably Victor Papanek in *Design for the Real World* (1971) and *Design for Human Scale* (1983), were also passionately arguing that designers should treat 'broadening constituencies' as a professional obligation; that is, that designing for non-standard users, from the short of stature to the partially sighted to people with learning disabilities, is a social and ethical duty.[49] Their perspectives anticipated and laid the ground for what is now termed 'universal design', which expands the definition of 'people with disabilities' to encompass anyone who is discriminated against by architecture. Not only does this expanded definition include people with a wider range of health conditions and physical abilities, it also includes small children, women and anyone with a child in a pushchair (the list is extensive).

We can track this shift again through Selwyn Goldsmith. In 1997 he published another edition of his seminal manual *Designing for the Disabled*, now pointedly subtitled *A New Paradigm* to announce his revised stance. In this work, he strongly rejected the 'treat as different' position of his previous work and embraced a 'treat as normal' one. This shift was informed by his work on mobility housing, which permits people with disabilities to live in adapted regular housing as opposed to special housing – the option they overwhelmingly prefer, according to Goldsmith's questionnaires. And it also reflected his own preferences as a person with severe disabilities. He said, 'I wish to be able . . . to use normal toilet facilities, and not to be told that a special toilet has been provided for people like me.'[50] (Or, as another user with disabilities put it simply, 'It should just be one word – toilet.'[51]) Goldsmith also began to contemplate the situations of others who experience discrimination in the built environment: 'Why is it', he asked, 'that we do not have an access regulation which ensures that when toilets are planned in public buildings the established practice of discrimination against women is outlawed?'[52] His curiosity piqued, Goldsmith and his wife embarked on a survey of public buildings across Britain that confirmed that a far greater number of men's amenities were provided than women's.

Of course, women's and feminist organizations had observed these inequalities for many years. Like disability campaigners, they had regularly been involved in campaigns to remove physical barriers to toilets and were also active in the 1960s and '70s: examples include a successful campaign in Britain against the use of turnstiles in public toilets which resulted in them being outlawed in 1963 (this ban was revoked in London in 2012, alas);[53] and a campaign against toilet user fees in the US. Even though the Committee to End Pay Toilets in America (CEPTIA) was a civil rights organization rather than a feminist one per se, the pay toilet was widely recognized as a form of discrimination that disproportionately affected women, because they had to pay every time they or their children wanted to use a facility. The American poet and activist Marge Piercy vividly evoked the scene in her poem 'To the Pay Toilet'. She angrily describes a mother with three children 'shrieking their simple urgency like gulls' who has to pay for each one to use a toilet and for the 'privilege of them not dirtying the corporate floor'.[54] Another memorable image from the 1960s is of Assembly member March Fong Eu, elegantly dressed and coiffed, smashing a toilet on the steps of the California State

Capitol with a sledgehammer in support of her bill to ban pay toilets. While her bill lost, other bills won, leading to the banning of pay toilets in Chicago in 1973, in New York in 1975 and others beyond.

But it is the question of how to alleviate the female queue for the loo that has received the most attention in recent years. The crux of the problem is this: even if an equal amount of space is allocated to women's facilities as to men's, this does not deliver equality in practice because women take longer to use toilets than do men – 90 seconds versus 45 seconds.[55] One response to the problem has been to try to increase provision for women by introducing female urinals. Efforts to introduce female urinals date back at least to the late nineteenth century in London, when a female public convenience was fitted with 'urinettes'. Smaller than conventional water closets and with curtains instead of doors, only a halfpenny was to be charged for their use.[56] Even though urinettes did not appear to catch on, this did not stop other manufacturers from developing models of female urinal over the years – Royal Doulton in the 1930s, American Standard in the 1950s – each time believing that they had unlocked the secret to selling them. Advertising for American Standard's female urinal, Sanistand, for instance, emphasized that 'it need not be touched in usage', implicitly acknowledging that most women do not actually sit on public toilet seats because of the fear of contagion. To drive home the link to superior hygiene, American Standard even had nurses stationed in their showrooms to talk to customers about the Sanistand's benefits.[57] Women, however, remained unconvinced.

Since then, many other efforts have been made to launch female urinals and some contemporary designs, such as the Dutch designer Marian Loth's Lady P for Gustavsberg Sphinx, are very elegant. Yet in spite of the abundant publicity they have received, these models tend to be installed individually in bars and nightclubs, settings in which they mainly serve as talking points, not as serious alternatives to water

closets. Where low-cost, temporary female urinals have been successfully adopted is at outdoor festivals such as Glastonbury in the UK or
Roskilde in Denmark, where women tend to be more open to new
experiences and, importantly, are keen to avoid long queues and dirty
portaloos.[58]

With this last (not insignificant) exception, it is hard to imagine at
present how female urinals could permanently replace the flush toilet
given the difficulties its use entails, much of it caused by clothing
(trouser zippers were designed to facilitate men's urination after all,
not women's). In face of these challenges, most campaigners have

Assembly member March Fong Eu breaks a porcelain potty with a sledge hammer on the steps
of the State Capitol Building in support of her bill to ban pay toilets, Sacramento, California,
1969.

Marian Loth, Lady P for Gustavberg Sphinx, 1999.

abandoned the idea of redesigning fixtures in any radical way and focused on simply getting more provided. This was the logic behind the adoption of US 'potty parity' laws in the 1980s and 1990s, which mandate that all new buildings provide two female toilets for every one male. But is this enough? According to his research, Goldsmith concluded that only *three* female toilets to every one male would be enough to right the balance, and he is not alone in this reckoning.

Even if the interest in women's toilet provision among proponents of universal design is not unprecedented, it is still significant. In fact,

Temporary female urinal, Pollee by UiWE, Roskilde Festival, Denmark, 2011.

the potential of universal design to bring together different special interest groups, its commitment to inclusiveness and its reminder of the social value of public conveniences are its most positive features. And these values have made an impact. Their influence is visible in the latest British Standard on public toilets, BS 6465-4, issued in 2010. Co-authored by one of today's most tireless and vocal toilet advocates, the planner Clara Greed, the new standard strongly emphasizes the needs of different user groups in line with the Equality Act 2010.[59] 'Different user groups' now very explicitly includes ethnic minorities, and BS 6465-4 exhibits new sensitivity to those whose religious beliefs shape bathroom habits, for instance by advising authorities to consider providing squat toilets in areas with large ethnic communities.[60]

When provided, however, squat toilets have provided fodder for the tabloids. The British paper *Daily Star*'s outraged story about their provision in the city of Rochdale, where one in five people is Asian, led with the headline: 'MUSLIM-ONLY PUBLIC LOOS: Council Wastes YOUR money on hole-in-ground toilets'.[61] With this, we are returned to the fact that toilets are sites where deeply rooted social conflicts and antagonisms play out; what suits one user may not suit another. This is important to remember. Despite the progress charted in this chapter, we should not gloss over the tensions that arise when various interests compete for scarce funding. Nor should we ignore the grim state of public toilet provision today. Over 50 per cent of public conveniences in Britain have actually been closed down since 1995:[62] most now sit abandoned, relics from a bygone era, although some have successfully found a second life as converted bars or community spaces, even as beauty salons. Ironically, these widespread closures can be attributed to the rise of disability legislation, as local authorities find it easier to close public conveniences, which they are under no legal obligation to provide, than make them accessible. Similarly, the reduction of public conveniences in both the UK and the USA has been blamed on the bans on turnstiles (which make it difficult to collect revenue) and on pay facilities.[63]

On a more philosophical level, some disability scholars voice concern about how people with disabilities are now expected to strive for total independence and normalcy in public space. They point out that accessible environments work to disguise dependence and flatten out other meaningful kinds of differences (especially gender differences) in ways that can be socially and ethically problematic. The increasing reliance on architectural supports and automated devices creates a hands-off attitude towards those who require assistance in public spaces and serve as a substitute for human exchanges, which have always been fundamental to care. Noting how 'the privileging of independence' can stigmatize 'reciprocity, caring, and cooperation', disability scholar David Serlin states: 'This has profound implications not only for how we understand the disabled toilet user but also for how we understand the social networks in which both the disabled and able-bodied are embedded.'[64] Furthermore, Serlin argues, by urging independence as a goal, the ideal of a society made up of fully functioning citizens remains unchallenged.

Ageing in place

If nothing else, the summary given here demonstrates how fraught questions of access are – and perhaps always will be – in the public realm. Where the concept of universal design has been less controversial and has made inroads is in homes for the aged, in countries from Britain to Brazil, Israel and China. The world is now in the midst of what is being referred to as 'an age wave', as many countries around the world are faced with rapidly ageing populations. Surveys repeatedly confirm that it is the overwhelming preference of older people to age 'in place' – that is, to live in their own homes for as long as possible or to live independently in retirement communities.[65] In this project, accessible bathrooms are essential, since research confirms over and over that they are the most difficult space for adults with any form of impaired mobility to negotiate.[66]

The problem of how to accommodate ageing users in the home has been the focus of important design research, notably the MetaForm project initiated by the American design firm Herman Miller's Research Corporation. Beginning in 1986, six cross-disciplinary design teams were charged with studying every aspect of domestic life to consider how it is affected by ageing, a process that included extensive testing of prototypes among a broad cross-section of users. Gianfranco Zaccai, from Design Continuum, was in charge of personal hygiene activities. Tellingly, he did not design individual fittings or a complete facility. Rather, like Kira (whose work he read closely), Zaccai favoured a modular approach, designing bathroom 'nodes', each of which incorporated all the equipment necessary to perform a particular hygiene activity. The sink node came with an integrated basin, lighted mirror, medicine cabinet, outlets and drawers; the shower node had a floor drain, support bar/accessory rail, and water/ventilation light column. All nodes were wheelchair accessible. Most radically, the toilet and sink nodes were height adjustable. In the case of the toilet, this meant that it could be raised from 10.5 to 24 inches (27 to 60 centimetres) to accommodate anyone, from a small child to an elderly person with disabilities; it also meant that a wheelchair user could transfer on to the toilet at the most convenient height (19.5 inches; about 50 centimetres) and then ride down to a semi-squat position for easier elimination. The toilet also had a built-in bidet sprayer/dryer and, after use, could be rotated into a wall cavity where it would be automatically washed and sanitized.[67]

MetaForm never made it into full-scale production, though the research of designers Bill Stumpf and Don Chadwick into seating

resulted in Herman Miller's famous Aeron Chair. But many of the basic principles established in Kira's criteria and in Zaccai's prototypes have become standard in recent initiatives like the UK-based Lifetime Homes, or Universal Design Demonstration Homes in America. The goal of these homes is adaptability, so that one may age in place without the need for drastic remodelling later in life. Universal design bathrooms incorporate many of Kira's bathroom criteria as a matter of course, from non-skid surfaces to easy-grip water controls, and sometimes even have height-adjustable sinks. (Height adjustability is rarely found in toilets, but it was incorporated into Twyford's futuristic 'concept' toilet, the Versatile Interactive Pan or VIP, in 2001.) Crucially, universal design circumvents the resistance to 'geriatric' design by insisting on 'invisible integration', thus reducing the visibility and the stigma of safety features. Manufacturers such as Kohler have not been slow to grasp the appeal of invisible integration to

MetaForm, man in wheelchair and young girl using sink node, 1986.

consumers and now offer a range of baths and toilets suitable for ageing in place.

In the creation of universal bathrooms, technology has an important role to play. Though Kira did not mention it, at the time he was writing, bidet seats for toilets, such as the Clos-O-Mat and the Air Wash Seat, did have limited acceptance in the Anglo-American world as a medical aid for those who required help with self-cleansing. And, as we saw with the Olsonite AD 2000 Comfort Control Center, companies had been trying for some time to market these devices to a wider public. The first to succeed was the Japanese sanitaryware maker TOTO, which introduced its Washlet G, an improved version of the American-made Air Wash Seat, in 1980.[68] Ironically, even though the company has never managed to sell the Washlet back to the American market, TOTO's offerings are ubiquitous in Japan, with sales of 20 million in a nation of 160 million.[69] Over the years, Washlets have become increasingly sophisticated, offering not only cleansing and drying features but night lights, heated seats, a choice of sprays (Wonderwave, oscillating, pulsating), sound effects, automatic flushing and air purifiers.

Given their widespread presence in homes and the continued use of specialized models in medical settings, it seems inevitable that Japan now looks to high-tech toilets to assist with elderly care – for instance to run tests on users' urine to monitor temperature, blood sugar, blood pressure and weight. And, as we saw with Sanyo's Harmony in Roll-lo Bathing, discussed in chapter Three, technology is being used positively to reshape the way the elderly bathe. But in other ways these examples highlight the chasm that still exists between high-tech environments and most people's bathrooms, especially those of the elderly, who very often have to make do with converted 5 by 7 foot models. While the age wave means that more attention is now being paid to bathrooms than in the past, universally designed bathrooms are still generally a luxury or novelty product. A Kohler toilet with bidet functions from their Aging in Place range is almost $4,000 – over ten times what a normal toilet might cost. Though exciting on paper, universal design still has a long way to travel before it becomes universal in reality.

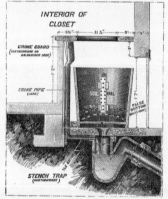

6 The Alternative Bathroom

The year is 1849, nine years before Joseph Bazalgette is given the go-ahead to construct London's sewer system. At this point a mere applicant for the post of Assistant Surveyor, Bazalgette proposes a city-wide network of public urinals and water closets for the relief of the populace. Well aware that the Metropolitan Commission of Sewers will never approve a scheme that is not self-sustaining, Bazalgette has come up with a plan: the construction and maintenance of the facilities will be financed through the sale of undiluted urine to farmers and market gardeners. Bazalgette surveys existing urinals at the Royal Exchange, Bank, National Gallery, Mansion House and Hyde Park and works out that between 26 and 90 users visit these facilities each half hour. On this basis, and assuming each user deposits a half-pint of urine, Bazalgette reckons that each urinal will yield a minimum of 408 pints (230 litres). Using the costing of Professor Cuthbert Johnson, leading manure expert (also a Commissioner of Sewers), Bazalgette predicts an overall profit of £600 a year.[1]

Bazalgette got the Assistant Surveyor job. His proposal impressed the Commissioners of Sewers enough that they ordered copies of Bazalgette's scheme to be printed at their own expense, even though it was never built. The episode remains instructive to consider here, however, because it underscores how open the sanitation situation was

Leaflet for a Turner and Robertshaw's patent Dividable Closet, or Improved Pail System toilet, c. 1881.

in 1850. For Bazalgette was hardly alone in his urine calculations. Even if the scheme may sound like something out of a sci-fi novel, urine harvesting and sewage farming were studied seriously throughout the nineteenth century. For much of the century, in major Western cities from Edinburgh to Munich, some alternative form of human waste disposal existed alongside or instead of waterborne sewerage. And it was by no means evident that waterborne waste disposal would come to dominate as it did – not even to the engineer whose name would become most closely associated with it.

Following the theories of the agricultural chemist Justus von Liebig, government officials, sanitarians, scientists and entrepreneurs dreamed of finding a way to utilize human manure. Most were driven by a sincere horror of how water closets polluted rivers and wasted the 'God-given' nutrients in human excreta. Most also believed, however, that reusing sewage could be lucrative – not an unreasonable idea in an age when there was still a working organic economy. The reasons flushing eventually won out will be considered in this chapter, but when it happened, many of the day's leading thinkers viewed it as a Pyrrhic victory at best. Karl Marx lamented: 'In London they can find no better use for the excretion of four and a half million human beings than to contaminate the Thames with it at heavy expense.'[2]

Why should this episode be of interest to us now? It is relevant because we are witnessing in our own time a massive push to try to approach the bathroom differently. This requires rethinking the system that supports it to try to unlock some of the assumptions and habits that have become deeply entrenched over the decades. As mentioned in the Introduction, this rethinking has been partially triggered by the realization that waterborne infrastructural systems cannot realistically be deployed to solve the sanitation crisis that affects the Global South today. While the situation is different in the Global North, which has a more or less universal water system, the status quo is also being questioned here in the face of environmental concerns and of ageing infrastructure. (In the US alone, the Environmental Protection Agency estimates that $200 billion to $400 billion is needed over the next two decades to ensure the sustainability of water and wastewater systems.[3]) While today's enthusiasm for reinventing the toilet can be seen as a piece of futurology, a visionary attempt to address current environmental and public health problems, it might equally be seen as an archaeological effort to reconnect with earlier modes of addressing waste. Urine harvesting is, once again, on the agenda.

'When thou wilt ease thyself abroad . . .'

Bazalgette's proposal for urine harvesting may seem extreme now, but would not have done in 1849 when people were accustomed to having their waste collected and used for agricultural purposes. Urban residents pre-Bazalgette still emptied waste into soil tanks or 'bog holes' at the end of their gardens or in cellars. Night-soil men periodically emptied the tanks, digging out the contents by hand or using pumps; the 'night' in 'night soil' referred to the fact that they worked by lanterns between midnight and five in the morning. Although some might dump their cargoes into nearby sewers, others removed them to night yards, enormous collective dung heaps scattered throughout London; a portion of these deposits would then be sent out of the city up Grand Union Canal by barge for use as fertilizer. This business, however, became far less profitable from the 1840s on due to competition from a rival fertilizer: cheap guano, or seabird droppings, imported from Peru.[4]

As discussed in chapter One, the perceived health dangers of cesspools resulted in their abolition and the creation of a modern sewer network, efforts that transformed the sanitary scene by the

1870s. And the story would seem to end there – with the triumph of flushing. But it was not so simple. Many passionately opposed the practice of disposing waste directly into natural bodies of water. In 1856 John Simon, Medical Officer of the General Board of Health, summed up the 'great dilemma' as follows: while most believed that the prevention of epidemics depended on universal house drainage, the cost was the pollution of rivers, which was not acceptable, at least to Simon, because its health effects were unknown.[5]

Bazalgette acknowledged the potential risks of water disposal, but argued that the benefits of drainage overrode them.[6] Other influential colleagues disagreed and the question of how best to dispose of London's sewage – in water or on land? – was constantly and acrimoniously debated by the Metropolitan Commission of Sewers.[7] Other powerful bodies threw their support behind land-based disposal, or 'conservancy', such as the General Board of Health (influenced, as ever, by the powerful sanitary reformer Edwin Chadwick). And following site visits to numerous sewage works and sewage farms in the UK and one in Italy, in 1858 the first Royal Commission on Sewage Disposal came out cautiously in favour of land: 'On the whole there can be no doubt that the sewage of a town . . . can be more profitably disposed of by direct application to land than by any other means.'[8]

The level of feeling that accompanied the debate over disposal must be seen in the context of contemporary European fears about soil exhaustion, the reduced fertility of farms, and the relentless global hunt for fertilizers by Britain and the United States. In this atmosphere of crisis, critics of all stripes had an almost visceral reaction to the wasting of human excrement. Their objections were framed in religious terms – flushing was an offence against the divinely ordained natural order – and economic ones – the failure to exploit such an abundant natural resource was a crime against capitalism. Liebig and his admirer Karl Marx spoke of the rise of waterborne sewerage and imported guano as nothing less than the rationalization of ecological destruction, creating a 'metabolic rift' between man and land.[9] Others framed their objections in patriotic terms, viewing the reliance of English farmers on 'foreign' guano as a threat to sovereignty. Indeed, the use of English sewage to grow food for the English people had an undeniably utilitarian and patriotic neatness.

These anxieties ensured that, even after the night-soil trade declined, sewage was still treated as a commodity to be bought and sold. The Public Health Act 1848 guaranteed that sewage might be 'collected for sale' and the right of local boards to make contracts with companies for its sale or distribution was always affirmed in later acts.[10] And there was no shortage of excremental wheeling and dealing. But these schemes all tended to turn on, and to fall down at, the level of the system: how could human waste best be harvested, collected and transported? How would it be valued and sold? And, importantly, could it make a profit? Based on the analyses of agricultural chemists, more accurate comparisons of the value of sewage and guano's fertilizing components began to be possible.[11] These figures convinced a large number of chemists, sanitary engineers, entrepreneurs and visionaries that human waste could make money. Working out how to unlock its value was the holy grail of the 1860s.

A number of different approaches were proposed. Accepting the reality of waterborne waste disposal, some sought to recover the valuable ingredients from diluted sewage: this recovery might be effected through mechanical and/or chemical methods, ideally resulting in something like a dry manure briquette that could be transported and sold. In light of the technical difficulties posed by waste recovery, others believed a simpler option was to apply sewage straight on to fields, in the 'Chinese' manner. Chadwick's own enthusiasm for sewage farming was inspired by the Craigentinny estate in Edinburgh, where 325 acres of flood meadows were irrigated by a third of the city's sinks, drains and privies, resulting in increased productivity of the land.[12] Chadwick saw no contradiction between his simultaneous advocacy of drainage *and* of sewage utilization because he believed that water most efficiently carried waste to land where it could be deployed as manure – a cost-effective way to bring 'the serpent's tail into the serpent's mouth'. Diluting sewage with water had the added benefit of making it far less 'offensive' to nearby residents in terms of smell.[13]

But even the staunchest supporters of sewage farms acknowledged that it was difficult to make them financially viable. The amount of space farms required meant that they had to be established far outside towns (1 acre, or 4,000 square metres, was thought necessary to handle the sewage of 100 to 300 people) and considerable infrastructural investment was needed for pumping stations, pipes or tubes, and storage reservoirs. Moreover, as waterborne sewage was so dilute, serious doubts remained about its viability as fertilizer. In the 1860s, agricultural scientists John Lawes and Joseph Gilbert undertook practical experimentation to attempt to settle the matter; they confirmed that sewage farming *could* be profitable, but only if the right crops were planted and the farm was not too far from market.[14] Such verdicts dampened the euphoric predictions of earlier years so that, by the late 1870s, sewage farming was no longer advocated on the grounds of productivity or profits. Instead, its ability to filter and purify urban waste more cheaply than chemical forms of treatment was emphasized, along with its ability to irrigate dry land during hot summer months.[15] In the wake of the Pollution of Rivers Act of 1876, which prohibited the discharge of crude sewage into natural watercourses, over 100 cities and large towns in Britain set up sewage farms.

In some places, however, waterborne waste disposal was sidestepped altogether in favour of dry systems. Certainly not all cities embraced the water closet enthusiastically: Manchester, for example, actively discouraged its use for many years.[16] This is why manufacturers like Walter Macfarlane & Co. offered wet and dry systems for sale simultaneously. If anything, Macfarlane gave more space in his catalogues to 'ordure closets', dry public latrines, which he introduced in the 1850s and extolled for economic and moral reasons: users of ordure closets would be providing manure for farmers as well as preventing the pollution of rivers.[17] Ordure closets were tilted troughs with an inclined discharge pipe under which a bucket would be placed; any residue was to be extracted with Macfarlane's specially designed 'ordure scraper'. The company also sold buckets and carts for transporting manure.

The obvious virtues of facilities like Macfarlane's were simplicity and cheapness. This was also true of the 'pail' system, which was in widespread use in Britain in the 1870s in major cities like Birmingham, Manchester and Nottingham as well as in smaller towns. People excreted in pails, then sprinkled ash on to it. The pails would then either be emptied into private privies or collected by the municipality for central treatment. For instance, in the mid-size town of Rochdale, excrement and urine, once collected and sorted, was emptied into a trench filled with fine ash. Sulphuric acid was added and the whole was mixed. After three weeks it would be dug over, screened and sold as manure. The pails, meanwhile, would be washed with aluminium chloride and returned to their owners. Some places used more sophisticated urine diverting pails, which separated urine from faeces, thus allowing the former to be used on its own as fertilizer or in manufacturing. Turner & Robertshaw's Patent Dividable Closet, for instance, was advertised as being suitable for 'factories', likely textile factories, where urine was used to remove the grease in wool.[18]

The best known of all dry systems, however, was the Reverend Henry Moule's earth closets and, in his aptitude and appetite for publicity, the Reverend deserves to be seen as the 'dry' counterpart to George Jennings. The evangelical Moule cited biblical authorities for his closets ('When thou wilt ease thyself abroad, thou shalt turn back and cover that which cometh from thee'; Deuteronomy 23:13) and, as he made clear in a steady stream of pamphlets written throughout the 1860s and '70s, he believed waterborne sewage was sinful.[19] Moule's patented closets replaced water with earth: here the flush handle was a lifting mechanism that released earth from a hopper into a bucket below the seat. In the bucket, soil and excrement would mix – in more elaborate models this mixing was done by a rotating screw turned by a hand crank – and the soil would dry and deodorize the faeces. Moule (inaccurately) claimed that the resulting mix was just as nourishing as the man-made fertilizers that had been available since the 1840s.[20]

As this brief survey highlights, there was no 'right way' of dealing with waste in Britain for most of the nineteenth century. The historian Christopher Hamlin remarks: 'For many sanitary problems, there were no obvious or unproblematic solutions, no consensus as to the rules of administrative and engineering practice.'[21] That the London model, complete with water closets and combined sewers, did eventually spread across the country is down to many factors. Dry systems then, as now, had obvious limitations as means of hygienically handling volumes of waste. Earth closets or pails were far more labour-intensive than water closets, requiring faithful maintenance to be kept clean and decent – hoppers had to be filled, pails scrubbed and disinfected and trenches dug. In the hierarchy of service, emptying the slops and maintaining privies and earth closets had long been the lowest of all jobs. Alison Light notes, 'Who emptied the sewage was a serious issue among the servants since it affected their earnings and their self-respect.' Beginning in the First World War, when servants were in short supply, it became increasingly hard to find those willing to take on the task: Light gives the example of Virginia Woolf's struggle to find a villager who would empty the earth closet at her country house in 1916.[22]

Even when no shortage of labour existed, engineers and health authorities preferred water systems, in large part because they knew that the job of emptying and collection was not always done safely, therefore increasing the likelihood of epidemics. Furthermore, unlike waterborne systems, dry systems were of little use in disposing of other refuse, such as the effluent from slaughterhouses or factories. Where they were viable was in rural areas, large estates and institutions, places that had substantial gardens and space for storage, and in those locations they continued to be used for many decades. Central pail collection reportedly continued in some areas into the 1960s.[23]

The British dream of sewage farming declined well before this. Volumes of sewage increased at a dramatic rate over the course of the nineteenth century as more people obtained water closets. As average water consumption rose, sewage farms became 'sewage sick' and it

Revd Henry Moule's earth closet, c. 1875.

was physically and financially impossible to meet the demand for land: Birmingham claimed to need an additional acre of land per week to keep up. At the same time, water disposal became a more palatable option thanks to the development of innovative new methods of sewage treatment from the 1890s on.

In London, the Metropolitan Board of Works began experimenting with these methods in an attempt to rectify one of the most pernicious legacies of Bazalgette's system: the increased pollution downriver of the outfalls at Barking and Crossness in the east and southeast of the city.[24] Under intense pressure to improve the water quality of the Thames, it introduced intermittent filtration, mechanical precipitation and biological waste treatment methods (the use of bacteria to destroy organic matter). Biological methods in particular would prove to be the way of the future: Davyhulme in Manchester was the first sewage works to introduce activated sludge treatment in 1914, which is now ubiquitous. The net result was that, after six decades of experimentation, hopes and fears, conservancy began to beat a long retreat.

Buckets, pails, vacuums and squats

This was where things stood in Britain, at least. No other country followed exactly the same path. America in some ways came closest in that it very quickly adopted water carriage systems; by the 1920s, coverage in cities was nearly universal. Americans seemed to be far less tortured than Europeans about disposing waste into natural bodies of water: by 1905, of the 28 million citizens with sewerage connections, 27 million discharged either directly into fresh water or the sea.[25] Though the outhouse continued to be a familiar feature of rural life, and a large percentage of Americans relied – as they still do – on onsite forms of treatment like septic tanks, collective efforts to recycle human waste were comparatively few and far between. The marked preference for water disposal was probably inevitable given that most major US cities were port or harbour cities, with large bodies of water in close proximity. However, it also reflected the American sanitary establishment's conviction that running water could self-purify, thus neutralizing the noxious component of sewage and making treatment unnecessary.[26]

By contrast, in Europe, countries or regions that were less urbanized or industrialized were less motivated to invest in sewerage and, outside urban centres, many did not. The historian Jean-Pierre Goubert notes, for instance, that in 1903 in France, 'of a total of 616 towns with a population of more than 5,000, only 294 had a sewage disposal system, most of which were inefficient, while 65 had a complete combined mains drainage system.'[27] Even in Paris it was not compulsory for private dwellings to connect to the mains drainage system until 1894. Up to that point, Haussmann's system carried limited amounts of sewage (though he would have preferred it to carry none at all) and the majority of human waste was still carted off by *vidange* crews to Montfaucon dump, where it was converted into compost.

Later in the century, strong support emerged for sewage farming. One of its most eloquent and vocal supporters was Victor Hugo who, like Marx, was an admirer of Liebig. In a famous passage from *Les Misérables*, Hugo passionately demanded:

> Do you know what those piles of ordure are [?] All this is a flowering field; it is green grass; it is mint; and thyme, and sage . . . it is perfumed hay; it is gilded wheat; it is bread on your table; it is warm blood in your veins; it is health; it is joy; it is life.[28]

Haussmann's Director of Sewers, Eugène Belgrand, was persuaded to set up a 6-hectare model irrigation farm at Gennevilliers in 1870; in 1889 the government passed a bill allowing sewage farming to expand. Soon, sewage farms occupied 5,000 hectares (12,500 acres) of land. Even in the mid-twentieth century, they still produced more than one-tenth of the vegetables for sale in Les Halles market. Significantly, the success of French sewage farms led to an even larger programme in Berlin, of over 17,000 hectares.[29]

France and Germany were not isolated examples. In many European cities the preference was to treat waste separately from stormwater. Dutch towns such as Groningen, Rotterdam, Leiden and Maastricht implemented tub or barrel systems with central collection. In 1842, Chadwick observed approvingly that tubs in the Netherlands were removed daily 'with as much care as our farmers remove their honey from the hives'.[30] These continued until after the Second World War. Several Dutch cities also experimented with the Liernur system, a pneumatic system invented by engineer Charles Thieme Liernur, consisting of toilets, funnels, conduits and a central collection reservoir. In this system, excrement was extracted daily with a vacuum created by steam pump, and then sold as manure. (The fact that the system required very little water to move waste also meant that the excrement was far less dilute and therefore more valuable to farmers.) After being trialled in Breda in 1867 and in Leiden in 1871, Amsterdam set up a demonstration project involving 1,700 people, which was expanded in 1879 to include about 90,000 people. The Liernur system was also set up on a trial basis in cities from the Czech Republic to France, apparently surviving in Trouville until the 1980s.[31]

Liernur was not the only pneumatic system available. One competitor was the Berlier, a vacuum system in use in parts of Paris and Lyons that maintained partial suction throughout the day, rather than operating only at set times as did Liernur's. And finally in England, the Shone Hydro-Pneumatic system was developed, which did not work by suction; rather, once sewage entered Shone's patented 'ejector stations' it was pushed into small, sealed pipes by means of compressed air from a central air-compressing station, ready to be delivered to an outfall or on to fields. By the end of the century, the Shone system was in operation in the Houses of Parliament, in British towns including Eastbourne and Winchester, and in colonial cities such as Durban, Rangoon and Bombay.[32] Its best publicized appearance, however, was in 1893 at the World's Columbian Exhibition in Chicago, where it was set up to demonstrate how sewage could be handled without polluting the Great Lakes. Visitors could go to see the precipitation tanks and two water-treatment plants processing the waste of 6,500 sinks and toilets per day.[33]

While pneumatic sewerage systems might now seem fantastical, this was a time when the value of air as a transmitting medium was well established – for instance in Post Office tubes. Chief among their advantages was the fact that their pipes were much smaller than conventional water pipes and could be used in areas where it was hard to

Night soil collection, Amsterdam, Netherlands, 1934.

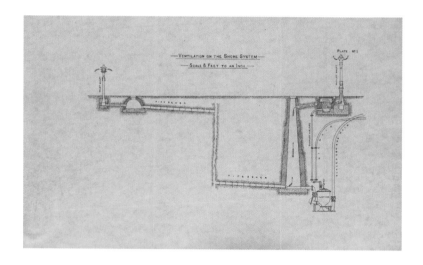

build sewers with a sufficient gradient to ensure proper flow.[34] Thus they were well suited to places like Amsterdam or Bombay, which were topographically challenging or had existing features, such as narrow streets or canals, which made conventional sewers unfeasible. These systems never did replace waterborne ones – sanitary engineers disliked the extra pipework and machinery they required – but vacuum sewage systems such as Qua-Vac continue to be widely used today in topographically challenging or ecologically sensitive terrain, from prisons and theme parks to historic city centres.[35]

Outside the US and Europe, large colonial cities were being endowed with drainage and sewerage systems, though these did not necessarily function exactly as their European counterparts did. As one handbook, *Oriental Drainage*, noted in 1902, 'To blindly accept in its entirely an English system is to court defeat in an Oriental city.'[36] Differences in climate, rainfall patterns and topography played a part, but social customs and habits were significant too. Consider Bombay. Though it had one of the most extensive colonial drainage systems of

Ventilation on the Shone Hydro-Pneumatic system in J. C. Carkeet, *Oriental Drainage* (revised edition, 1917).

the nineteenth century, houses were not directly connected to it and water closets were not widespread. Rather, privies were usual in houses and even chawls (four-to-five-storey dwellings, sometimes containing hundreds of tenants). Waste fell down a shaft into a privy receptacle, which opened on to an alleyway and was emptied into a basket by Untouchable sweepers. These baskets, weighing about 40 pounds (18 kilograms) each, would then be carried on the head to a depot connected to the sewers where they would be deposited.[37] The resulting system was a hybrid, an example of a modern infrastructure being grafted on to a traditional social system.

This was a common pattern. Even after sewerage was available in parts of most large Indian cities by the early 1900s, water closets did not follow for the urban poor. There were usually good technical reasons for this: in Bombay, for instance, due to rain patterns (the city was dry for much of the year followed by an intense rainy season), it was difficult to fully clear sewers of foul matter, making it imperative to keep night soil out of the system, where it would otherwise fester.[38] But, even when such real difficulties existed, administrators insisted that water closets would never catch on because the 'habits of the people are in many ways not suited to them and caste prejudices often interpose'.[39] The caste system was an undeniably powerful factor in shaping toilet use and preferences. In technical manuals, sanitary engineers were transformed into anthropologists as they tried to instruct colleagues about the intricacies and implications of caste. For instance, they noted that if a toilet handle had come into contact with an Untouchable, it became polluted and could not be used by people of higher castes. The same problem of defilement did not exist with rivers, which was why open defecation was – and often still is – preferred to flush toilets.[40]

To colonists, however, the fundamental conviction that 'natives' were innately dirty confirmed their otherness and justified their

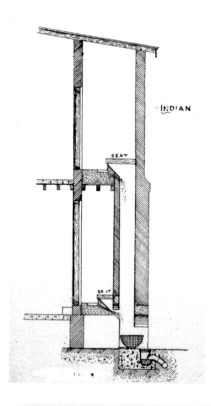

Diagram of an Indian privy in J. A. Turner, *Sanitation in India* (1914).

'Sweeper's Gully with Basket Privies and Open Drains', in J. A. Turner, *Sanitation in India* (1914).

subjugation; it was constantly asserted that, without education and training, they were incapable of using sanitary fittings correctly. In a guide for Europeans moving to the tropics, colonial medical officer J. Balfour Kirk warned, 'In the absence of constant European supervision these places [i.e. latrines] are apt to become unutterably filthy.' Kirk pointed to religious beliefs as the main source of problems. For instance, he explained, water closet blockages often occurred because Muslim male servants, eager to avoid soiling their robes and defiling them, applied pebbles to their penises to absorb the last drops of urine; these pebbles then stopped the drains. (Avoiding the backsplash of urine, which rendered Muslims ritually unclean, was another acknowledged challenge for the designers of tropical sanitary appliances.[41]) While Kirk felt traditional rituals should be respected – he suggested asking that male servants use paper instead of pebbles – he also believed that sanitary infractions should be dealt with firmly: 'If you find that the floor has been fouled, insist upon its being cleaned up there and then. Don't take a servant's word that it will be done – see it done.'[42]

The belief that, left to their own devices, locals could not appreciate such facilities also meant that they were often provided with a lower standard of sanitary provision than were Americans or Europeans. Thus, a very clear differentiation in toileting and hygiene habits emerged and largely continues to this day in former colonies: colonists and upper-class locals used throne-style water closets in their homes while the lower classes used communal facilities with buckets or latrines, or were left to carry on with open defecation. In fact, toilet habits are an example par excellence of how rich and poor develop very differing patterns of life, decried by the economist E. F. Schumacher as one of the most 'disruptive' features of societies developing countries.[43]

When water closets were provided for locals, they were almost always squats with porcelain pans. Waste fell into a channel that was automatically flushed with water several times a day. Administrators took steps to ensure appliances were used properly: in India, the practice was to hang a small looking glass or an outspread red hand (a symbol of plenty) 3 feet from the ground so that users would face the correct direction.[44] Segregation was a normal feature of colonial sanitary arrangements. When fancier convenience accommodation was provided, for instance in city business districts, white people and 'natives' were each provided with a closet for their own use – natives had a stand pipe which provided them with water for their ablutions.[45] In Durban, South Africa, separate public facilities were supplied for Europeans (of both sexes) and for Coloureds (the local African and Indian populations). Here, however, the town engineer, Englishman John Fletcher, broke ranks and reported that the Coloured had used them 'in such a manner and with such satisfaction' as to disprove the notion that they were naturally unsuited to use of modern conveniences.[46]

Alongside these modernized systems, of course, age-old modes of dealing with waste continued to flourish, especially in rural locations. East Asian countries – Japan, Korea and China – had been using sewage for thousands of years to fertilize their fields, but China attracted the lion's share of interest in Europe. With ambivalence typical of the day, Bazalgette remarked:

> The Chinese, sacrificing to a large extent the delicacy and comfort so highly prized by more civilized nations, but with a sound appreciation of the town refuse, apply it in the most direct and rude manner to the reproduction of their growing crops.[47]

Farmers often did apply waste to their fields or fed it to their pigs – many rural latrines opened directly onto pigpens – but in cities, human waste was collected by a system that was no less 'rude' than European pail or bucket systems. In Beijing, scavengers removed

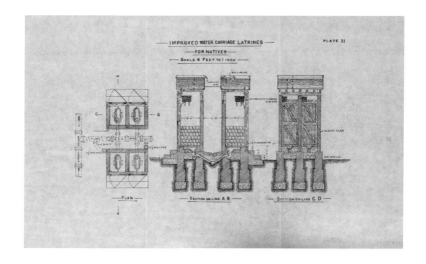

faecal material, took it to fields outside the city and then dried it into cakes for sale as fertilizer.[48] Night soil was also collected for sale in Shanghai where, despite the prevalence of electricity, gas supply and telephones from the 1920s on, few people had fixed sanitary fittings. Instead they had night stools, drum-shaped buckets with wooden lids, some of which were exquisitely decorated. These stools were placed outside every night for the 'Emptying Master'. After removing the waste, the night-soil man would take it to the docks, mix it with water and sell it on to farmers for the equivalent of about US$1 per cart. (Shanghai night soil was especially prized because of the locals' superior diets.) Gangsters controlled this lucrative business. The most celebrated were the 'Royalty of Nightsoil' – Sister Ah Gui and her son, Ma Hongeen – who, with 400 carts and thousands of workers, ran the night-soil trade from the French Concession docks.[49]

Following collectivization in the 1950s, the Chinese communist government took back the night-soil business, encouraging the people to 'turn all waste into treasure'.[50] Initially each person was meant to carry

'Improved Water Carriage Latrines for Natives', in J. C. Carkeet, *Oriental Drainage* (1917).

their own buckets, but the government soon began to employ sanitary workers instead, who brought waste to depots for biological treatment – mostly aerobic composting. Under this centrally organized means of collection it was estimated that, by 1956, 90 per cent of human waste in China was used as fertilizer.[51] Well into the 1980s, the night stool remained a feature of everyday life for the 60 per cent of Shanghai families without sanitary fittings, though communal cesspools and 'excavator' vacuum trucks came to replace the Emptying Master.[52]

Closing the loop

Considering the methods described above, it becomes evident that methods for dealing with human waste remained diverse throughout

'Faeces Collector in Peking', in J. C. Scott, *Health and Agriculture in China* (1952).

the nineteenth and twentieth centuries, with huge variations depending on local conditions and customs. We might speak generally of a split between places that adhered to a wet system of sanitation and those that adhered to a dry one, but this in itself does not correspond to any particular underlying attitude towards waste. Some places with wet systems still tried to utilize waste for agricultural purposes and some places with dry systems did not, preferring, for instance, to simply leave waste in a pit latrine and dig another. In those countries that did have waterborne systems, concerns about water pollution never entirely went away, but they roared to the front of public debate again in the 1970s thanks to the environmental movement.

At this point in Europe, much sewage did undergo treatment before hitting the waterways; in America, treatment became mandatory following the Clean Water Act in 1972. Conventional treatment generally consisted of a primary stage in which solids were removed through grit screens and in settling tanks, and a secondary stage, in which effluent was cleaned through oxidation and chlorination. Treated effluent was released back into waterways. Yet was this adequate to deal with everything that was being dumped into sewers? In the wake of Rachel Carson's book *Silent Spring* (1962) there was a greater awareness of toxic chemicals, PCBs (polychlorinated biphenyls) and pesticides like DDT, which entered the sewerage system through industry drains or as run-off from farms. Even chlorine, an essential part of sewage treatment and water purification since the early 1900s, became suspect, charged with damaging aquatic life and producing carcinogenic chemical compounds. And what became of the by-product of the sewage treatment process: the sludge that accumulated at the bottom of settling tanks? It might be dumped at sea, buried as landfill, incinerated, gasified, or repackaged and sold as fertilizer with enticing names like Fond de Green. But what guarantee was there that sludge was free of bacteria, pathogens, chemicals and heavy metals found in sewage? Were these being introduced via sludge back into the food chain or into groundwater?[53] These fears still thrive today, despite the rebranding of sludge as the more respectable-sounding 'biosolids'.[54]

Rather than continuing to rely on centralized water treatment, those in the environmental movement sought natural and less energy-intensive alternatives, such as municipal composting or the construction of wetlands. In 1975 the first 'natural' waste-treatment environment of water hyacinth, duckweed, bulrush and water iris was designed by environmental scientist Bill Wolverton, whose previous research had established the capacity of aquatic systems to filter and purify toxic herbicides (specifically Agent Orange). The site for Wolverton's wetland was NASA's John C. Stennis Space Center in Mississippi and was built as part of the agency's research into closed-loop ecological systems in which all resources are recycled in order to sustain astronauts on the Moon long-term.[55] NASA's studies inspired earthbound activists, who began to advocate sewage treatment in ponds, or a combination of ponds and land irrigation, showing the dream of sewage farming had not died. But the problems that dogged nineteenth-century proposals had not died, either: the land required was often too extensive and, critics claimed, engineers were too invested in complex engineering systems to test natural alternatives.[56] In face of these obstacles, many environmental activists chose to opt out of the 'life-support' of modern infrastructural systems altogether.

Like their forebears, this generation of environmentalists was outraged by water pollution and tantalized by waste's fertilizing potential. But now they were also specifically driven by a desire to conserve water and energy, as the costs of centralized sewerage were becoming more apparent. Beginning in the early 1970s, a series of pamphlets and books appeared that championed alternative sanitation. The McGill University Minimum Cost Housing Group, under the direction of Alvaro Ortega and Witold Rybczynski, produced *Stop the Five Gallon Flush*, a still eye-opening menu of toilet technologies around the world (pit, pour-flush, composting, septic, buckets, cartage, waterborne) which might flush, dehydrate, incinerate, compost, package, macerate or freeze waste. The book was first published in 1973 and, to its authors' surprise, sold 6,000 copies and went through many subsequent editions. Later publications on sanitation included the Rodale organization's *Goodbye to the Flush Toilet* (1977), Uno Winblad and Wen Kilama's *Sanitation without Water* (1978) and Sim Van der Ryn's *The Toilet Papers* (1978). While diverse in terms of their audience and approach, all were united in the belief that waterborne sanitation would not work in large swathes of the world, from Sub-Saharan Africa to water-stressed northern California.

In addition to these dedicated guides, alternative sanitation was covered extensively in source books like the *Mother Earth News*, *Undercurrents* and the Buckminster Fuller-inspired *Whole Earth Catalog*. These publications aimed to support the creation of autonomous houses, fuelled only by 'sun, wind, rain, muck and muscle'.[57] In addition to producing energy by means of solar panels or windmills, autonomous houses usually harvested rainwater and used greywater, household waste water from sinks or tubs, to water gardens or to flush toilets. They did not, of course, use standard flush toilets, which in this period still averaged a shocking 5 gallons, or 20 litres, per flush (versus 1.6 gallons or 6 litres today). *Stop the Five Gallon Flush* featured several low-flush toilets in its pages, as well an early dual-flush model from Ideal-Standard.[58] It also had a water-conserving toilet of its own design, the Minimum Sanitary Unit, inspired by an existing TOTO model, where a hand-washing basin was integrated into the cistern and greywater was used for flushing.[59] The Minimum Cost Housing Group also revived and extended Fuller's research into atomization to promote a more water-efficient means of personal cleansing. Their

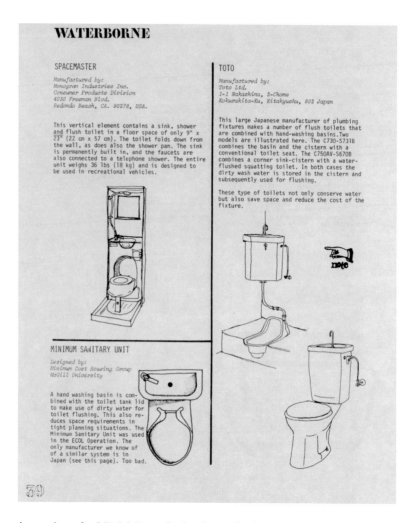

WATERBORNE

SPACEMASTER

Manufactured by:
Monogram Industries Inc.
Consumer Products Division
4030 Freeman Blvd.
Redondo Beach, CA. 90278, USA.

This vertical element contains a sink, shower and flush toilet in a floor space of only 9" x 23" (22 cm x 57 cm). The toilet folds down from the wall, as does also the shower pan. The sink is permanently built in, and the faucets are also connected to a telephone shower. The entire unit weighs 36 lbs (18 kg) and is designed to be used in recreational vehicles.

TOTO

Manufactured by:
Toto Ltd.
1-1 Nakashima, 2-Chome
Kokurakita-Ku, Kitakyushu, 802 Japan

This large Japanese manufacturer of plumbing fixtures makes a number of flush toilets that are combined with hand-washing basins. Two models are illustrated here. The C730-S731B combines the basin and the cistern with a conventional toilet seat. The C750AV-S670B combines a corner sink-cistern with a water-flushed squatting toilet. In both cases the dirty wash water is stored in the cistern and subsequently used for flushing.

These type of toilets not only conserve water but also save space and reduce the cost of the fixture.

MINIMUM SANITARY UNIT

Designed by:
Minimum Cost Housing Group
McGill University

A hand washing basin is combined with the toilet tank lid to make use of dirty water for toilet flushing. This also reduces space requirements in tight planning situations. The Minimum Sanitary Unit was used in the ECOL Operation. The only manufacturer we know of of a similar system is in Japan (see this page). Too bad.

invention, the Mini-Mister, built of standard components for less than $2, only required 1 litre of water.[60]

Despite the availiability of low-flush options, the most irreproach-able toilets from an ecological standpoint were composting ones. Many autonomous homesteaders opted to build their own, but composting toilets also began to be manufactured commercially, mostly in Scandinavia where there is a strong interest in 'ecological sanitation'. These

Space Master, Minimum Sanitary Unit and TOTO combined hand basin-toilet models, in Witold Rybczynski, ed., *Stop the Five Gallon Flush*, Minimum Cost Housing Group, School of Architecture, McGill University (1980).

Mini-Mister, in Alex Morse, Vikram Bhatt and Witold Rybczynski, *Water Conservation and the Mist Experience*, Minimum Cost Housing Group, School of Architecture, McGill University (1978).

models were more high-tech than their home-grown equivalents, with electric heaters and fans for dehydrating compost.[61] The Swedish engineer Rikard Lindstrom's 'Clivus Multrum' aerobic composting toilet, manufactured from 1964 onwards, was the best known.[62] The Clivus consisted of a large, sloped, fibreglass box which could compost the sewage and organic kitchen waste of a family of six; its air conduit system meant that householders did not have to turn or rake the compost themselves. It remains on the market today, installed in various Swedish spots of natural beauty and even in the Bronx Zoo.

All projects for on-site waste recycling can be seen as political at some level, for surely there is no more potent way of criticizing capitalism than to transform waste back into something productive. Their political implications, however, were stressed most explicitly in Britain; rather than the more neutral 'alternative technology', the British preferred the term 'radical technology' to emphasize their commitment to structural social change. This was the aim of architect Graham Caine's Street Farm House (1972), an urban rather than rural autonomous house. Street Farm House was a closed loop of energy and food production: it consisted of solar collectors, windmill, sod roof, fishpond, hydroponic greenhouse and waste-recycling system. All grey- and blackwater drained into a primary digester where it was partially digested before passing to a second tank. This tank had a glass side that was exposed to the sun to encourage algal growth and to harness the 'pathogenicidal' properties of ultraviolet light.[63] The matter was passed into a third digester where it was converted, via anaerobic digestion, to methane gas, for household cooking. The final sludge effluent then passed to the greenhouse for use as fertilizer.[64]

Street Farm's closed-loop system meant that it was not a building in a conventional sense: rather, it was a biotechnical system, in which humans and technology sustained each other. Caine acknowledged:

> Within the ecological house . . . the individual is not only involved in its production, he is directly involved within the biological cycles that constitute so much of its life support systems. ONE RELATES TO ONE'S OWN SHIT.[65]

Architect Lydia Kallipoliti, in an insightful analysis of Caine's relationship to his home, confirms that his excrement became 'an indispensable biological part of the house he built'. He was required to 'feed' the digesters daily with his waste, a relationship he captured visually in the 'Diagram of Basic Inter-dependencies', in which a shitting man sits at the centre of various interlinked organic cycles, like a spider in a web.[66]

As a result of his role in maintaining the house's health, Kallipoliti notes, Caine became obsessed with 'managing, retaining, and reorganizing his excrements', a process that involved him studying the shape and form of the toilet itself.[67] For this he turned to Kira's criteria, and built a low-flush, semi-squat, fibreglass toilet with pad supports, elongated bowl and bidet water-jet (to eliminate the use of toilet paper).[68] Caine's attentiveness to Kira was unusual: though people in the ecological movement knew of *The Bathroom*, they criticized Kira for showing little interest in what happens to waste after it is flushed.[69] But Caine highlighted that Kira's work was in fact highly relevant to

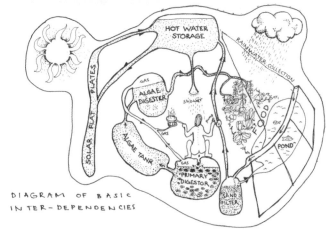

Graham Caine, 'Diagram of Basic Interdependencies', Street Farm, London, 1972.

the project of self-sufficiency because, in autonomous homes, healthy excreting was necessary to produce fuel, fertilizer and food. Caine's understanding of closed-loop ecologies here was deeply influenced by NASA's interest in waste recycling: as well as the wetlands experiment, the agency had also tried to reclaim potable water from urine and to grow food hydroponically using dilute urine.[70] (Kira had also done consulting for NASA, but the research he was involved with – personal hygiene conditions on manned space flights – focused less on recycling waste than on containing it to avoid contamination.[71])

Caine's domestic biogas plant is significant for another reason. Methane gas is the natural by-product of the anaerobic digestion process and the principle of harnessing it was by no means unknown in Europe.[72] Even so, biogas did not yet seem to be fully on the radar of environmentalists, certainly not for home use, and was barely mentioned in *Stop the Five Gallon Flush*. This would soon change, as the oil crisis of 1973 made 'home-made' fuels more attractive and the research and designs of the Indian engineer Ram Bux Singh became better known. Singh had spent two decades at the Gobar Gas Research Station in northern India experimenting with biogas and developing small, low-cost digesters, mostly processing chicken and cow manure. Singh always stressed that he had not invented the idea of using biogas, pointing to other examples of its use in Algeria, South Africa, Korea, Hungary and elsewhere, but he was probably most responsible for raising its profile in the developed world thanks to the design manuals he published and the coverage he received in journals like *Whole Earth Catalog*.[73] In 1972, *Mother Earth News* went one better and invited Singh to design a homestead-sized methane generator, adapted for cold weather, for its headquarters in Madison, Ohio.[74]

Methane digesters and composting methods in general – which were also very much informed by research in India and China at this time – are an important example of developed countries learning from

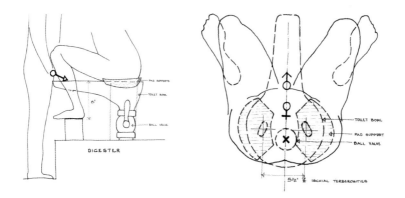

the developing world, examples of reverse technology transfer.[75] Far more typically, technology and expertise flowed in the opposite direction, as when governments provided drainage and sewerage to their colonies, and this was felt to be the correct way of doing things into the postcolonial period. Describing the attitude among European and American aid agencies in the 1960s, E. F. Schumacher noted, 'Discussions on economic development almost invariably tended to take technology simply as "given"; the question was how to transfer the given technology to those not yet in possession of it.' Schumacher described this as 'unintentional neocolonialism' and pointed to its corrosive social effects: as exported technologies primarily benefitted a developing country's urban elites (certainly the case with modern sewerage systems and flush toilets), they further contributed to the emergence of a 'dual economy' – the split between modern and non-modern populations that Schumacher found so toxic.[76] In *Small is Beautiful* (1973) he proposed another approach: the development of 'appropriate technology', small-scale and locally produced technologies that could work within the actual conditions of poverty and stabilize the lives of the poor.

Graham Caine, toilet bowl drawings, Street Farm, London, 1972. The drawing on the right is adapted from Kira's 'Plan View of Sitting Position on a Conventional Water Closet', reproduced in both editions of *The Bathroom* (1966; 1976).

At the same time as Schumacher was writing, a remarkable organization was set up in India that seemed to justify his faith in the socially liberating power of appropriate technologies: Sulabh Sanitation Movement. Inspired by Mahatma Ghandi's mission to better the lives of those in the lowest caste, Sulabh's founder, Dr Bindeshwar Pathak, identified simple, well-built toilets as essential to achieving this goal, because they freed manual scavengers from the job of handling fresh human waste.[77] For households, Sulabh designed a twin-pit, pour-flush toilet which is in widespread use today. Washed down the ceramic pan by a 2-litre flush, waste accumulates in one pit until it is full (usually this takes three years), whereupon the hole is sealed off and the other pit put into use. At the end of three years, the compost from the first pit is ready to be removed – even if dug out manually it is safe to handle and pathogen-free – and can be used as fertilizer.

Another facet of Sulabh's operations is pay-and-use toilet and bath complexes, of which there are presently 7,500 across India at some of the country's most sacred and most touristic spots. More recently, the organization has designed and built biogas plants with ultraviolet-ray effluent treatment to address one of the country's most dire problems: the proportion of raw sewage that is returned straight into India's water supplies (only 232 of India's 4,800 towns have sewerage systems).[78] These biogas plants transform excrement into energy, which is used, for instance, for street lighting, and its treated effluent can be safely used as fertilizer. And Sulabh has also developed a thermophilic aerobic composter which it claims can create compost in eight to ten days 'without any manual handling'.[79] As this example shows, Sulabh's goal of improving the lives of scavengers remains integral to its development of technology; 'appropriate technology' is always implicitly socially liberating technology.

A trigger for social awakening

Despite the early example of Sulabh, the message about the need for appropriate sanitation technologies and the related social benefits took a long time to reach those at the front line of development. Sanitation has always been an unloved and underfunded cause in comparison to water, its sexier and cleaner companion. This situation is only now changing, thanks to studies that demonstrate that sanitation has a very significant impact on child survival rates and well-being.[80] (It also costs less than most other interventions, which is why toilets are regularly referred to by NGOs as 'the cheapest vaccine' or 'the cheapest medicine'.) The research and effort to put sanitation on the global agenda has been well documented by Maggie Black and Ben Fawcett in *The Last Taboo* (2008), and their account makes clear what an arduous uphill battle it has been.[81] Not all countries ignored sanitation between the 1960s and 1980s: indeed some, like India, invested heavily in it. But these top-down government programmes tended not to pay sufficient attention to local conditions or do enough to inform people about how to use their new facilities. As the pioneering sanitation advocate Uno Winblad warned: 'The mere provision of a latrine is no guarantee that it will be used, or used properly.'[82]

It took decades of failures in sanitation programmes, however, before this truth began to be absorbed. In particular, the thousands of sturdily built but unused latrines that dot India's countryside are often cited today as a monument to top-down 'development folly'.[83] The failures of this and many other schemes made clear the need to educate users and to fully explain the health benefits of toilets and good hygiene practices, which are legion. Rose George grimly lists some of the 50 infections that are transmitted by faeces: 'salmonella, schistosomiasis and cholera. Cryptosporidiosis and campylobacter. Giardia, meningitis, shigellosis (which leads to dysentery). Hookworms, roundworms, tapeworms.

Dengue, leptospirosis, hepatitis A. Typhoid, scabies and botulism.'[84] Yet the realities of faecal transmission are still poorly understood in many communities. Visual aids have been devised to communicate the risks and the many pathways for infection: in the widely used 'F-diagram', for instance, Faeces is linked to Fluids, Fields, Flies and Fingers, which are linked in turn to Food.

Recently, however, the messages and techniques have shifted. Rather than focusing on health education alone, programmes now also target people's sense of shame about open defecation practices or appeal to their desire for respectability and status. Most important of all, the process now begins well before the toilets even arrive, and the whole community is actively involved in their implementation, either by agreeing to pay for toilets or building them themselves.[85] This is described as 'social mobilization', or sometimes even 'social awakening'.[86]

The radical shift away from top-down approaches is exemplified by the rise in the last decade of Community-led Total Sanitation (CLTS) programmes. CLTS not only demands that all villagers participate in sanitation improvements but that they drive them. This is encouraged through a method called participatory rural appraisal (PRA), pioneered by development specialist Dr Kamal Kal in Bangladesh. PRA is a rather fancy sounding term for a very simple technique. As Kal describes it, facilitators arrange for locals to 'visit the dirtiest and filthiest areas of the neighbourhood. Appraising and analysing their practices shocks, disgusts and shames people.'[87] So dramatic are the results that some villagers are reported to vomit once they confront evidence of how much faeces is deposited and transmitted through their community.[88] The collective shock triggers a desire to become 'open defecation free'. Without any financial incentive or support (CLTS believes the lack of subsidies is essential to success), villagers then construct their own toilets using improvised techniques and available materials such as plastic soft-drink bottles for piping.[89] And, once built, they ensure that the toilets are used, by developing reward systems or shaming tactics, such as equipping children with whistles to blow when they spot somebody defecating in the open, or flagging piles of shit with the offender's name.

Insofar as there is a new orthodoxy, CLTS is it, and it is spreading rapidly to NGO projects throughout South and Southeast Asia, Africa, Latin America and the Middle East. Even though its newness as a method means that its long-term efficacy has not been fully established, initial feedback from practitioners suggests that it achieves good results in rural areas. It seems to be less effective, however, in urban or peri-urban informal settlements, which are some of the most challenging places to deliver sanitation. Thanks to exploding population growth and dense environments where land tenure is uncertain, neither conventional sewage nor dry toilets are realistic possibilities in these environments.[90] Government agencies, NGOs and social enterprises have responded by installing various kinds of communal provision (converting shipping containers into community ablution blocks, for instance), these are usually pay facilities with caretakers to ensure a higher level of maintenance and to provide local employment. Another approach is to provide informal settlements with simplified sewerage systems that are built and maintained in and by the community – the pioneering initiative here was the Orangi Pilot Project in Pakistan.[91]

If the utilization of sewage was the 'holy grail' of the nineteenth century, the holy grail of sanitation today is to find a means of provision that can be reliably scaled up; that is, can improve the lives not of thousands but of millions of people. Thus the search for a perfect self-contained toilet goes on. The goal of the Gates Foundation's 'Reinvent the Toilet' challenge, for instance, is the production of a low-cost toilet that can be used anywhere in the world; it should generate energy and

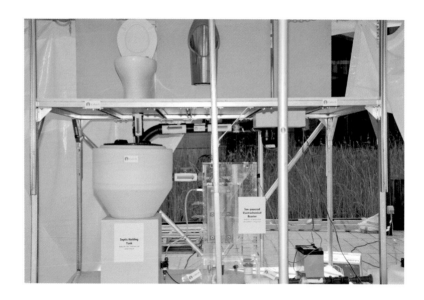

reclaim water and waste nutrients, but not require water supply or sewerage.[92] The foundation is also funding a pilot project that seeks to establish a market for the urine separated in urine-diverting toilets, much as Bazalgette proposed to do 160 years ago.[93] Like Bazalgette's scheme, this project is driven by the geopolitics of fertilizer, specifically now the search for a viable alternative source of non-renewable phosphorus.[94] Parallel efforts to find a productive use for excrement and urine are also thriving: for instance, one communal pay toilet system in Madagascar by the UK-based company Loowatt integrates both energy production – biogas which can be used to charge mobile phones – and fertilizer creation. Such projects refuse to accept human waste as 'waste', the useless but inevitable by-product of conventional sewer systems. (As Winblad reminds us, 'The human body does not produce sewage. Sewage is the product of a particular technology.'[95]) This is as radical a proposition as it ever was.

In some ways, the Reinvent the Toilet challenge, with its focus on hardware, might appear to stand at the opposite end of the CLTS approach, which focuses far more on what we might call the 'software' –

California Institute of Technology, 'A solar-powered toilet that generates hydrogen and electricity', at 'Reinvent the Toilet Fair', Bill & Melinda Gates Foundation, Seattle, 2012.

people's hygiene habits, behaviours and beliefs. But this is deceptive. Across the spectrum, even the most technologically driven projects today tend to have a far greater appreciation of the social benefits of sanitation. In the first instance, there are obvious environmental and health benefits, but others naturally follow on from these: healthier people tend to be better educated, for instance, because they miss fewer days of school. And, as NGOs increasingly stress, the provision of clean, safe school toilets helps ensure that young women stay in education beyond puberty.[96] Overall, toilets create safer and more equitable societies by reducing female labour (as women tend to be the ones who carry water) and chances of sexual assault.[97] Rose George's observation in *The Big Necessity* is worth repeating here. Sanitation, she observes, is 'the most difficult entry point and the one that people are least likely to agree on, but once they do, anything is possible'.[98]

Toilet user entering Loowatt facility under the eyes of the entrepreneur/attendant in Madagascar, Africa, 2012.

Conclusion

As this book began with one bathroom pilgrimage, it seemed right to end it with another. One place in particular beckoned: Therme Vals, Switzerland, a bath complex designed by Peter Zumthor between 1994 and 1997 and widely acknowledged to be one of the most significant works of architecture of the last twenty years. I went, hoping to learn something about bathing culture today.

If bathing is performed either with the aim of external ablution or of regeneration, as Sigfried Giedion maintained, Therme Vals is assuredly on the side of regeneration.[1] It has a lightness of touch I was not expecting as I knew the Therme to be a work of high architecture with all of the seriousness that this term implies. And in the precision of the architecture, the care taken with lighting and detailing, a certain solemnity is established. Nestled in the Alps, the building's simple weave of stone, bronze, concrete, light, water and sound give it a timeless air. But the playfulness of the baths themselves prevents the mood from getting too reverent; a balance between Apollo and Bacchus is struck. Tucked away in hollowed-out columns between the two main baths is a series of wondrous surprises. One moves between the Flower, Fire, Ice and Sound Baths, revelling in the different temperatures, moods and atmospheres.

In this garden of sensory delight, bathers are encouraged to roam; there is no fixed path or order to the experience. Although never

Peter Zumthor, Therme Vals, Switzerland, 1994–7.

overly literal, the spaces freely evoke earlier bathing traditions, from the caldarium of Rome to German 'water cure' establishments. The douche evokes the latter most directly: like Catharine Beecher and countless other water cure enthusiasts, I, too, had the bizarrely exhilarating experience of being pounded with water falling from a great height. And the water at Vals is for drinking as well, in a room that is in some ways the most mystical of all. In a darkened space, a steady trickle of water falls into a dramatically lit pool that roils up like an egg yolk or an orange sun (Olafur Eliasson's art installation *The Weather Project* comes to mind). The pool is surrounded by a gleaming bronze cage to which conical cups are attached. After holding out the cup to catch the water, one drinks.

But despite these strong echoes of the past, Vals is, of course, not at all like a traditional water cure establishment. Few people today would expect a medically correct way of bathing to be prescribed to them. 'Taking the baths' is now primarily a personal and pleasure-led experience, designed not to cure specific ailments per se but to provide the elusive thing called 'wellness', and what I later overheard referred to as 'healthstyle'. Spa culture, which Therme Vals elegantly embraces, is central to healthstyle and it has now come home, shaping the domestic bathroom in the form of features and fixtures that enhance wellbeing. Some of these are new (chromotherapy) and some are more familiar (steam baths and hydrotherapy baths). But the greatest icon of the rise of wellness today is the bath itself: those with money and space use free-standing baths to display their devotion to relaxation.

In 1994, the same year that Zumthor won the competition for Therme Vals, Axor Hansgrohe released a new bath suite designed by Philippe Starck. Axor claimed the design was revolutionary because it was the first to treat the bathroom holistically, as a 'meditative living bathroom'. Even though the idea of a living bathroom was not as revolutionary as Axor claimed, Starck's design did seem to announce a shift in modern

bathing culture, one that Zumthor would come to embody as well. Like Zumthor, Starck was openly inspired by 'archetypal' forms connected to bathing, in his case, the zinc bucket, tin washbowl and water pump. The iconic 'joystick' shape of his taps, for instance, emerged from his study of the curved pump handle and to drive home the link, Axor's sumptuous catalogues typically feature Starck Classic taps beside an image of a cast-iron water pump. In seeking formal inspiration from vernacular forms and traditional materials, Starck and Zumthor both seemed to be channelling an older bathing culture and adopting a quasi-spiritual approach to rejuvenation.

There is no doubt that Starck has left an indelible impact on high-end bathroom design. Luxury homes, hotels, restaurants and nightclubs now trip over each other in an effort to produce the latest jaw-dropping bathrooms.[2] They are larger and more mechanically sophisticated than ever (under-floor heating and advanced lighting

Philippe Starck bathroom, Axor-Hansgrohe, 1994.

are now common), with features such as walk-in rain showers. Exhibitionism, narcissism and voyeurism all come to the fore in these 'naked' spaces, which quite often boast vitrine-like showers or even toilets in their push towards exposure and display.[3] 'The important thing', one architect sums up, 'is to create an attractive, sexy bathing environment.'[4]

Additionally, top-end bathrooms now offer at least one special element to generate a wow factor, for instance a privileged or unique view that can only be obtained while seated on the toilet. The ultimate example is Patrick Jouin's extraordinary black toilet cubicles at Mix restaurant in Las Vegas, which have floor-to-ceiling windows overlooking the city (there is something decidedly imperial about offering one of the finest views in the city to patrons as they evacuate).[5] These are spectacular, decadent and knowing spaces. And they are notably well designed. Since Starck, the line-up of architects who have created sanitary fittings includes Zaha Hadid, David Chipperfield, Norman Foster and Antonio Citterio, along with industrial designers including Marc Newson, Karim Rashid, Patricia Urquiola and Ron Arad.

These products and environments are very exclusive, but they are matched for quality by a handful of projects sited in the public realm. Some local authorities, having seen the value of well-designed public facilities, have decided they are worth investing in or are pushed to do so by citizens' groups or campaigners.[6] An early but still unsurpassed example is CZWG's Westbourne Grove Public Toilets in London (1993). This wedge-shaped, aquamarine building, with its distinctive glass canopy and florist's kiosk, was a clever and practical insertion in Notting Hill at a moment when the area was starting to undergo gentrification: its transformation of the static pictograms depicting 'men' and 'women' into dancing figurines at once captured the area's rakish vibe and nodded to the area's annual

Carnival. Above all, the Westbourne Grove Public Toilets demonstrated that such small-scale insertions into the urban fabric could improve its quality in myriad ways, from animating a leftover public space (in this specific case a traffic island) to providing much-needed public amenities.

CZWG, Westbourne Grove Public Toilets, London, 1993.

When architects are commissioned to design public toilets today, they tend to produce statement buildings: unlike Westbourne Grove's more whimsical aesthetic, most favour dramatic profiles, edgy, deconstructivist forms and rugged natural or industrial materials. Some of the best known examples include the sharply angled public toilets in Gravesend, Kent, by Plastik architects, the tensile, white-canopied Aire de Merle restroom built along the French A54 motorway by Gilles Béguin and Jean-André Macchini, and the rustic, Cor-ten steel-plate Trail Restroom by Miró Rivera Architects in Austin, Texas.[7] Overall, however, the most creative public facilities are those created for Japanese open spaces, such as the seventeen origami-crane-inspired pavilions by Future Studio in Hiroshima Park. More than any other Japanese architect, Shuhei Endo has set the standard in this field, for instance, with a remarkable public toilet in Hyogo, covered by a ribbon-like (perhaps toilet roll-inspired) structure of corrugated sheet metal.[8]

Shuhei Endo, Sprintecture H, Hyogo, Japan, 1998.

What unites these very different projects is that they all work to challenge the idea that toilets should be discreet features of the land-scape or of the urban streetscape. They refuse invisibility. Some even chose to upend the normally implicit rules of toilet design and use. This is especially true of artist-produced public conveniences, which share Duchamp's original provocative impulse but with one signifi-cant difference: they are meant to be used. Take, for instance, Monica Bonvicini's *Don't Miss A Sec*, a public toilet of one-way glass which has been installed in various urban locations since 2003. Although one knows oneself to be hidden when inside the toilet, the trans-parency of the walls makes passers-by startlingly visible, leaving one feeling vulnerable (nervous, or excited?). The unit takes the teasing game of exposure and concealment, which features in so many bathrooms, to its furthest limit.

Or consider Atelier Van Lieshout, the studio led by the artist Joep van Lieshout, which has created bathrooms of all degrees of

Monica Bonvicini, *Don't Miss a Sec*, 2003–4. Exterior of two-way mirror structure.

Monica Bonvicini, *Don't Miss a Sec*, 2003–4. Interior of two-way mirror structure.

functionality. Some are working facilities produced in collaboration with architects like MDRDV and Rem Koolhaas: for instance, the Atelier's 'sanitary spaces' at the Grand Palais in Lille (1994). Much of Lieshout's work, however, is experimental. In the 1980s and '90s the artist produced polyester bathroom furniture and units, which slyly signalled their departure from strict technological rationalism by means of gold-plated taps. *The Mobile Home for Kröller Müller* (1995) also wittily subverts the rationalist legacy: here the bathroom pod is a womb-like 'slave unit' that projects parasitically from its 'master' – playfully reversing the usual dichotomy that sees 'feminine' services hidden within a 'masculine' structure. Most recently, Lieshout has been experimenting with composting toilets and the creation of biogas. The resulting projects do not treat these technologies or processes as a solution to environmental woes but seek to re-embed them

Atelier Van Lieshout, *The Mobile Home for Kröller Müller*, aka The Master and Slave Unit, Otterlo, Netherlands, 1995. Sanitary Slave Unit in yellow.

in the cycles of human use. Take *Huize Organus* (2008) at the Zuiderzeemuseum in Enkhuizen, a multifunctional, squidgy installation that 'houses the complete digestive system from tongue to rectum'. The clip-on composting toilet appears at one end; the female reproductive organs appear at the other.[9]

Surveying these eclectic, dynamic examples or visiting some recent temple-like bathroom showrooms, such as the Zaha Hadid-designed space at Roca London Gallery, one is tempted to conclude that a new era of bathroom design is indeed here. But the moment one makes this claim, doubts begin to set in. To borrow Bruno Latour's phrase, when it comes to bathing, 'have we ever been modern?' When we consider the washbasin and bath, can we claim to have ever moved that far from the archetypal container-like forms with which we began? Is Starck's bath so different from the parallel-ended baths of the nineteenth century or, come to that, the baths at Knossos? Under scrutiny, the claim that Zumthor represents something different is perhaps the

Atelier Van Lieshout, *Huize Organus*, Enkhuizen, Netherlands, 2008. Clip-on composting toilet in pink.

more persuasive one. As Markus Frenzl points out in a thoughtful review of recent bath design, Therme Vals has ushered in a more general shift towards natural materials (copper, bronze, marble, unsealed stone and wood) along with a turn away from obsessive waterproofing. Frenzl interprets this as a sign that we are at last giving up our compulsion to suppress and control water in pursuit of a more authentic bathing experience.[10]

Frenzl's argument is interesting, if somewhat counter-intuitive. For one way in which much contemporary bathroom technology *is* undeniably different from what has come before is that it attempts to conserve water. Water-efficient devices are no longer confined to the realm of the DIY or the wonky green scene: all sanitaryware companies today trumpet their eco-friendly designs. Contemporary showerheads mix water with air to provide a satisfying shower with

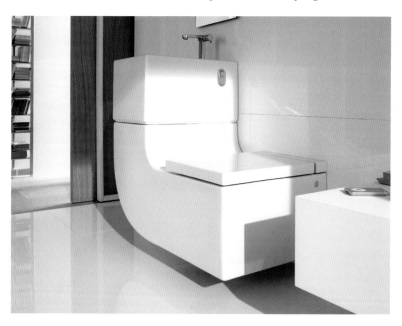

W+W Roca combined sink and toilet that uses greywater from hand washing to flush the toilet, 2012.

less flow – a principle not so far removed from Fuller's fog gun or the McGill Minimum Cost Housing Group's Mini-Mister. Waterless urinals are found in public conveniences everywhere; they are standard in McDonald's across Europe. Dual-flush toilets are now common in the home and toilets with integrated hand basins and greywater flush, such as Roca's W+W unit, may well come to conquer the domestic market too. And innovative systems like Hansgrohe's Pontos AquaCycle uses greywater from showers and baths to flush toilets at a collective scale. Yet Frenzl's comments about the return to natural materials and finishes suggests that the environmental restraint of modern bathroom fixtures has, paradoxically, increased our desire to see erosion, watermarks and patinas. Perhaps it is

Ron Arad, Hotel Puerta América, Madrid, 2005.

because we are more invested than ever before in controlling water that we are beginning to fetishize evidence of its traces. We want the appearance and feeling of endless flow, even though this illusion requires increasing technological ingenuity to sustain.

Of course, this trend towards the natural bath is just one of many. One suspects that a large number of consumers would still be reluctant to accept bathrooms with unsealed materials and water stains. Certainly, it seems fair to say that at least an equal number are going the opposite direction, embracing the possibilities of non-porous materials such as glass or compounds of resin, stone and acrylic. The acrylic stone Hi-Macs, for instance, was used by both Zaha Hadid and Ron Arad to create their (very different) integrated bathroom units at that 'cornucopia of superstar architecture', the Hotel Silken Puerta América in Madrid.[11] Such materials produce bathrooms that are all translucent sheen, seamless surface and sinuous contours. The results are slick and sometimes even alien – not a naturalistic detail in sight. And whatever the colour of the walls, the majority of bath fittings are still white. The purity of the bathroom remains (even if in a softer and more textured guise), sealants are liberally applied, and we continue to be shielded from the traces of our use. Indeed, this is precisely what most sanitaryware manufacturers promise: their products will save water and we won't notice a thing.

The subject of water conservation is too vast to enter into here in a detailed way. Yet it seems necessary to conclude this book by at least asking if changes in the way we flush and bathe eventually need to reach deeper than they do at present. Are technological fixes enough or will our hard-wired water consumption habits have to change as well? To leave the present system unchanged seems increasingly unsustainable in terms of cost as well as the environment. As I write this book, Thames Water, which controls London's water and sewerage systems, has embarked on what will be one of the biggest infrastructural projects in

Britain: the Thames Tideway Tunnel. The proposed tunnel, to be built at a cost of £3.6 billion, aims to correct a problem inherited from the Victorian period. Unlike modern sewerage systems that deal with foul water and rainwater separately, Bazalgette's system is a combined one that deals with everything in a single pipe. This combined system was designed to overflow every time there was a severe rainfall so that buildings and streets would not be flooded. This overflow is discharged straight into the Thames via 57 combined sewage overflows (CSOs).

In Bazalgette's time, overflows did not occur with any frequency: usually only when there was a major storm (and it should not be forgotten that the sewage went into a river that was biologically dead). As London's population has grown and as hard surfaces have proliferated, the overflows now happen far more regularly – weekly, in fact. This means that untreated sewage passes through CSOs into the Thames on a regular basis – some 39 million cubic tonnes of sewage annually. To give a sheer sense of the volume of these discharges, Thames Water says that they effectively fill the equivalent one Olympic size swimming pool in about two minutes. They can carry on for several days.

These overflows seriously impact the quality of Thames water, threaten aquatic life and violate the European Urban Wastewater Treatment Directive. The proposed tunnel, ranging from 35 to 65 metres in depth, will essentially provides storage for overflows, intercepting the contents of the CSOs before they discharge into the Thames. All the intercepted matter will be directed along a tunnel which will carry all material east to Beckton Sewage Treatment Works, the largest in Europe, where it will be pumped out and treated. This process will clear the discharge completely in 48 hours, ready to begin again. It is predicted that the Thames Tunnel will catch 96 per cent of discharges from the most polluting CSOs, solving the problem for the next hundred years (which raises the question: what then?).[12]

The sheer scale, expense and complexity of this infrastructural project brings home the point that we live in a time when 'hard engineering' projects and technological fixes are a must. In a sea-level city like London, which faces increased rainfall and risks of flooding on the one hand and droughts and water shortages on the other, big-system solutions in some form will likely always be necessary. But it is also clear that 'soft engineering' solutions must also be considered: we need to rethink our own behaviours and patterns of water consumption in the years to come. This challenge is one that the bathroom and its designers and users are only just beginning to face.

Yet this history offers some hope. While it often feels as if change is unthinkable – that people's beliefs and behaviours are as deeply entrenched and immovable as infrastructure – this history has shown time and time again that our ideas about and our methods of dealing with water and waste are much less uniform, inevitable and fixed than we usually realize. Bathrooms, like sewers, are relatively recent inventions and they constantly evolve and adapt in the face of shifting social, medical, economic, political and environmental factors. This suggests that they will certainly change again in future. To what specific pressures will they respond? How will spaces and customs be affected in turn? And as we face these challenges, will we do so with any more confidence than did metropolitan dwellers 150 years ago?

References

Introduction

1 François Truffaut, *Hitchcock: The Definitive Study of Alfred Hitchcock by François Truffaut*, revd edn (New York, 1983), p. 320.

2 Matthew Gandy, 'Rethinking Urban Metabolism: Water, Space and the Modern City', *City*, VIII/3 (December 2004), pp. 363–79; Stephen Graham and Simon Marvin, *Splintering Urbanism: Networked Infrastructures, Technological Mobilities and the Urban Condition* (London, 2001).

3 'Slavoj Žižek on Toilets and Ideology', www.youtube.com, accessed 31 January 2012; see also Slavoj Žižek, *The Plague of Fantasies* (London, 2008), pp. 4–5.

4 Mary Douglas, *Purity and Danger: An Analysis of the Concepts of Pollution and Taboo* [1966] (London, 1996), p. 2.

5 Alison Moore, 'Colonial Visions of "Third World" Toilets: A Nineteenth-century Discourse that Haunts Contemporary Tourism', in *Ladies and Gents: Public Toilets and Gender*, ed. Olga Gershenson and Barbara Penner (Philadelphia, 2009), pp. 105–25.

6 Svetlana Boym, 'Obscene Homes', in *Ruins*, ed. Brian Dillon (London, 2011), pp. 68–9.

7 David Inglis, 'Dirt and Denigration: The Faecal Imagery and Rhetorics of Abuse', *Postcolonial Studies*, V/2 (July 2002), pp. 208–9.

8 See, for instance, Scott Baldauf, 'On Eve of World Cup, South Africa's "Toilet Wars" Reveal Volatile Politics', *Christian Science Monitor* (10 June 2010), at www.csmonitor.com.

9 James Forman, *Sammy Younge, Jr: The First Black College Student to Die in the Black Liberation Movement* (New York, 1968).

10 See Sheila Cavanagh, *Queering Bathrooms: Gender, Sexuality, and the Hygienic Imagination* (Toronto, 2010).

11 Sharon LaFraniere, 'For Chinese Women, a Basic Need, and Few Places Attend to It', *New York Times* (29 February 2012), at www.nytimes.com.

12 'Flushing Away Unfairness', *The Economist* (8 July 2010), at www.economist.com.

13 For a more detailed discussion, see Olga Gershenson and Barbara Penner, 'Introduction', in *Ladies and Gents*, pp. 21–2.

14 Louise Norton, 'The Buddha of the Bathroom', *The Blind Man*, 2 (May 1917), pp. 5–6.

15 Wendell Berry, 'Foreword', in Sim Van der Ryn, *The Toilet Papers: Recycling Waste and Conserving Water* [1978] (n.p., 1995), n.p.

16 Eran Ben-Joseph, *The Code of the City: Standards and the Hidden Language of Place Making* (Cambridge, MA, 2005), pp. 80, 92–5.

17 Harvey Molotch, 'On Not Making History: What NYU Did with the Toilet and What It Means for the World', in *Toilet: Public Restrooms and the Politics of Sharing*, ed. Harvey Molotch and Laura Norén (New York, 2010), pp. 255–72.

18 Harvey Molotch, *Where Stuff Comes From: How Toasters, Toilets, Cars, Computers and Many Other Things Come to Be as They Are* (New York, 2005), pp. 100–01.

19 Molotch, 'On Not Making History', p. 256.

20 Quoted in Daniel Max Gerling, 'American Wasteland: A Social and Cultural History of Excrement, 1860–1920', PhD dissertation (University of Texas at Austin, 2011), p. 6.

21 Warwick Anderson, 'Excremental Colonialism: Public Health and the Poetics of Pollution', *Critical Inquiry*, XXI/3 (Spring 1995), pp. 640–69; and Colin McFarlane, 'Governing the Contaminated City: Infrastructure and Sanitation in Colonial and Post-colonial Bombay', *International Journal of Urban and Regional Research*, XXXII/2 (June 2008), pp. 415–35.

22 Rose George, *The Big Necessity: Adventures in the World of Human Waste* (London, 2008), p. 51; Jun'ichirō Tanizaki, *In Praise of Shadows* [1933], trans. Thomas J. Harper and Edward G. Seidensticker (Stony Creek, CT, 1977), pp. 3–6.

23 James L. Watson, *Golden Arches East: McDonald's in East Asia* (Stanford, CT, 2006), p. 33.

24 Oliver August, 'China Scrubs Up to Impress Global Elite of Sanitation', *The Times* (17 November 2004), p. 40; Dominique Laporte, *History of Shit* [1978], trans. Nadia Benabid and Rodolphe el-Khoury (Cambridge, MA, 1993), pp. 28–9.

25   For a sobering assessment of these inequities and the challenges ahead, see *Report of the Special Rapporteur on the Human Right to Safe Drinking Water and Sanitation, Catarina de Albuquerque: Mission to the United States of America*, UN General Assembly, Human Rights Council, 18th Session A/HRC/18/33/Add.4 (2 August 2011).

26 See www.showusyourlongdrop.co.nz, accessed 31 January 2012, and 'Christchurch Earthquakes – Compost Toilets', www.waterscape.co.nz, 21 September 2011.

27 Asa Briggs, *Victorian Cities* (Berkeley, CA, and Los Angeles, 1993), pp. 16–17; 'Greatest Medical Milestone Revealed', www.inthenews.co.uk, 18 January 2007.

28 'Will We Ever Invent Anything this Useful Again?', *The Economist* (12–18 January 2013), cover.

29 Dominique Coughlin, 'Bath to Happiness', *The Times* (20 October 2002), at www.thetimes.co.uk.

30 Clara Greed, *Inclusive Urban Design: Public Toilets* (Oxford, 2003), p. 55. See also 'The Lament of the Public Bathroom', www.architizer.com, 22 June 2011.

1 The Civilizing Bathroom

1 This left a profit of £1,769 18*s*. 6*d*. 'First Report of the Commissioners for the Exhibition of 1851 to the Right Hon. Spencer Horatio Walpole, Appendix XXX', in *Official Descriptive and Illustrated Catalogue of the Great Exhibition* (London, 1851), vol. IV, pp. 151–2.

2 Public Health Act 1848, 11 & 12 Vict., c. 63, s. 57; 'Town and Country Talk', *The Examiner*, 2235 (30 November 1850).

3 Roger-Henri Guerrand, *Les Lieux: Histoire des commodités* (Paris, 1985), pp. 88–95.

4 'Report to the Hon. Commissioners of the City of London upon Sites Proposed for Public Urinals within the City of London by William Haywood, Surveyor to the Commission, 18th February 1851', in *Surveyors and Other Reports: Miscellaneous* (Corporation of London, 1848–57), vol. I , CLLA/006/AD/07/36, London Metropolitan Archives [henceforth LMA].

5 Michael Leapman, *The World for a Shilling: How the Great Exhibition of 1851 Shaped a Nation* (London, 2001), p. 93.

6 'Jennings's Inventions', in *Prospectuses of Exhibitors* (London, 1851), n.p. This is an advertising prospectus Jennings produced for the Great Exhibition. It has been bound up with other prospectuses in a volume at the National Art Library at the Victoria & Albert Museum.

7 Deborah Brunton, 'Evil Necessaries and Abominable Erections: Public Conveniences and Private Interests in the Scottish City', *Social History of Medicine*, XVIII/2 (2005), p. 189.

8 'First Report of the Commissioners', pp. 151–2.

9 'Public Waiting-rooms', *The Morning Chronicle*, 26349 (26 May 1851).

10 Quote from Captain Henry C. Owen, 'Waiting Room Report', in the *Minutes of Council* (May 1852–June 1853), vol. IV, p. 209, AD/MA/100/12/178, Royal Society of Arts Archive, London.

11 David J. Eveleigh, *Privies and Water Closets* (London, 2008), p. 35.

12 See the case of *Tinkler* v. *Board of Works for the Wandsworth District* [1857–8], in Jamie Benidickson, *The Culture of Flushing: A Social and Legal History of Sewage* (Vancouver, 2007), pp. 85–9.

13 Public Health Act 1848, 11 & 12 Vict., c. 63, ss. 41–59.

14 They were designed by John Phillips, Chief Surveyor for the Metropolitan

Commission of Sewers. 'Plans of Public Conveniences, etc.' [1847–1854], MCS/P/013, LMA.

15 Common Lodging Houses 1851, 14 & 15 Vict., c. 28, s. 9.

16 Joseph Bazalgette, 'On the Main Drainage of London, and the Interception of the Sewage from the River Thames' [1865], in *Thames Tunnel to Channel Tunnel: 150 Years of Civil Engineering*, ed. W. Howie and M. Chrimes (London, 1987), p. 283.

17 Quoted in Steven Johnson, *The Ghost Map: A Street, A City, An Epidemic and the Hidden Power of Urban Networks* (London, 2006), p. 120.

18 J. E. Wakefield, *Statement of the Works and Improvements Carried Out by the Board in the Metropolis, from the Passing of the Metropolis Local Management Act in 1855, up to the End of the Year 1882* (London, 1883), p. 2.

19 J. B. Lakeman, 'A Lecture on Health in the Workshop', in *International Health Exhibition, London, 1884* (London, 1884), vol. III, pp. 159, 168–9.

20 Henry Jephson, *The Sanitary Evolution of London* (London, 1907), p. 96.

21 See the summary in William Woodward, 'The Sanitation and Reconstruction of Central London', in *Essays on the Street Re-alignment, Reconstruction, and Sanitation of Central London* (London, 1886), pp. 46–64.

22 Edwin Chadwick, *Report on the Sanitary Condition of the Labouring Population of Great Britain* [1842], ed. M. W. Flinn (Edinburgh, 1965), esp. pp. 98, 112.

23 Henry Roberts, *The Dwellings of the Labouring Classes: Their Arrangement and Construction; Illustrated by a Reference to the Model Houses of the Society for Improving the Condition of the Labouring Classes* (London, 1850), p. 2.

24 David J. Eveleigh, *Bogs, Baths and Basins: The Story of Domestic Sanitation* (Stroud, 2002), pp. 155–6.

25 See Mark Wigley, 'Untitled: The Housing of Gender', in *Sexuality and Space*, ed. Beatriz Colomina (New York, 1992), pp. 326–89.

26 Roberts, *The Dwellings of the Labouring Classes*, p. 37.

27 Marilyn Thornton Williams, *Washing 'The Great Unwashed': Public Baths in Urban America, 1840–1920* (Columbus, OH, 1991), pp. 6–10.

28 William Paul Gerhard, *Modern Baths and Bath Houses* (New York, 1908), p. 6.

29 Alain Corbin, *The Foul and the Fragrant*, trans. M. Koshan (London, 1994), p. 105.

30 Michel Foucault, *Discipline and Punish: The Birth of the Prison*, trans. A. Sheridan (London, 1991), pp. 171–2.

31 *The Sanitary Record: Bird's-eye Guide and Handbook to the International Health Exhibition* (London, 1884), p. 27.

32 Christopher Silver, *Renkioi: Brunel's Forgotten Crimean War Hospital* (Sevenoaks, 2007), pp. 66, 82–3, 97–8; Alex Attewell, ed., *Lessons from Renkioi* (London, 2005), pp. 6–9; Isambard Kingdom Brunel, *The Life of Isambard Kingdom Brunel: Civil Engineer* (London, 1870), p. 464.

33 Florence Nightingale, *Notes on Hospitals*, 3rd edn (London, 1863), pp. 43, 72–3.

34 'Report of *The Lancet* Sanitary Commission on the State of Londesborough

Lodge & Sandringham, in Relation to the Illness of H.R.H. The Prince of Wales', *The Lancet* (9 December 1871), pp. 828–9.

35 Quoted in S. S. Hellyer, *The Plumber and Sanitary Houses*, 4th edn (London, 1887), p. 1.

36 Ibid.

37 Ibid., p. 11. The seminal account of the domestic sanitation movement and the role of women within it is Annmarie Adams, *Architecture in the Family Way: Doctors, Houses, and Women, 1870–1900* (Montreal, 1996), pp. 36–102.

38 Adams, *Architecture in the Family Way*, pp. 26–35, 48.

39 Ibid., p. 34.

40 'The Parkes Museum', *The Lancet* (2 August 1879), p. 165; and Lawrence Wright, *Clean and Decent: The Fascinating History of the Bathroom and the Water-Closet* (London, 1960), p. 208.

41 'Sanitary Appliances: Report of International Jury of 1889', *The Lancet* (30 April 1892), p. 994; and Hellyer, *The Plumber and Sanitary Houses* ('copious flushes'), p. 5.

42 Jephson, *The Sanitary Evolution of London*, p. 330.

43 Liberal MP Francis Mowatt, in *Hansard Parliamentary Debates*, 3rd ser., vol. CXXII (1852), col. 3, at 853. See also Vanessa Taylor and Frank Trentmann, 'Liquid Politics: Water and the Politics of Everyday Life in the Modern City', *Past and Present*, CCXI/1 (May 2011), pp. 199–241.

44 Letter from R. J. Butler, in Metropolitan Commission of Sewers, *Works Committee Minute & Report Book* (23 July 1849), MCS/195, LMA.

45 Barbara Penner, 'A World of Unmentionable Suffering: Women's Public Conveniences in Victorian London', *Journal of Design History* XIV/1 (2001), pp. 35–52.

46 Quoted in The Mayor's Committee (William Gaston Hamilton, Moreau Morris, William Howe Tolman), *Report on Public Baths and Public Comfort Stations* (New York, 1897), p. 10.

47 Quoted in David Pinkney, *Napoleon III and the Rebuilding of Paris* (Princeton, NJ, 1958), p. 127.

48 Stephen Halliday, *The Great Stink of London: Sir Joseph Bazalgette and the Cleansing of the Victorian Metropolis* (Stroud, 1999), pp. 12–14.

49 Peter Payer, *Unentbehrliche Requisiten der Grossstadt* (Vienna, 2000), pp. 74–6.

50 The Mayor's Committee, *Report on Public Baths*, pp. 18–19, 68–134, 142–62 (quote on Paris p. 142, quote in praise of London p. 174).

51 'Calcutta Drainage (Cowie) Committee 1856–57: Report and Appendices (Including Evidence), Calcutta, 1857', p. 2, IOR/V/26/842/1, Asia, Pacific and Africa Collections, British Library, London.

52 Evan Maconochie quoted in Niall Ferguson, *Empire: How Britain Made the Modern World* (London, 2003), p. 209.

53 Ira Klein, 'Urban Development and Death: Bombay City, 1870–1914', *Modern Asian Studies*, XX/4 (1986), pp. 725–54.

54 Daniel Max Gerling, 'American Wasteland: A Social and Cultural History of Excrement, 1860–1920', PhD dissertation (University of Texas at Austin, 2011), p. 6.

55 Warwick Anderson, 'Excremental Colonialism: Public Health and the Poetics of Pollution', *Critical Inquiry*, XXI/3 (Spring 1995), pp. 666–7.

56 Jennings's career is summarized with reference to 'A Pioneer in Sanitary Engineering', *The Sanitary Record* (23 April 1897), pp. 368–72; David J. Eveleigh, 'Jennings, (Josiah) George (1810–1882)', in *Oxford Dictionary of National Biography*, www.oxforddnb.com, May 2009; and Lucinda Lambton, *Temples of Convenience and Chambers of Delight* (London, 1998), pp. 20–25, 66–7, 98–9.

57 Wallace Reyburn, *Flushed with Pride: The Story of Thomas Crapper* (London, 1969), pp. 38–43.

58 City of Sydney, 'Water, Water, Every Where: A Virtual Historical Exhibition', www.cityofsydney.nsw.gov.au, 2 February 2006.

59 'Sanitary Appliances', *The Lancet* (1892), p. 994.

60 Adolf Loos, 'Plumbers', trans. Harry Francis Mallgrave, in *Plumbing: Sounding Modern Architecture*, ed. Nadir Lahiji and D. S. Friedman (New York, 1997), p. 15.

61 May N. Stone, 'The Plumbing Paradox: American Attitudes toward Late Nineteenth-century Domestic Sanitary Arrangements', *The Winterthur Portfolio*, XIV/3 (Autumn 1979), p. 286.

62 Lambton, *Temples of Convenience*, pp. 84–5.

63 Adrian Forty, *Objects of Desire: Design and Society since 1750* (London, 1986), pp. 11–41.

64 To see how widely these structures were spread across Britain, see the Scottish Ironwork Foundation at www.scottishironwork.org, accessed 2 June 2010.

65 Walter Macfarlane, 'A New System of Sewerage, and Other Sanitary Arrangements, for Converting the Excrementary Refuse, Dry Garbage, Ashes &c., of Towns into their Proper and Most Valuable Purposes', in Walter Macfarlane & Co., *Catalogue of Macfarlane's Cast Iron Manufactures*, 4th edn (Glasgow, 1862), vol. II, p. 10.

66 Brunton, 'Evil Necessaries', pp. 188, 191.

67 Ibid., p. 189.

68 Macfarlane, 'A New System of Sewerage', p. 40.

69 George Jennings quoted in Wright, *Clean and Decent*, p. 200.

70 James Denley, 'A History of Twyford's, 1680–1982', p. 56, at www.twyfordbathrooms.com, accessed 3 June 2010.

71 Joseph Hatton, *Twyfords: A Chapter in the History of Pottery* (London, 1897), p. 22.

72 C. C. James, *Oriental Drainage: A Guide to the Collection, Removal and Disposal of Sewage in Eastern Cities* (Bombay, 1902), p. 7.

2 The Iconic Bathroom

1 Hermann Muthesius, *The English House* [1904–5], ed. Dennis Sharp, trans. Janet Seligman and Stewart Spencer (London, 2007), vol. III, p. 235.
2 Le Corbusier, *The Decorative Art of Today* [1925], trans. James I. Dunnett, (Cambridge, MA, 1987), p. 90.
3 Alison Light, *Mrs Woolf and the Servants* (London, 2007), p. 35.
4 See, for instance, Clarence Cook, *The House Beautiful* [1881] (New York, 1995), pp. 269–71.
5 David J. Eveleigh, *Bogs, Baths and Basins: The Story of Domestic Sanitation* (Stroud, 2002), pp. 74–5.
6 'James Barlow's Price Current and Illustrated Catalogue of Illuminators', in *Prospectuses of Exhibitors* (London, 1851).
7 Quoted in 'International Exhibition, Class 31', *The Ladies' Monthly Magazine*, 465 (1 September 1862), n.p.
8 Eveleigh, *Bogs, Baths and Basins*, pp. 74–81; Lawrence Wright, *Clean and Decent: The Fascinating History of the Bathroom and the Water-closet* (London, 1960), pp. 193–8.
9 Calvert Vaux, *Villas and Cottages* (New York, 1864), pp. 54–5, 100, 153–4.
10 On the evolution of the American bathroom, see Daniel Max Gerling, 'American Wasteland: A Social and Cultural History of Excrement, 1860–1920', PhD dissertation (University of Texas at Austin, 2011), pp. 99–108.
11 S. S. Hellyer, *The Plumber and Sanitary Houses*, 4th edn (London, 1887), p. 236.
12 Maureen Ogle, *All the Modern Conveniences: American Household Plumbing, 1840–1890* (Baltimore, MD, 1996), pp. 61–2.
13 Richard Blodgett, *A Sense of Higher Design: The Kohlers of Kohler* (Lyme, CT, 2003), pp. 40–41.
14 Jane C. Nylander, *Our Own Snug Fireside: Images of the New England Home, 1760–1860* (New Haven, CT, 1994), p. 146.
15 'Benham & Sons, 19, Wigmore Street, Cavendish Square, London', in *Prospectuses of Exhibitors* (London, 1851), n.p.
16 A. P. Herbert, 'About Bathrooms', in *The Penguin Book of Twentieth-century Essays* [1921], ed. Ian Hamilton (London, 1999), p. 60.
17 Sigfried Giedion, *Mechanization Takes Command: A Contribution to Anonymous History* (New York, 1948), p. 690.
18 Ibid., p. 692.
19 Wright, *Clean and Decent*, p. 202.
20 Wallace Reyburn, *Flushed with Pride: The Story of Thomas Crapper* (London, 1969), pp. 13–15.
21 Vanessa Taylor and Frank Trentmann, 'Liquid Politics: Water and the Politics of Everyday Life in the Modern City', *Past and Present*, CCXI/1 (May 2011), p. 215.
22 Eveleigh, *Bogs, Baths and Basins*, p. 135.

23 David J. Eveleigh, *Privies and Water Closets* (London, 2008), pp. 45–56.

24 Eveleigh, *Bogs, Baths and Basins*, p. 136.

25 Harriette Merrick Hodge Plunkett, *Women, Plumbers, and Doctors; or, Household Sanitation* (New York, 1885), p. 119.

26 Ibid.

27 Adrian Forty, *Objects of Desire: Design and Society since 1750* (London, 1986), p. 115.

28 Margaret Morgan, 'The Plumbing of Modern Life', in *Surface Tension: Problematics of Site*, ed. Ken Ehrlich and Brandon Labelle (n.p., 2003), p. 139.

29 Muthesius, *The English House*, vol. III, p. 238.

30 Nancy Newhall, ed., *The Daybooks of Edward Weston* (Rochester, NY, 1973), vol. I, p. 132.

31 Le Corbusier, *The Decorative Art of Today*, p. 17.

32 Josiah C. Wedgwood, *Staffordshire Pottery and Its History* (London, 1913), p. 207.

33 Joseph Hatton, *Twyfords: A Chapter in the History of Pottery* (London, 1897), pp. 20–21, emphasis added.

34 Ibid.

35 S. E. Thrower, 'Sanitary Appliances', *Architect and Building News* (21 July 1955), pp. 82–3.

36 Eveleigh, *Bogs, Baths and Basins*, pp. 96–7.

37 Alfred H. Barr, 'Foreword', in Philip Johnson, *Machine Art* (New York, 1934), n.p.

38 Colin Rowe quoted in Nadir Lahiji and D. S. Friedman, 'At the Sink: Architecture in Abjection', in *Plumbing: Sounding Modern Architecture*, ed. Lahiji and Friedman (New York, 1997), p. 35.

39 Muthesius, *The English House*, vol. III, p. 239.

40 Ibid., pp. 238–9.

41 Le Corbusier, 'Other Icons: The Museums' [1924], in *Museum Studies: An Anthology of Contexts*, ed. Bettina Messias Carbonell (London, 2003), p. 404.

42 Le Corbusier, quoted in Tim Benton, 'The Art of the Well-tempered Lecture: Banham and Le Corbusier', in *The Banham Lectures: Essays on Designing the Future*, ed. Jeremy Aynsley and Harriet Atkinson (Oxford, 2009), p. 24.

43 Richard Pommer and Christian F. Otto, *Weissenhof 1927 and the Modern Movement in Architecture* (Chicago, 1991), p. 85, fig. 129.

44 Full discussions of these spaces can be found in Mary McLeod, 'New Designs for Living: Domestic Equipment of Charlotte Perriand, Le Corbusier, and Pierre Jeanneret, 1928–29', in *Charlotte Perriand: An Art of Living*, ed. Mary McLeod (New York, 2003), pp. 36–67; Arthur Rüegg, 'Transforming the Bathroom: Perriand and Le Corbusier, 1927–57', in *Charlotte Perriand*, ed. McLeod, pp. 114–29.

45 Helen Molesworth, 'Bathrooms and Kitchens: Cleaning House with Duchamp', in *Plumbing*, ed. Lahiji and Friedman, pp. 82–3, 88–9.

46 Louise Norton, 'The Buddha of the Bathroom', *The Blind Man*, 2 (May 1917), pp. 5–6.

47   Roy Palmer, *The Water Closet: A New History* (Newton Abbot, Devon, 1973), p. 74.
48   James Denley, 'A History of Twyford's, 1680–1982', pp. 66, 73, www.twyfordbathrooms.com, accessed 3 June 2010.
49   Jeffrey L. Rodengen, *The History of American Standard* (Fort Lauderdale, FL, 1999), p. 34; Giedion, *Mechanization Takes Command*, p. 705.
50   Forty, *Objects of Desire*, p. 8.
51   Alexander Kira, *The Bathroom* (Ithaca, NY, 1966); Bernard Rudofsky, *Now I Lay Me Down to Eat: Notes and Footnotes on the Lost Art of Living* (New York, 1980), p. 109.
52   Gio Ponti, 'Industrial Design', in *In Praise of Architecture*, trans. Giuseppina and Mario Salvadori (New York, 1960), pp. 176–9.
53   Charlotte Perriand, 'Wood or Metal?' [1929], reprinted in *Charlotte Perriand*, ed. McLeod, p. 251.
54   Emma M. Jones, *Parched City: A History of London's Public and Private Drinking Water* (Winchester, 2013), pp. 116–18; Christopher Hamlin, 'William Dibden and the Idea of Biological Sewage Treatment', *Technology and Culture*, XXIX/2 (April 1988), pp. 189–218.
55   F. C. Stockman, *A Practical Guide for Sanitary Inspectors*, 2nd edn (London, 1904), p. 112.
56   Richard Smyth, *Bum Fodder: An Absorbing History of Toilet Paper* (London, 2012), pp. 55–61.
57   Le Corbusier, *Towards a New Architecture*, trans. Frederick Etchells (New York, 1931), p. 277.
58   Ibid., p. 122.
59   'Instrument of health' was used to describe the Pioneer Health Centre (1930) in Peckham, London: Elizabeth Darling, *Re-forming Britain: Narratives of Modernity Before Reconstruction* (London, 2007), pp. 58–66.
60   Standard Sanitary Manufacturing Company, *The Bathroom: A New Interior* (Pittsburg, PA, 1931), p. 4.
61   A. Lawrence Kocher, Albert Frey and Joseph Rosa, 'The Aluminaire House, 1930–31', *Assemblage*, 11 (1990), pp. 61–2.
62   Muthesius, *The English House*, vol. III, p. 238.
63   Florence Nightingale, *Notes on Hospitals*, 3rd edn (London, 1863), p. 73.
64   Mary Douglas, *Purity and Danger: An Analysis of the Concepts of Pollution and Taboo* (London, 1966); Forty, *Objects of Desire*, pp. 115–18 (quote on hygiene p. 117); Mark Wigley, *White Walls, Designer Dresses* (New York, 1995), p. 5.

3 The Rational Bathroom

1   R. Buckminster Fuller, *Nine Chains to the Moon* (Philadelphia, 1938), p. 10.
2   R. Buckminster Fuller, 'The Cardboard House', *Perspecta*, 2 (1953), pp. 28–35.
3   R. Buckminster Fuller, 'I Figure', in *The Buckminster Fuller Reader*, ed. James

Meller (London, 1970), p. 100; Fuller, 'Influences on my Work', in *The Buckminster Fuller Reader*, ed. Meller, p. 64.

4 Mark Wigley, 'Foreword', in Federico Neder, *Fuller Houses: R. Buckminster Fuller's Dymaxion Dwellings and Other Domestic Adventures* (Baden, 2008), p. 12.

5 Regina Lee Blaszczyk, *Imagining Consumers: Design and Innovation from Wedgwood to Corning* (Baltimore, MD, 2000), p. 202.

6 Sigfried Giedion, *Mechanization Takes Command: A Contribution to Anonymous History* (New York, 1948), p. 697.

7 Lisa Pfueller Davidson, 'Early Twentieth Century Hotel Architecture and the Origins of Standardization', *Journal of Decorative and Propaganda Arts*, 25 (2005), pp. 82–7

8 Gwendolyn Wright, *Building the Dream: A Social History of Housing in America* (New York, 1981), p. 168.

9 Jeffrey L. Rodengen, *The History of American Standard* (Fort Lauderdale, FL, 1999), p. 44.

10 Giedion, *Mechanization Takes Command*, p. 700.

11 Lewis Mumford quoted in Rosalyn Baxandall and Elizabeth Ewen, *Picture Windows: How the Suburbs Happened* (New York, 2000), p. 21.

12 Ellen Lupton and J. Abbott Miller, *The Bathroom, The Kitchen, and the Aesthetics of Waste: A Process of Elimination* (New York, 1992), pp. 25–31.

13 Susan Henderson, manuscript for *Building Culture: Ernst May and the New Frankfurt Initiative, 1926–1931* (forthcoming).

14 Ibid.

15 Ibid.

16 In an early twentieth-century French catalogue devoted to public facilities, for instance, a choice of *sièges à l'anglaise* or *sièges à la turque* was offered as a matter of course, though the company recommended the former for upper-class accommodation and the latter for lower-class facilities. G. Larivière & Cie, *Urinoirs: Publics et privés, kiosques et chalets de nécessité, sièges et cabinets communs* (Paris, c. 1910), p. 49.

17 Quoted in Paul Breton, ed., *L'Art Ménager Français* (Paris, 1952), p. 533.

18 'Master's Bath', *Industrial Design*, VIII/6 (1961), pp. 78–9; Arthur Rüegg, 'Transforming the Bathroom: Perriand and Le Corbusier, 1927–57', in *Charlotte Perriand: An Art of Living*, ed. Mary McLeod (New York, 2003), pp. 119–29; Catherine Clarisse, Gabriel Feld, Mary McLeod and Marth Teall, 'Charlotte Perriand and the Alps: Skiing for the Masses', in *Charlotte Perriand*, ed. McLeod, pp. 192–3.

19 For instance, the British Standard concerning toilets is BS 6456 on Sanitary Installations (in four parts) and is linked to the Part G and Part M Building Regulations.

20 Eran Ben-Joseph, *The Code of the City: Standards and the Hidden Language of Place Making* (Cambridge, MA, 2005), esp. pp. xiii–xxi.

21 Robert Marks and R. Buckminster Fuller, *The Dymaxion World of Buckminster Fuller* (New York, 1973), p. 66.

22 Fuller, 'Influences on my Work', pp. 64–5.

23 Marks and Fuller, *The Dymaxion World*, p. 67.

24 Fuller, 'I Figure', p. 100.

25 See, for instance, Alister MacDonald, 'Sanitary Installations and Appliances: Their Place in Good Building Design', *Royal Society for the Promotion of Health Journal*, LXXVII/4 (April 1957), pp. 150–60.

26 'The Prefabricated House', *Architectural Forum* (January 1943), p. 62.

27 Marks and Fuller, *The Dymaxion World*, p. 32.

28 Dietrich Neumann, ed., *Richard Neutra's Windshield House* (Cambridge, MA, 2001), pp. 47–8.

29 This account of the Dymaxion is drawn primarily from Joachim Krausse and Claude Lichtenstein, eds, *Your Private Sky: R. Buckminster Fuller, the Art of Design Science* (Baden, 1999), pp. 30–31, 202–11; Marks and Fuller, *The Dymaxion World*, pp. 32–4, 94–100.

30 'Unit Bathroom Panels', *Architectural Forum* (May 1933), p. 34.

31 Christine Taylor Klein, 'The Quiet Dissemination of American Modernism: George Sakier's Designs for American Radiator', *Design Issues*, XXVIII/1 (Winter 2012), pp. 88–9.

32 Guy Rothenstein, the architect of the 'fixturepanel' system, had formerly worked with Le Corbusier. See 'Prefab Bathroom with Flexibility', *Architectural Forum* (1950), pp. 152–4.

33 For other projects, see 'The Prefabricated House', *Architectural Forum*, pp. 62–4; Eugenio Gentili, 'Cucina-bagno, cuore meccanico della casa', *Domus*, 212 (August 1946), pp. 24–9; Alexander Pike, 'Product Analysis 5: Heart Units', *Architectural Design* (April 1966), pp. 204–12.

34 William R. Pogue, *How do You Go to the Bathroom in Space?* (New York, 1999), pp. 70–75.

35 Marks and Fuller, *The Dymaxion World*, pp. 21–2.

36 Arthur Quarmby, *The Plastics Architect* (London, 1974), p. 46.

37 Reyner Banham, 'The Dymaxicrat', in *A Critic Writes*, ed. Mary Banham, Paul Barker, Sutherland Lyall and Cedric Price (Berkeley, CA, 1996), p. 94; Hadas Steiner, *Beyond Archigram: The Structure of Circulation* (New York and London, 2009), pp. 116–48.

38 'Spray Plastic House Project', 1961, at The Archigram Archival Project, http://archigram.westminster.ac.uk, accessed 2 July 2011.

39 For examples see Quarmby, *The Plastics Architect*, pp. 138–42. See also Gontran Goulden, *Bathrooms: A Design Centre Publication* [1967], revd edn (London, 1970), pp. 61–3; Alexander Pike, 'Product Analysis 3: Baths', *Architectural Design* (February 1966), pp. 104–6; Pike, 'Product Analysis 5', pp. 204–12.

40 '*This* is a House?', *Mechanix Illustrated* (September 1956), pp. 61–3; Dirk van

den Heuvel and Max Risselada, eds, *Alison and Peter Smithson: From the House of the Future to a House of Today* (Rotterdam, 2004), pp. 78–91.

41 Gilles Ivain [Ivan Chtcheglov], 'Formulary for a New Urbanism' (1953), at Situationist International Online, Pre-Situationist Archive: Lettrist International, www.cddc.vt.edu/sionline.

42 Breton, ed., *L'Art Ménager Français*, p. 549.

43 David J. Eveleigh, *Bogs, Baths and Basins: The Story of Domestic Sanitation* (Stroud, 2002), p. 166.

44 See, for instance, Mass Observation, *An Enquiry into People's Homes* (London, 1943), pp. xiii–xiv; Arnold Whittick, 'The Small House of the Future: Progress and the People's Wants', *Building*, XIX/2 (February 1944), pp. 40–42.

45 Breton, ed., *L'Art Ménager Français*, pp. 545–61.

46 Mary McLeod, 'New Designs for Living: Domestic Equipment of Charlotte Perriand, Le Corbusier, and Pierre Jeanneret, 1928–29', in *Charlotte Perriand*, ed. McLeod, p. 271, n. 71; Breton, ed., *L'Art Ménager Français*, pp. 545–51.

47 'Modern Living: Bathrooms for Living', *Time* (22 December 1975), at www.time.com.

48 Quarmby, *The Plastics Architect*, p. 141.

49 Peter Buchanan, 'High-Tech: Another British Thoroughbred', *Architectural Review* (July 1983), p. 17.

50 Stephen Bell, 'Tower of Bathrooms', *Design* (April 1968), pp. 51–2; 'Bathroom Tower, Paddington, London', *Architectural Design* (November 1966), p. 577; 'The Farrell/Grimshaw Partnership's Bathroom Tower Conversion', *Architectural Design* (October 1968), pp. 490–94; Murray Fraser with Joe Kerr, *Architecture and the 'Special Relationship': The American Influence on Post-war British Architecture* (London, 2007), p. 327.

51 Kenneth Powell, *Lloyd's Building: Richard Rogers Partnership* (London, 1994), p. 33.

52 Ibid., p. 33.

53 Colin Davies, *The Prefabricated Home* (London, 2005), pp. 175–8; 'Venesta: Toilet Panels', www.venesta.co.uk, accessed 12 August 2011.

54 'RB Farquhar: Finish', www.rbf.digitalface.co.uk, accessed 13 August 2011.

55 Email from Guillaume Aper, Direction de la Communication, JCDecaux (13 April 2012).

56 For instance, Cemusa won the contract to supply New York City's street furnishing by projecting that at least $1 billion in revenue would be supplied to the city over twenty years – a fee the company pays the city in exchange for permission to advertise. Under the deal, Cemusa supplies all street furnishings without charge. Winnie Hu, 'Deal Is Reached to Put Toilets on City Streets', www.nytimes.com, 22 September 2005.

57 Julienne Hanson, Jo-Anne Bichard and Clara Greed, *The Accessible Toilet Resource* (London, 2007), p. 90, see also p. 148.

58 'Power Surge Explodes "Superloo"', www.bbc.co.uk/news, 4 February 2004.

59 David Bass, 'Towering Inferno: The Metaphoric Life of Building Services',
    AA Files, 30 (Autumn 1995), p. 26.
60 For the clash between JCDecaux and the disabled community in New York City,
    see '"We Won't Go Back": The ADA on the Grass Roots Level', *Disability &*
    Society, XI/2 (1996), pp. 277–9.
61 Simon Akam, 'A Sidewalk Oasis if You Can Find One', www.nytimes.com,
    30 August 2009.
62 Fuller, 'Architecture Out of the Laboratory' [1955], quoted in Krausse and
    Lichtenstein, eds, *Your Private Sky*, p. 205.
63 Marks and Fuller, *The Dymaxion World*, pp. 99–100.
64 Quarmby, *The Plastics Architect*, pp. 141–2.

4 The Soft Bathroom

1   In 1970, 30 per cent of British homes had central heating versus 79 per cent in
    1990 and 96 per cent today. 'What We Spend: Past, Present and Future',
    Which? (October 2012), p. 16.
2   David Hicks, *On Bathrooms* (Britwell Salome, Oxon, 1970), p. 9, emphasis added.
3   Sigfried Giedion, *Mechanization Takes Command: A Contribution to*
    Anonymous History (New York, 1948), p. 628.
4   Françoise de Bonneville provides an excellent in-depth overview of the upper-
    class bathroom's history. See Françoise de Bonneville, *The Book of the Bath*
    (London, 1997).
5   Barbara A. White, *The Beecher Sisters* (New Haven, CT, 2003), pp. 77–8.
6   Catharine Beecher [1841], quoted in Jane C. Nylander, *Our Own Snug Fireside:*
    Images of the New England Home, 1760–1860 (New Haven, CT, 1994), p. 144.
7   Lucinda Lambton, *Temples of Convenience and Chambers of Delight* (London,
    1998), p. 139.
8   Countess Drohojowska, quoted in Lucy Worsley, *If Walls Could Talk: An*
    Intimate History of the Home (London, 2010), p. 129.
9   Monique Éleb, 'La Mise au propre en architecture', *Techniques & Culture*, 54–55
    (2010), at www.tc.revues.org/783.
10 Marquise de Pompeillan, quoted in Bonneville, *The Book of the Bath*, p. 109.
11 Ibid., pp. 109–16.
12 Éleb, 'La Mise au propre en architecture', translation author's own.
13 Mark Girouard, *The Victorian Country House* (London, 1979), pp. 280–82.
14 Jeffrey L. Rodengen, *The History of American Standard* (Fort Lauderdale, FL,
    1999), p. 45.
15 Fiona Leslie, *Designs for 20th-century Interiors* (London, 2000), pp. 59–60.
16 Beatriz Colomina, *Privacy and Publicity* (Cambridge, MA, 1998), pp. 260–64.
17 Jan Jennings, 'Le Corbusier's "Naked": "Absolutely Honesty" and (Exhibitionist)
    Display in Bathroom Settings', *Interiors*, II/3 (2011), pp. 323–4.

18 Sergio Los, *Carlo Scarpa: An Architectural Guide*, trans. Antony Shugaar (Venice, 1995), p. 112.

19 Penny Sparke, *So Long as it's Pink* (London, 1995), pp. 166, 194.

20 Emily Post, *The Personality of a House* [1930], quoted in Sarah A. Leavitt, *From Catharine Beecher to Martha Stewart: A Cultural History of Domestic Advice* (Chapel Hill, NC, 2002), p. 146.

21 Regina Lee Blaszczyk, *Imagining Consumers: Design and Innovation from Wedgwood to Corning* (Baltimore, MD, 2000), pp. 194–206; Richard Blodgett, *A Sense of Higher Design: The Kohlers of Kohler* (Lyme, CT, 2003), pp. 70–73.

22 Ibid., pp. 201–2. For the British industry standard colours, see Terence Conran, *The Bed and Bath Book* (London, 1978), p. 197.

23 Blaszczyk, *Imagining Consumers*, pp. 206–7.

24 David J. Eveleigh, *Bogs, Baths and Basins: The Story of Domestic Sanitation* (Stroud, 2002), p. 136.

25 See Barbara Penner, 'Doing It Right: Postwar Honeymoon Resorts in the Pocono Mountains', in *Architecture and Tourism: Perception, Performance and Place*, ed. D. Medina Lasansky and Brain McLaren (Oxford, 2004), p. 214.

26 Roland Barthes, 'Soap-powders and Detergents' [1957], in *Mythologies*, trans. Annette Lavers (London, 2009), pp. 32–3.

27 Margaret Withers, 'Plastics in the Modern Bathroom', *The Architect* (August 1977), p. 40.

28 Ibid., p. 39.

29 Disposable sanitary napkins had been available since 1921, when Kimberly-Clark (also the maker of Kleenex) put Kotex on the market. These were kept in place by a belt. Adhesive pads such as those in use today were only launched in 1970. Tampax, the first tampon brand, was invented in 1933. See also Janice DeLaney, Mary Jane Lupton and Emily Toth's *The Curse: A Cultural History of Menstruation* [1976], revd edn (New York, 1988), pp. 138–50.

30 Anthony Snow and Graham Hopewell, *Planning Your Bathroom: A Design Centre Book* (London, 1978), p. 50. See also 'Rethinking the Purpose of a Bathroom', *Building Trades Journal* (5 April 1974), pp. 16–18, 23–6.

31 Rita Reif, 'After 10 Years, Revised Look at Bathroom Says Something about Society, Too', *New York Times* (12 January 1976), p. 46.

32 R. W. Kennedy, quoted in Alexander Kira, *The Bathroom*, revd edn (New York, 1976), p. 170.

33 Beatriz Preciado, 'Pornotopia', in *Cold War Hothouses: Inventing Postwar Culture, from Cockpit to Playboy*, ed. Beatriz Colomina, Annmarie Brennan and Jeannie Kim (New York, 2004), p. 245.

34 Mary Josephson [1971], quoted in Penner, 'Doing It Right', p. 211.

35 All quotes in this paragraph from Penner, 'Doing It Right', pp. 210–17.

36 Gretchen Edgren, *Inside the Playboy Mansion: If You Don't Swing, Don't Ring* (London, 1998), p. 211. The term 'pornotopia' is drawn from Beatriz Preciado's article of that name, pp. 216–53.

37 Margo Miller, 'Living: Do You Bathe or Shower?', *Boston Globe* (3 July 1976), p. 8.

38 The Housing Development Group (UK Department of the Environment), 'Spaces in the Home: Bathrooms and WCs', *Design Bulletin*, XXIV/1 (London, 1972), pp. 2–4.

39 'Bathrooms for Living', www.time.com, Monday 22 December 1975.

40 Rita Reif, 'For the Bathroom that Already has Everything', *New York Times* (21 October 1966), p. 69.

41 Conran, *The Bed and Bath Book*, pp. 252–3.

42 For the Wohnbad, see 'Bathrooms for Living', Time.com; and Kira, *The Bathroom*, revd edn, pp. 172–3.

43 Kira, *The Bathroom*, p. 172.

44 Reif, 'For the Bathroom that Already has Everything', p. 69.

45 Mary Daniels, 'Small in Space, Big in Pleasure: The New Bath', *Chicago Tribune* (7 September 1980), p. S-A5.

46 Conran, *The Bed and Bath Book*, pp. 202–3; Blodgett, *A Sense of Higher Design*, pp. 173–4.

47 Michael Evamy, *Ideal-Standard: The First 100 Years* (Kingston upon Hull, 1996), pp. 28–31.

48 Conran, *The Bed and Bath Book*, p. 159.

49 For sales figures, see Joseph Giovannini, 'A Combination of Gym and Bath, the Latest in Home Amenities', *New York Times* (23 January 1986), pp. C1, C6.

50 Conran, *The Bed and Bath Book*, p. 161.

51 Norma Skurka and Oberto Gili, *Underground Interiors* (New York, 1972), p. 1.

52 Ettore Sottsass, 'Design as Postulation', in *Italy: The New Domestic Landscape*, ed. Emilio Ambasz (Italy, 1972), p. 162.

53 Joan Kron and Suzanne Slesin, *High-Tech: The Industrial Style and Source Book for the Home* (New York, 1978), p. 1.

54 Peter Buchanan, 'High-Tech: Another British Thoroughbred', *Architectural Review* (July 1983), p. 16.

55 Penny McGuire, 'Flat, Belsize Park, North London', *Architectural Review* (July 1983), pp. 65–8.

56 Peter Greenaway, *Inside Rooms: 26 Bathrooms, London & Oxfordshire, 1985* (Artifax, 1985).

57 Conran, *The Bed and Bath Book*, p. 193.

58 Kron and Slesin, *High-Tech*, pp. 188–9.

59 Henry Dreyfuss, *Designing for People* [1955] (New York, 2012), pp. 78–8, 93, 192, 273; Philippe Daverio, Enrico Finzi, Anna Lombardi and Vitaliano Pesante, *Hic Licet: Bathrooms and Wellness, the Story of Pozzi-Ginori* (Spilimbergo, 2004), pp. 53, 88–9.

60 Lisa Licitra Ponti, *Gio Ponti: The Complete Work, 1923–1978* (London, 1990), pp. 162–3; Marco Romanelli, *Gio Ponti: A World* (Milan, 2002), p. 74.

61 Jonathan Glancey, *Douglas Scott* (London, 1988), pp. 81–3.

62 Evamy, *Ideal-Standard*, pp. 32, 38.
63 Enzo Biffi Gentili, *Antonia Campi: Antologia Ceramica, 1947–1997* (Laveno and Milan, 1998), p. 91.
64 Leslie, *Designs for 20th-century Interiors*, p. 115; and Snow and Hopewell, *Planning Your Bathroom*, p. 9.
65 Evamy, *Ideal-Standard*, p. 33
66 David Heathcote and Sue Barr, *The 70s House* (Chichester, 2006), p. 84.
67 Leslie, *Designs for 20th-century Interiors*, p. 117.

5 The Inclusive Bathroom

1 Selwyn Goldsmith, *Designing for the Disabled: The New Paradigm* (London, 1997), pp. 14–18.
2 Taunya Lovell Banks, 'Toilets as a Feminist Issue: A True Story', *Berkeley Women's Law Journal*, VI/2 (1990), p. 287.
3 Judith Plaskow, 'Embodiment, Elimination, and the Role of Toilets in Struggles for Social Justice', *Cross Currents* (22 March 2008), p. 1.
4 Erika Diane Rappaport, *Shopping for Pleasure: Women in the Making of London's West End* (Princeton, NJ, 2000), p. 79.
5 *Twenty-third Annual Report of the Ladies' Sanitary Association* [1881], quoted in Barbara Penner, 'A World of Unmentionable Suffering', *Journal of Design History*, XIV/1 (2001), pp. 39, 42–5.
6 See, for instance, the concerns over 'auto-intoxication' (constipation) in United States Department of Labor Women's Bureau, *The Installation and Maintenance of Toilet Facilities in Places of Employment* (Washington, DC, 1933), pp. vii–viii.
7 Ibid., esp. pp. 4–15. See also Terry S. Kogan, 'Sex Separation: The Cure-All for Victorian Social Anxiety', in *Toilet: Public Restrooms and the Politics of Sharing*, ed. Harvey Molotch and Laura Norén (New York, 2010), pp. 156–63.
8 Denise Scott Brown, 'Planning the Powder Room', *AIA Journal* (April 1967), p. 81.
9 *Architects Journal* [1953], quoted in Sue Cavanagh and Vron Ware, *At Women's Convenience: A Handbook on the Design of Women's Public Toilets* London, 1990), p. 9.
10 See The Housing Development Group (UK Department of the Environment), 'Spaces in the Home: Bathrooms and WCs', *Design Bulletin*, XXIV/1 (London, 1972), pp. 2–4; Marilyn Langford, *Personal Hygiene Attitudes and Practices in 1000 Middle-class Households* (Ithaca, NY, 1965).
11 See Jane Rendell, Barbara Penner and Iain Borden, eds, *Gender Space Architecture: An Interdisciplinary Introduction* (London, 2000).
12 Scott Brown, 'Planning the Powder Room', p. 83.
13 Walter Macfarlane & Co., *Catalogue of Macfarlane's Cast Iron Manufactures*, 4th edn (Glasgow, 1862), vol. II, p. 33.

14 Advertisement for Scott's Advisory Service in *Architectural Record* (4 April 1958), p. 305.

15 Alexander Pike, 'Product Analysis 4: Supply Showers and Fittings', *Architectural Design* (March 1966), p. 157.

16 Le Corbusier, *Precisions on the Present State of Architecture and City Planning* [1930], trans. Edith Schreiber Aujame (Cambridge, MA, 1991), p. 108.

17 Selwyn Goldsmith, *Universal Design* (Oxford, 2000), p. 22.

18 Lance Hosey, 'Hidden Lines: Gender, Race, and the Body in *Graphic Standards*', *Journal of Architectural Education*, LV/2 (November 2001), pp. 104, 110 n. 32.

19 Scott Brown, 'Planning the Powder Room', p. 81.

20 Julius Panero and Martin Zelnik, *Human Dimension and Interior Space* (New York, 1979), pp. 301–2.

21 Langford, *Personal Hygiene Attitudes and Practices.*

22 Alexander Kira, *The Bathroom,* (Ithaca, NY, 1966), pp. 90–92.

23 Ibid., p. 75.

24 Ibid., p. 6.

25 Jonathan Glancey, *Douglas Scott* (London, 1988), p. 23; Michael Evamy, *Ideal-Standard: The First 100 Years* (Kingston-Upon-Hull, 1996), pp. 32–5.

26 Goldsmith, *Designing for the Disabled*, p. 6.

27 Raymond Lifchez and Barbara Winslow, *Design for Independent Living: The Environment and Physically Disabled People* (New York, 1979), pp. 78–81.

28 Margaret Agerholm, Elizabeth M. Hollings and Wanda M. Williams, eds, *Equipment for the Disabled* (London, 1960), vol. II, Section 10 ('Personal Toilet'), A-J.

29 Goldsmith, *Designing for the Disabled*, pp. 23, 48.

30 Ibid., p. 24.

31 This was BS 5810 Code of Practice for Access for the Disabled to Buildings.

32 These were the Part M Building Regulations. Goldsmith, *Designing for the Disabled*, p. 40.

33 For a full account, see Clara Greed, *Inclusive Urban Design: Public Toilets* (Oxford, 2003), pp. 155–72.

34 P.J.R. Nichols and E. R. Wilshere, eds, *Equipment for the Disabled: Personal Care* (Oxford, 1978), p. 1.

35 See, for instance, Anthony Snow and Graham Hopewell, *Planning Your Bathroom: A Design Centre Book* (London, 1978), p. 42.

36 Jeffrey L. Rodengen, *The History of American Standard* (Fort Lauderdale, FL, 1999), p. 80.

37 Kira, *The Bathroom*, revd edn (New York, 1976), back cover.

38 Ibid., p. 49.

39 F. A. Hornibrook, *The Culture of the Abdomen* [1933], quoted in Kira, *The Bathroom*, revd edn, p. 116; F. A. Hornibrook, 'AJ Technical Study SfB (74): The Case for the Health Closet', *Architects Journal* (July 1963), pp. 231–2.

40 On Le Corbusier's designs, see Arthur Rüegg, 'Transforming the Bathroom: Perriand and Le Corbusier, 1927–57', in *Charlotte Perriand: An Art of Living*, ed. Mary McLeod (New York, 2003), p. 129; Kira, *The Bathroom*, revd edn, p. 129, fig. 40. It was the bible of household taste, *L'Art Ménager Français*, which said that *sièges à la turque* were no longer in fashion: Paul Breton, ed., *L'Art Ménager Français* (Paris, 1952), p. 533.

41 Rita Reif, 'The Bathtub Gradually Takes on a 20th-century Look', *New York Times* (13 January 1969), p. 24.

42 Kira, *The Bathroom*, revd edn, p. vii.

43 Gio Ponti, 'Industrial Design', in *In Praise of Architecture*, trans. Guiseppina and Mario Salvadori (New York, 1960), pp. 178–9.

44 Enzo Biffi Gentili, *Antonia Campi: Antologia Ceramica, 1947–1997* (Laverno and Milan, 1998), p. 91.

45 Philippe Daverio, Enrico Finzi, Anna Lombardi and Vitaliano Pesante, *Hic Licet: Bathrooms and Wellness, The Story of Pozzi-Ginori* (Spilimbergo, 2004), pp. 108–9.

46 'Fitting Out', *Building Design* (19 November 1976), pp. 18–19; 'Designing a Logical Bathroom – With a Glance at the New Streamlined Units', *House and Garden*, XXX/3 (April 1977), pp. 156–9.

47 Daniel Lametti, 'Don't Just Sit There! How Bathroom Posture Affects Your Health', www.slate.com, 26 August 2010.

48 Vivian Brown, 'Bathroom Designs Needs More Thought', *The Hartford Courant* (15 February, 1976), p. 10D.

49 Victor Papanek, *Design for Human Scale* (New York, 1983), pp. 13–29.

50 Goldsmith, *Designing for the Disabled*, p. vii.

51 Shane, quoted in Rob Kitchin and Robin Law, 'The Socio-spatial Construction of (In)accessible Public Toilets', *Urban Studies*, 38 (February 2001), p. 295.

52 Goldsmith, *Designing for the Disabled*, p. vii.

53 Greed, *Inclusive Urban Design*, p. 52.

54 Marge Piercy, 'To the Pay Toilet', in *Living in the Open* (New York, 1976), p. 82.

55 11.2.3.4, 'Time a Person Takes to Use the Facilities', BS 6465-4:2010, p. 23; Harvey Molotch, 'The Rest Room and Equal Opportunity', *Sociological Forum*, III/1 (1988), pp. 128–33.

56 George David and Frederick Dye, *A Complete and Practical Treatise upon Plumbing and Sanitation Embracing Drainage and Plumbing Practice etc.* (London, 1898), pp. 171–2.

57 Rodengen, *The History of American Standard*, pp. 74–5; see photograph on p. 75.

58 For just one recent example, see 'Pollee by UiWE', www.dezeen.com, 15 July 2011.

59 British Standard 6465-4 strongly reflects Greed's research as laid out in Greed, *Inclusive Urban Design*, as well as the expertise of another strong planner-campaigner, Michelle Barkley.

60 10.5.1, 'Squat Toilets', BS 6465-4: 2010, p. 20.

61 Emily Hall, 'Fury at Muslim-only Shop Loos: Squat Holes to Aid "Cultural Cohesion"', *Daily Star* (15 July 2010), pp. 1 and 11.

62 Greed, *Inclusive Urban Design*, p. 55.

63 Banks, 'Toilets as a Feminist Issue', p. 273.

64 David Serlin, 'Pissing without Pity: Disability, Gender, and the Public Toilet', in *Toilet*, ed. Molotch and Norén, p. 174.

65 Jeffrey P. Rosenfeld and Wid Chapman, *Home Design in an Aging World* (New York, 2008), pp. xvi–xvii, 3, 6.

66 For instance, see Ernesto Morales, Jacqueline Rousseau and Romedi Passini, 'Bathrooms in Retirement Residences: Perceptions and Experiences of Seniors and Caregivers', *Physical & Occupational Therapy in Geriatrics*, XXX/1 (2012), pp. 1–21.

67 John R. Berry, *Herman Miller: The Purpose of Design* (New York, 2004), pp. 164–71; Gianfranco Zaccai, 'Bringing Convenience to the Whole Family', *Innovation* (Fall 1992), pp. 94–8.

68 Allen Chun, 'Flushing in the Future: The Supermodern Japanese Toilet in a Changing Domestic Culture', *Postcolonial Studies*, V/2 (July 2002), p. 159.

69 Rose George, *The Big Necessity: Adventures in the World of Human Waste* (London, 2008), p. 48. George provides a thorough history of Japanese toilets, pp. 44–71.

6 The Alternative Bathroom

1 Joseph Bazalgette, *Letter of Mr J. W. Bazalgette on Establishment of Public Conveniences throughout the Metropolis: Printed by Order of Court, 22nd March, 1849* (London 1849), p. 367.

2 Quoted in John Bellamy Foster, 'Marx's Ecology in Historical Perspective', *International Socialism Journal*, 96 (Winter 2002), at www.socialistreviewindex.org.uk.

3 *Report of the Special Rapporteur on the Human Right to Safe Drinking Water and sanitation, Catarina de Albuquerque: Mission to the United States of America*, UN General Assembly, Human Rights Council, 18th session A/HRC/18/33/Add.4 (2 August 2011), p. 6.

4 Stephen Halliday, *The Great Stink of London: Sir Joseph Bazalgette and the Cleansing of the Victorian Metropolis* (Stroud, 1999), p. 41.

5 John Simon, 'Report on the Last Two Cholera-Epidemics of London as Affected by the Consumption of Impure Water' (London, 1856), p. 13.

6 Joseph Bazalgette, 'On the Main Drainage of London, and the Interception of the Sewage from the River Thames' [1865], in *Thames Tunnel to Channel Tunnel*, ed. W. Howie and M. Chrimes (London, 1987), pp. 283–5.

7 See Halliday, *The Great Stink*, pp. 113–17.

8 *Preliminary Report of the Commission Appointed to Inquire into the Best Mode of Distributing the Sewage of Towns and Applying it to Beneficial and Profitable Uses* (London, 1858), p. 19.

9 John Bellamy Foster, *Marx's Ecology: Materialism and Nature* (New York, 2000), pp. 149–63.

10 Public Health Act 1848, 11 & 12 Vict., ch. 63, s. 46.

11 Halliday, *The Great Stink*, p. 109.

12 Edwin Chadwick, *Report on the Sanitary Condition of the Labouring Population of Great Britain* [1842], ed. M. W. Flinn (Edinburgh, 1964), pp. 121–3; *Preliminary Report of the Commission*, pp. 14–17.

13 John Sheail, 'Town Wastes, Agricultural Sustainability and Victorian Sewage', *Urban History*, XXIII/2 (August 1996), pp. 192, 196.

14 Ibid., p. 202.

15 Ibid., p. 203.

16 Halliday, *The Great Stink*, p. 45.

17 Walter Macfarlane & Co., *Catalogue of Macfarlane's Cast Iron Manufactures*, 4th edn (Glasgow, 1862), vol. II, pp. 33–48.

18 David J. Eveleigh, *Bogs, Baths, and Basins: The Story of Domestic Sanitation* (Stroud, 2002), pp. 56–8.

19 See, for instance, Revd Henry Moule, *The Advantages of the Dry Earth System in the Disposal of Sewage and Excreta* (London, [186?]), and *Manure for the Million* (London, 1870).

20 Eveleigh, *Bogs, Baths, and Basins*, pp. 45–51; Sheail, 'Town Wastes', p. 195.

21 Christopher Hamlin, 'William Dibdin and the Idea of Biological Sewage Treatment', *Technology and Culture*, XXIV/2 (April 1988), p. 189.

22 Alison Light, *Mrs Woolf and the Servants* (London, 2007), pp. 136, 175.

23 Eveleigh, *Bogs, Baths, and Basins*, pp. 45–51.

24 Hamlin, 'William Dibdin', pp. 196–200.

25 Jamie Benidickson, *The Culture of Flushing: A Social and Legal History of Sewage* (Vancouver, 2007), pp. 115–19.

26 Ibid.

27 Jean-Pierre Goubert, *The Conquest of Water*, trans. Andrew Wilson (Princeton, NJ, 1989), p. 62.

28 Victor Hugo, quoted in *The Shone Hydro-Pneumatic System of Sewerage: Scientific and Sanitary Drainage versus Flat Gradient, Foul Tunnel Sewers of Deposit* (Liverpool, 1885), p. 21.

29 Donald Reid, *Paris Sewers and Sewermen: Realities and Representations* (Cambridge, MA, 1991), pp. 58–70.

30 Chadwick, *Report on the Sanitary Condition*, p. 123.

31 Frank W. Geels, 'The Hygienic Transition from Cesspools to Sewer Systems (1840–1930): The Dynamics of Regime Transformation', *Research Policy*, XXXV (2006), pp. 1076–8.

32 'The Shone Hydro-Pneumatic System of Sewerage', *The Manufacturer and*

Builder, XIX/5 (May 1887), p. 104; 'Recent Sewer Construction', *The Sanitary Engineer and Construction Record* (2 April, 1887), pp. 456–8; and C. C. James, *Oriental Drainage: A Guide to the Collection, Removal and Disposal of Sewage in Eastern Cities* (Bombay, 1902), pp. 14–32.

33 Eran Ben-Joseph, *The Code of the City: Standards and the Hidden Language of Place Making* (Cambridge, MA, 2005), pp. 88–90.

34 'The Shone Hydro-Pneumatic System', pp. 9–12.

35 'Qua-Vac: History', www.quavac.com, accessed 25 November 2012.

36 James, *Oriental Drainage*, p. 1.

37 John Andrew Turner, *Sanitation in India* (Bombay, 1914), pp. 170–75.

38 Hector Tulloch, *The Drainage and Sewerage of Bombay* (London, 1872), pp. 9–12.

39 James, *Oriental Drainage*, p. 119.

40 Daniel R. Headrick, *The Tentacles of Progress: Technology Transfer in the Age of Imperialism, 1850–1940* (Oxford, 1988), p. 153.

41 See also the discussion in James, *Oriental Drainage*, pp. 10, 103.

42 J. Balfour Kirk, *Hints on Equipment & Health for Intending Residents in the Tropics* (London, 1926), pp. 83–6.

43 E. F. Schumacher, *Small is Beautiful: A Study of Economics as if People Mattered* [1973] (London, 1993), p. 135.

44 James, *Oriental Drainage*, pp. 97–8.

45 Ibid., p. 105. See also Moran E. Gregory and Sian James, *Toilets of the World* (London, 2006), pp. 146–7.

46 Harri Mäki, 'John Fletcher and the Development of Water Supply and Sanitation in Durban, 1889–1918', *Journal of Natal and Zulu History*, 27 (2009), p. 52.

47 Bazalgette, 'On the Main Drainage of London', p. 280.

48 James Cameron Scott, *Health and Agriculture in China: A Fundamental Approach to Some of the Problems of World Hunger* (London, 1952), pp. 64–71.

49 Hanchao Lu, *Beyond the Neon Lights: Everyday Shanghai in the Early Twentieth Century* (Berkeley, CA, 1999), pp. 189–98.

50 Sim Van der Ryn, *The Toilet Papers: Recycling Waste and Conserving Water* [1978] (n.p., 1995), p. 23.

51 Uno Winblad and Wen Kilama, *Sanitation without Water*, revd edn (Stockholm, 1980), pp. 24–9.

52 Lu, *Beyond the Neon Lights*, p. 193, p. 372 n. 12.

53 For a good summary of the anxieties concerning water pollution, see Barbara Ward and René Dubois, *Only One Earth: The Care and Maintenance of a Small Planet* (Middlesex, 1972), pp. 113–127.

54 Rose George, *The Big Necessity: Adventures in the World of Human Waste* (London, 2008), pp. 167–94; Joseph Jenkins, *The Humanure Handbook: A Guide to Composting Human Manure*, 3rd edn (Grove City, PA, 2005), pp. 97–101; John Stauber and Sheldon Rampton, *Toxic Sludge is Good for You!*

Lies, Damn Lies and the Public Relations Industry (Monroe, LA, 1995), pp. 99–122.

55 'NASA Spinoff: Plants Clean Air and Water for Indoor Environments', www.spinoff.nasa.gov, 2007; B. C. Wolverton and John D. Wolverton, *Growing Clean Water: Nature's Solution to Water Pollution* (Picayune, MS, 2001), pp. 38, 42–6, 50–53, 63–7.

56 Van der Ryn, *The Toilet Papers*, pp. 103–11; Wolverton and Wolverton, *Growing Clean Water*, p. 5.

57 Peter Harper, 'Autonomy', in *Radical Technology*, ed. Godfrey Boyle and Peter Harper (London, 1976), p. 137.

58 Minimum Cost Housing Group, School of Architecture, McGill University, *Stop the Five Gallon Flush: A Survey of Alternative Waste Disposal Systems*, ed. Witold Rybczynski, 5th edn (Montreal, 1980), pp. 34–9.

59 Ibid., p. 39; and Alvaro Ortega, Witold Rybczynski, Samir Ayad, Wajid Ali and Arthur Acheson, *The Ecol Operation: Ecology + Building + Common Sense* (Montreal, 1972), p. 84.

60 Alex Morse, Vikram Bhatt and Witold Rybczynski, *Water Conservation and the Mist Experience* (Montreal, 1978), pp. 37–42.

61 Minimum Cost Housing Group, *Stop the Five Gallon Flush*, pp. 11–20.

62 Ibid., p. 42; Van der Ryn, *The Toilet Papers*, pp. 39–40; Harper, 'Autonomy', p. 14; Winblad and Kilama, *Sanitation without Water*, pp. 40–44.

63 Brenda and Robert Vale, *The Autonomous House: Design and Planning for Self-sufficiency* (London, 1975), pp. 119–20.

64 Philip Steadman, *Energy, Environment and Building* (Cambridge, 1975), pp. 241–2, 276–7.

65 Graham Caine quoted in Lydia Kallipoliti, 'From Shit to Food: Graham Caine's Eco-House in South London, 1972–1975,' *Buildings and Landscapes*, XIX/1 (Spring 2012), p. 91. See also Lydia Kallipoliti, 'Clearings in a Concrete Jungle', *Journal of the Society of Architectural Historians*, LXX/2 (June 2011), pp. 240–44; Lydia Kallipoliti, 'Return to Earth: Feedback Houses,' *The Cornell Journal of Architecture*, 8: re (2011), pp. 25–35.

66 Kallipoliti, 'From Shit to Food', pp. 90–91.

67 Ibid., pp. 92–3.

68 Steadman, *Energy, Environment and Building*, p. 242.

69 See, for instance, Van der Ryn, *The Toilet Papers*, p. 121.

70 Kallipoliti, 'From Shit to Food', pp. 92, 96, 106 n. 28–9; Wolverton and Wolverton, *Growing Clean Water*, pp. 43–6.

71 Grumman Aerospace Corporation, 'Study of Personal Hygiene Concepts for Future Manned Missions: Final Report', *Prepared for National Aeronautics and Space Administration* (New York, 1970), Accession Number N70-40806; NASA Number CR-108607.

72 Steadman, *Energy, Environment and Building*, pp. 230–31.

73 See, for instance, Ram Bux Singh, *Bio-Gas Plant: Designs with Specifications* (Ajitmal, 1973).

74 'The Plowboy Interview: Ram Bux Singh', *Mother Earth News*, 18 (November/December 1972), at www.journeytoforever.org, accessed 24 September 2012; Steadman, *Energy, Environment and Building*, p. 235; Robert Vale, 'Plant your Own Power', in *Radical Technology*, ed. Boyle and Harper, p. 63.

75 For a good summary of composting research, see Steadman, *Energy, Environment and Building*, pp. 222–9.

76 Schumacher, *Small is Beautiful*, pp. 156, 160.

77 The illegality of caste discrimination was affirmed in India's Constitution (written in 1950), however, it is widely acknowledged to persist in many parts of the country.

78 Sulabh International Social Service Organisation, Sulabh Sanitation Movement promotional literature (n.p.p., [2008?]), p. 49.

79 Ibid., p. 70.

80 See, for instance, S. A. Esrey, J. B. Potash, L. Roberts and C. Shiff, 'Effects of Improved Water Supply and Sanitation on Ascariasis, Diarrhoea, Dracunculiasis, Hookworm Infection, Schistosomiasis, and Trachoma', *Bulletin of the World Health Organization*, LXIX/5 (1991), pp. 609–21. See also United Nations University Institute for Water, Environment and Health, *Sanitation as a Key to Global Health: Voices from the Field* (2010), at www.inweh.unu.edu.

81 Maggie Black and Ben Fawcett, *The Last Taboo: Opening the Door on the Global Sanitation Crisis* (London, 2008), pp. 71–7.

82 Winblad and Kilama, *Sanitation without Water*, p. 4.

83 Black and Fawcett, *The Last Taboo*, p. 77.

84 George, *The Big Necessity*, p. 198.

85 For the example of the success of 'motivators' in extending sanitation in Midnapur, India, see Black and Fawcett, *The Last Taboo*, pp. 88–90.

86 Kamal Kar with Robert Chambers, *Handbook on Community-led Total Sanitation* (London, 2008), p. 8.

87 George, *The Big Necessity*, pp. 211–18.

88 Ibid., p. 213; and Kal and Chambers, *Handbook on Community-led Total Sanitation*, pp. 26, 36.

89 George, *The Big Necessity*, p. 218.

90 Yvonne Rydin et al., 'Shaping Cities for Health: Complexity and the Planning of Urban Environments in the 21st Century', *The Lancet* (2 June 2012), pp. 2087–91.

91 Black and Fawcett, *The Last Taboo*, pp. 53–5.

92 'Flushed with Pride', *The Economist Technology Quarterly* (1 September 2012), p. 8.

93 Marine Veith, 'Urine for Sale? Durban's in the Market', *Mail & Guardian*, www.mg.co.za, 7 November 2010.

94 David A. Vaccari, 'Phosphorus Famine: The Threat to Our Food Supply', *Scientific American* (June 2009), pp. 54–9.

95 Andreas Schönborn, 'Don't Mix! Interview with Uno Winblad', *EcoEng Newsletter*, 2 (2000), www.iees.ch/EcoEng003/downloads/EcoEng003_Interv.pdf, accessed 29 March 2013.

96 The problem of safely disposing of menstrual products, however, is only just beginning to be addressed by bodies like the World Toilet Organization.

97 Claudia Mitchell, 'Geographies of Danger: School Toilets in Sub-Saharan Africa', in *Ladies and Gents: Public Toilets and Gender*, ed. Olga Gershenson and Barbara Penner (Philadelphia, 2009), pp. 62–74; *Kenya: Insecurity and indignity: Women's Experiences in the Slums of Nairobi, Kenya*, Amnesty International Report, AFR 32/002/2010 (7 July 2010), pp. 17–23; United Nations University Institute for Water, Environment and Health, *Sanitation as a Key to Global Health*, esp. pp. 11–15.

98 George, *The Big Necessity*, p. 206.

Conclusion

1 Sigfried Giedion, *Mechanization Takes Command: A Contribution to Anonymous History* (New York, 1948), p. 628.

2 For good overviews of recent developments, see Jennifer Hudson, *Restroom: Contemporary Design* (London, 2008), and Cristina del Valle Schuster, *Public Toilet Design* (Richmond Hill, 2005).

3 'Naked', www.intypes.cornell.edu, accessed 6 June 2012.

4 The architect William T. Georgis, quoted in Charles Wardell and Wendy Talarico, 'Mastering the Master Bathroom', *Architectural Record* (April 2000), p. 148.

5 Hudson, *Restroom*, pp. 108–9.

6 Portland-based campaigners PHLUSH have even drawn up public restroom design principles to help guide urban planners and city governments. See 'Urban Restroom Design', www.phlush.org, 20 February 2009.

7 'Gravesend Public Toilets by Plastik Architects', www.dezeen.com, 2 January 2008; Hudson, *Restroom*, pp. 23–5; 'Elevating the Discourse: Public Toilets Pt 1', www.bruteforcecollaborative.com, 23 August 2010.

8 'Hiroshima Park Restrooms by Future Studio', www.dezeen.com, 23 May 2011; and Hudson, *Restroom*, pp. 38–41.

9 *Atelier Van Lieshout: A Manual* (Rotterdam, 1998), pp. 67–71, 112–15, 124–31, 140–43; 'The Technocrat, 2003', 'Modular Bathroom Units 2004' and 'Huize Organus, 2008', www.ateliervanlieshout.com, accessed 8 June 2011.

10 Markus Frenzl, 'The Comeback of Copper and Limescale Edging', www.stylepark.com, 13 March 2009.

11 Hudson, *Restroom*, p. 85.

12 This account is drawn from a conference paper given by Thames Water's External Affairs and Sustainability Director, Richard Aylard. 'London's

Sewerage: A Three Hundred Year View', *London Water: Past, Present, Future* (18 January 2011). With additional reference to documents produced by Thames Water as part of the Thames Tideway Tunnel public consultation process.

Select Bibliography

Adams, Annmarie, *Architecture in the Family Way: Doctors, Houses, and Women, 1870–1900* (Montreal, 1996)

Anderson, Warwick, 'Excremental Colonialism: Public Health and the Poetics of Pollution', *Critical Inquiry*, XXI/3 (Spring 1995), pp. 640–69

At your Convenience: Public Toilets from Around the World (London, 2001)

Barthes, Roland, 'Soap-powders and Detergents', in *Mythologies* [1957], trans. Annette Lavers (London, 2009), pp. 31–3

Bazalgette, Joseph, *Letter of Mr J. W. Bazalgette on Establishment of Public Conveniences throughout the Metropolis: Printed by Order of Court, 22nd March, 1849* (London, 1849)

Ben-Joseph, Eran, *The Code of the City: Standards and the Hidden Language of Place Making* (Cambridge, MA, 2005)

Benidickson, Jamie, *The Culture of Flushing: A Social and Legal History of Sewage* (Vancouver, 2007)

Black, Maggie, and Ben Fawcett, *The Last Taboo: Opening the Door on the Global Sanitation Crisis* (London, 2008)

Blair, Munroe, *Ceramic Water Closets* (Risborough, Bucks, 2000)

Blaszczyk, Regina Lee, *Imagining Consumers: Design and Innovation from Wedgwood to Corning* (Baltimore, MD, 2000)

Blodgett, Richard, *A Sense of Higher Design: The Kohlers of Kohler* (Lyme, CT, 2003)

Bonneville, Françoise de, *The Book of the Bath* (London, 1997)

Breton, Paul, ed., *L'Art Ménager Français* (Paris, 1952)

Cavanagh, Sheila, *Queering Bathrooms: Gender, Sexuality, and the Hygienic Imagination* (Toronto, 2010)

Cavanagh, Sue, and Vron Ware, *At Women's Convenience: A Handbook on the Design of Women's Public Toilets* (London, 1990)

Chadwick, Edwin, *Report on the Sanitary Condition of the Labouring Population of Great Britain* [1842], ed. M. W. Flinn (Edinburgh, 1965)

Clayton, Antony, *Subterranean City: Beneath the Streets of London,* (London, 2000)

Conran, Terence, *The Bed and Bath Book* (London, 1978)

Cooper, Patricia, and Ruth Oldenziel, 'Cherished Classifications: Bathrooms and the Construction of Gender/Race on the Pennsylvania Railroad during World War II', *Feminist Studies*, XXV/1 (1999), pp. 7–41

Corbin, Alain, *The Foul and the Fragrant*, trans. M. Koshan (London, 1994)

Daverio, Philippe, Enrico Finzi, Anna Lombardi and Vitaliano Pesante, *Hic Licet: Bathrooms and Wellness. The Story of Pozzi-Ginori* (Spilimbergo, 2004)

Delaney, Janice, Mary Jane Lupton and Emily Toth, *The Curse: A Cultural History of Menstruation* [1976] revd edn (New York, 1988)

Denley, James, 'A History of Twyford's: 1680–1982', www.twyfordbathrooms.com, accessed 3 June 2010

Douglas, Mary, *Purity and Danger: An Analysis of the Concepts of Pollution and Taboo* [1966] (London, 1996)

Éleb, Monique, 'La Mise au propre en architecture', *Techniques & Culture*, LIV/55 (2010), pp. 588–609

Evamy, Michael, *Ideal-Standard: The First 100 Years* (Kingston upon Hull, 1996)

Eveleigh, David J., *Bogs, Baths, and Basins: The Story of Domestic Sanitation* (Stroud, 2002)

–, *Privies and Water Closets* (London, 2008)

Forty, Adrian, *Objects of Desire: Design and Society since 1750* (London, 1986)

Foucault, Michel, *Discipline and Punish: The Birth of the Prison*, trans. A. Sheridan (London, 1991)

Gandy, Matthew, 'Rethinking Urban Metabolism: Water, Space and the Modern City', *City*, VIII/3 (December 2004), pp. 363–79

George, Rose, *The Big Necessity: Adventures in the World of Human Waste* (London, 2008)

Gerhard, William Paul, *Modern Baths and Bath Houses* (New York, 1908)

Gerling, Daniel Max, 'American Wasteland: A Social and Cultural History of Excrement, 1860–1920', PhD dissertation (University of Texas at Austin, 2011)

Gershenson, Olga, and Barbara Penner, eds, *Ladies And Gents: Public Toilets and Gender* (Philadelphia, 2009)

Giedion, Sigfried, *Mechanization Takes Command: A Contribution to Anonymous History* (New York, 1948)

Goldsmith, Selwyn, *Designing for the Disabled: The New Paradigm* (London, 1997)

Goubert, Jean-Pierre, *The Conquest of Water*, trans. Andrew Wilson (Princeton, NJ, 1989)

Goulden, Gontran, *Bathrooms: A Design Centre Publication* [1967], revd edn (London, 1970)

Greed, Clara, *Inclusive Urban Design: Public Toilets* (Oxford, 2003)

Gregory, Moran E., and Sian James, *Toilets of the World* (London, 2006)

Guerrand, Roger-Henri, *Les Lieux: Histoire des commodités* (Paris, 1985)

Halliday, Stephen, *The Great Stink of London: Sir Joseph Bazalgette and the Cleansing of the Victorian Metropolis* (Stroud, 1999)

Hanson, Julienne, Jo-Anne Bichard and Clara Greed, *The Accessible Toilet Resource* (London, 2007)

Hatton, Joseph, *Twyfords: A Chapter in the History of Pottery* (London, 1897)

Hebel, Dirk, and Jörg Stollmann, eds, *Bathroom Unplugged: Architecture and Intimacy* (Basel, 2005)

Hellyer, Samuel Stevens, *The Plumber and Sanitary Houses*, 4th edn (London, 1887)

Hicks, David, *On Bathrooms* (Britwell Salome, Oxon, 1970)

Hoagland, Alison K., 'Introducing the Bathroom: Space and Change in Working-class Houses', *Buildings & Landscapes*, XVIII/2 (Fall 2011), pp. 15–42

Hudson, Jennifer, *Restroom: Contemporary Design* (London, 2008)

James, Charles Carkeet, *Oriental Drainage: A Guide to the Collection, Removal and Disposal of Sewage in Eastern Cities* (Bombay, 1902)

Jenkins, Joseph, *The Humanure Handbook: A Guide to Composting Human Manure* 3rd edn (Grove City, PA, 2005)

Jephson, Henry, *The Sanitary Evolution of London* (London, 1907)

Jones, Emma M., *Parched City: A History of London's Public and Private Drinking Water* (Winchester, 2013)

Kira, Alexander, *The Bathroom* (New York, 1966)

–, *The Bathroom*, revd edn (Ithaca, NY, 1976)

Lahiji, Nadir, and D. S. Friedman, eds, *Plumbing: Sounding Modern Architecture* (New York, 1997)

Lambton, Lucinda, *Temples of Convenience and Chambers of Delight* (London, 1998)

Laporte, Dominique, *History of Shit*, trans. Nadia Benabid and Rodolphe el-Khoury [1978] (Cambridge, MA, 1993)

Leslie, Fiona, *Designs for 20th-century Interiors* (London, 2000)

Lupton, Ellen, and J. Abbott Miller, *The Bathroom, The Kitchen, and the Aesthetics of Waste: A Process of Elimination* (New York, 1992),

Marks, Robert, and R. Buckminster Fuller, *The Dymaxion World of Buckminster Fuller* (New York, 1973)

The Mayor's Committee (William Gaston Hamilton, Moreau Morris, William Howe Tolman), *Report on Public Baths and Public Comfort Stations* (New York, 1897)

Minimum Cost Housing Group, School of Architecture, McGill University, *Stop the Five Gallon Flush: A Survey of Alternative Waste Disposal Systems*, ed. Witold Rybczynski, 5th edn (Montreal, 1980)

Molotch, Harvey, *Where Stuff Comes From: How Toasters, Toilets, Cars, Computers, and Many Other Things Come to Be as They Are* (New York, 2005)

–, and Laura Norén, eds, *Toilet: Public Restrooms and the Politics of Sharing* (New York, 2010)

Muthesius, Hermann, *The English House* [1904/5], ed. Denis Sharp, trans. Janet Seligman and Stewart Spencer (London, 2007)

Ogle, Maureen, *All the Modern Conveniences: American Household Plumbing, 1840–1890* (Baltimore, MD, 1996)

Palmer, Roy, *The Water Closet: A New History* (Newton Abbot, 1973)

Payer, Peter, *Unentbehrliche Requisiten der Grossstadt* (Vienna, 2000)

Penner, Barbara, 'A World of Unmentionable Suffering: Women's Public
    Conveniences in Victorian London', *Journal of Design History*, XIV/1 (2001),
    pp. 35–52
Reid, Donald, *Paris Sewers and Sewermen: Realities and Representations* (Cambridge,
    MA, 1991)
Reyburn, Wallace, *Flushed with Pride: The Story of Thomas Crapper* (London, 1969)
Rodengen, Jeffrey L., *The History of American Standard* (Fort Lauderdale, FL, 1999)
Routh, Jonathan, *The Good Loo Guide: Where to go in London* (London, 1965)
–, *The Better John Guide: Where to Go in New York* (London, 1966)
–, *Guide Porcelaine to the Loos of Paris* (London, 1966)
Rüegg, Arthur, 'Transforming the Bathroom: Perriand and Le Corbusier, 1927–57',
    in *Charlotte Perriand*, ed. Mary McLeod (New York, 2003), pp. 114–29
Schumacher, Ernst Friedrich, *Small is Beautiful: A Study of Economics as if People
    Mattered* [1973] (London, 1993)
Schuster, Cristina del Valle, *Public Toilet Design* (Richmond Hill, Ontario, 2005)
Scott Brown, Denise, 'Planning the Powder Room', *AIA Journal* (April 1967),
    pp. 81–3
Sheail, John, 'Town Wastes, Agricultural Sustainability and Victorian Sewage', *Urban
    History*, XXIII/2 (August 1996), pp. 189–210
Shove, Elizabeth, *Comfort, Cleanliness and Convenience: The Social Organization of
    Normality* (Oxford, 2003)
Snow, Anthony, and Graham Hopewell, *Planning Your Bathroom: A Design Centre
    Book* (London, 1978)
Sparke, Penny, *So Long as It's Pink* (London, 1995)
Steadman, Philip, *Energy, Environment and Building* (Cambridge, 1975)
'The Toilet Issue', *Postcolonial Studies*, V/2 (July 2002)
Vliet, Bas van, Gert Spaargaren, and Peter Oosterveer, *Social Perspectives on the
    Sanitation Challenge* (Dordrecht, 2010)
Walter Macfarlane & Co., *Catalogue of Macfarlane's Cast Iron Manufactures*, 4th edn
    (Glasgow, 1863)
Wedgwood, Josiah C., *Staffordshire Pottery and Its History* (London, 1913)
Wigley, Mark, *White Walls, Designer Dresses* (New York, 1995)
Williams, Marilyn Thornton, *Washing 'The Great Unwashed': Public Baths in Urban
    America, 1840–1920* (Columbus, OH, 1991)
Winblad, Uno, and Wen Kilama, *Sanitation without Water*, revd edn (Stockholm,
    1980)
Wright, Lawrence, *Clean and Decent: The Fascinating History of the Bathroom and
    the Water-Closet* (London, 1960)

Acknowledgements

Research for this book has taken me to many weird and wonderful places: the Paris sewers, the Gladstone Pottery Museum in Stoke-on-Trent, Deephams Waste Treatment facility in north London, the Kohler Factory in Wisconsin, Hansgrohe's Aquademie in the Black Forest, the Centre for Alternative Technology in Wales, the Shanghai World Expo, the World Toilet Summit in Durban, and Therme Vals in Switzerland. I have seen sophisticated Japanese toilets in Tokyo and basic urine-diverting models in South Africa. And I literally immersed myself in my research when I waded through one of Joseph Bazalgette's intercepting sewers under London – an incredible if unnerving experience.

As well as having been hugely instructive, most of this research has been great fun, but it could never have happened without the generous support of many family members, friends and colleagues. With good humour and minimal resistance, my family indulged my endless plotting to fit in bathroom-related excursions and road trips on holidays. I would like to thank Irmgard, Paul and Sophia especially for their constant love, care and willingness to say 'yes' just one more time. I would also like to acknowledge my friends who joined me on my various journeys and patiently listened to me enthusing about my latest discoveries. Particular thanks go to Charles Rice, for sharing the Paris sewers with me (and always saving me a seat in the British Library), the Rupp family for supplying me with books and encouragement, and Iona Brindle for so diligently reading and commenting on this manuscript at draft stage. I cannot think of a better reader.

My students and colleagues at the Bartlett School of Architecture and in other UCL departments have been unstinting in their support. In particular, I would like to thank Jan Birksted, Iain Borden, Ben Campkin (a fellow traveller in dirty subjects), Julio Davila, Elizabeth Dow, Jonathan Hill, Yeoryia Manolopoulou, Murray Fraser, Jann Matlock, Peg Rawes, Jane Rendell and Tse-Hui Teh. Philip Steadman and Sophie Handler both very kindly read chapters, for which I am grateful. I have enjoyed the fact-checking abilities and friendship of Sarah Bell. And my colleague Adrian Forty's scholarship has been a constant companion and inspiration.

A heartfelt thanks is also due to my comrades in sanitation. This is a bigger community than one might think, filled with people from diverse disciplines: engineers, public health and development specialists, entrepreneurs, academics and activists. I have been genuinely inspired by the forthright (though never moralistic) way in which this community tackles taboos. At the 2012 World Toilet Summit, many of the conversations taking place, particularly around the subject of menstruation, female education and social justice, were some of the most radical I've heard in seventeen years as an academic. Although I cannot name all of those whose thoughts and research have influenced this project, I'd particularly like to mention Chris Buckley, Michelle Barkley, Jo-Anne Bichard, Sheila Cavanagh, Olga Gershenson, Clara Greed, Harvey Molotch, Olivia Muñoz-Rojas Oscarsson, Elisa Roma, Jack Sim, and the amazing Portland-based activist organization PHLUSH, especially Abigail Brown and Carol McCreary.

For generously responding to specific questions or for helping me with images, I thank Ann Agee, Vikram Bhatt, Willem de Bruijn, Graham Caine, David J. Eveleigh, Virginia Gardiner, Susan Henderson, Mary Johnson, Lydia Kallipoliti, Marian Loth, Isabelle Priest, David Roberts, Arthur Rüegg, Witold Rybczynski, Alex Schweder and Hadas Steiner. A very great debt is also owed to Emma M. Jones, reader, cheerleader and researcher extraordinaire, who worked tirelessly to track down some of the more elusive images and facts contained in these pages, all the while working on her own book, *Parched City* (Winchester, 2013), about London's drinking water and fountains. We thus found ourselves in the fortuitous position of considering the same subject from different ends, so to speak, which enriched this book immeasurably. And with good cheer and unflagging resourcefulness Danielle Willkens stepped in to help finalize image permissions for which I am most appreciative.

These acknowledgements would not be complete without mention of the Bartlett's Architecture Research Fund, which helped this project in many ways, most substantially through funding the image permissions. This book quite simply would not have happened without this support. Two grants from UCL Grand Challenges also helped sponsor research on the way. I am grateful that Nancy Levinson, the remarkable editor of the online journal *Places*, has encouraged me to debut numerous bathroom-themed pieces online. And, finally, sincere thanks to my editor, Vivian Constantinopoulous, and the entire production team at Reaktion, who saw the potential of this project and calmly and competently helped to usher it into the world.

Photo Acknowledgements

The author and publishers wish to express their thanks to the below sources of illustrative material and/or permission to reproduce it:

Alvar Aalto Saatio Tiilimaki: p. 112; Amsterdam City Archives: p. 251; Arcaid Images/Alamy: p. 190; from *Architectural Forum*, LVII/1 (January 1933): p. 126; Archive of the Royal Commission for the Exhibition of 1851: p. 48; Archives Charlotte Perriand: p. 128; © ARS, NY and DACS, London 2013, photo courtesy of Through the Flower Archives: p. 26; Association Chaplin (Modern Times © Roy Export S.A.S.): p. 24; courtesy Atelier van Lieshout: pp. 283, 284; author's collection: p. 39; Axor-Hansgrohe: p. 277; photo courtesy of Jenny Baier: p. 16; used by permission of Bantam Books, a division of Random House, Inc.: pp. 184, 212, 213, 222; courtesy of Maria Ida Biggi: p. 172; courtesy of the Bill & Melinda Gates Foundation, photo © Bill & Melinda Gates Foundation: p. 272; from *Bride's Magazine* (1965): p. 177; courtesy of Graham Caine, image courtesy of Lydia Kallipoliti: pp. 265, 267; courtesy Cardiff Council: p. 167; Collection Centre Canadien d'Architecture/Canadian Centre for Architecture, Montreal: 145 (top), 262, 263; Collection of City of London, London Metropolitan Archives: pp. 41 (photo courtesy of the *West Middlesex Chronicle*), 47, 63, 75; Corbis Images: pp. 20, 36, 56, 279; DACS 2013, photos by Jannes Linders, courtesy of Galerie Max Hetzler, Berlin, © VG Bildkunst, Bonn: pp. 281, 282; Design Council Slide Collection/Manchester Metropolitan University: p. 220; Endo Shuhei Architect Institute: p. 280; © Fondation Le Corbusier/ADAGP, Paris and DACS, London 2013: pp. 103, 109; courtesy of the Free Library of Philadelphia Foundation: p. 74; courtesy of The Estate of R. Buckminster Fuller: pp. 121, 133; courtesy of General Research and Reference Division, Schomburg Center for Research in Black Culture, The New York Public Library, Astor, Lenox and Tilden Foundations, New York City: p. 19; Getty Images, photo Allan Grant: p. 180; Gio Ponti Archives: pp. 193, 224; from Selwyn Goldsmith, *Designing for the Disabled: The New Paradigm* (Oxford, 1997): pp. 218, 219; courtesy David Greene: p. 143; courtesy of Nicholas Grimshaw: p. 152; W. Heath Robinson and K.R.G. Browne, *How to Live in a Flat* (London: Hutchinson & Co., n.d. [1936]): p. 90; from S. Stevens Hellyer, *The Plumber and Sanitary Houses: A Practical*

Treatise on the Principles of Internal Plumbing Work; or, The Best Means for Effectually Excluding Noxious Gases from our Houses (London: B.T. Batsford, n.d. [1887]): pp. 67, 96; from the Collections of The Henry Ford Archives, Dearborn, Michigan: pp. 12, 235; courtesy of Hotel Silken Group, photo © Rafael Vargas: p. 286; from Philip Johnson, *Machine Art* (New York: The Museum of Modern Art/W. W. Norton & Co., Inc., 1934): p. 107; from Alexander Kira, *The Bathroom* (New York: The Viking Press, Inc., 1976): pp. 184, 222; from Alexander Kira, *The Bathroom: Criteria for Design* (Ithaca, NY: Centre for Housing and Environmental Studies, Cornell University [Research Report No. 7], n.d. [1966]) 212, 213; courtesy of the John Michael Kohler Arts Center, Sheboygan, Wisconsin: pp. 6, 175, 185, 195; Library of Congress, Washington, DC (Prints and Photographs Division): p. 17; Liverpool Record Office: p. 62; © 2012 Loowatt Ltd: p. 273; courtesy of Marian Loth: p. 230; from A. C. Martin and John H. Henwood, *The Modern Practical Plumber*, vol. III (London, [1929]): pp. 89, 97; Mary Evans Picture Library: p. 60; from *Mechanix Illustrated*: pp. 144 (December, 1947), 145 foot (September, 1956); from *Mott's Illustrated Catalog of Victorian Plumbing Fixtures for Bathrooms and Kitchens*: pp. 98, 99; courtesy The Museum of Modern Art, New York: p. 107; © National Aeronautics & Space Administration/Science & Society Picture Library: p. 140; © National Railway Museum/Science & Society Picture Library: p. 138; Perth Museum and Art Gallery: p. 79; from Mrs H. M. Plunkett, *Women, Plumbers and Doctors; Household Sanitation* (New York, 1885): p. 11; Press Association Images: pp. 23, 229; reproduced courtesy of the artist (Lars Ø Ramberg): p. 157; from Charles George Ramsay and Harold Reeve Sleeper, *Architectural Graphic Standards* (New York and London, 1951): p. 204; RIBA Library Photographs Collection: pp. 34, 114, 126, 136, 170, 171; from Henry Roberts, *The Dwellings of the Labouring Classes, their Arrangement and Construction . . .* (London: The Society for Improving the Condition of the Labouring Classes, 1851): p. 58; courtesy of Roca: p. 285; photos © Roger Viollet/Topfoto: pp. 44, 46; courtesy of Robert Rubin, photo courtesy of Mark Lyon: p. 189; from Witold Rybczynski, *Stop the Five Gallon Flush: A Survey of Alternative Waste Disposal Systems*, 5th edn (Montréal, 1980): p. 262; courtesy of SANYO Electric Co., Ltd: pp. 149, 150; courtesy of Alex Schweder: p. 28; © Science Museum/Science & Society Picture Library: pp. 66, 86, 87, 247; from James Cameron Scott, *Health and Agriculture in China* (London: Faber and Faber, 1952): p. 258; from *Shanks Public Appliances Section 'F' General Cat[alogue] List No. 805* (n. p., n.d. [1930s?]): p. 223; courtesy of Society of Lloyd's: p. 154; Stoke-on-Trent Archives: pp. 77, 111; Succession Marcel Duchamp/ADAGP, Paris and DACS, photo © Tate, London, 2013: p. 25; reproduced by permission of Taylor & Francis Books UK: pp. 218, 219; courtesy of Twyford Bathrooms, Stoke-on-Trent: p. 82; courtesy of UiWE: p. 231; VIEW Pictures Ltd, photo © Zooey Braun/Artur: p. 274; courtesy Villeroy & Boch: p. 198; courtesy of Wellcome Library, London: pp. 21, 117, 216, 238, 252, 254, 257; Whitney Museum of American Art, photo courtesy of the Oldenburg van Bruggen Studio: p. 162; reproduced with Permission of John Wiley & Sons, Inc.: p. 204; courtesy William Heath Robinson Trust: p. 90.

Index